Advance Praise

"The maintenance of nervous system health will **revolutionize acting training** by providing tools to manage the habitual trauma reactions that can be triggered by the work. I wish I had this knowledge as a young actor and will be using these techniques in the classroom for years to come."

— Adrianne Krstansky, *Head of Acting, Brandeis University*

"Ruby's work has **changed my life.** That sounds like a big statement, yet it doesn't fully convey the deep, positive impact it has had. I've felt my nervous system change, felt myself move up the polyvagal ladder, and noted my set point permanently shifted from her work and classes. I feel incredibly fortunate to have found a way for my body and mind to make sense of past experiences in theater. **I wish this work was around 15+ years ago,** but I'll share it with every artist I know now because they need it. If you have found your way to Ruby, I hope you give yourself the gift of sitting with the work, applying it to your life, and returning to it whenever this journey gets tough."

— Novalee Wilder, *Actor & Writer*

"The process of discovery through MuscleMusic is meant to guide you toward long-term resilience, not towards some abstract notion of 'ultimate or instant success.' It is also **emphatically anti-culty,** encouraging self-knowledge and putting you in touch with your own experience. So refreshing! For me, perhaps this venture's greatest asset is that it is led by an incredible and experienced artist who truly understands the artist's dilemma, with all its vast riches, rewards, obstacles, challenges, and even traumas. In my experience, you get vast value out of MuscleMusic."

— Eszter Balint, *Musician, Actor, Violinist*

"When I came across Ruby's work a few years ago, I knew that working with and learning from her was what I needed to support the next step in my musical and human journey. Ruby opened so many doors for me, filled in so many gaps, and helped me understand how creativity, performance, and the mind-body-spirit connection work together. She helped me realize that **my real instrument is my nervous system.** I'm forever grateful."

— Be Bard, *Singer-Songwriter*

"This methodology isn't asking individuals to bend to a set of rules but to tune into their own rules on a core level. Not only does it feel **empowering to apply** this work myself, but it's work I feel can benefit anyone, no matter their starting point or life experience. Since beginning this nervous system work through MuscleMusic, I feel I have been able to name and unshame many sources of my artistic dysregulation with a specificity I was lacking before. As an artist, it has been **transformative to tune into the idea that 'I am my canvas,'** and my canvas is shifting how I create art in a way that, put simply, feels better."

— Marina Blue, *Performer/Director*

"**MuscleMusic has transformed my life** in so many ways—professionally, creatively, and personally. I am grateful for Ruby every single day. Every artist can benefit from this work."

— Lyzz Zinn, *Singer-Songwriter and Music Therapist*

"Ruby's MuscleMusic has bridged the gap in my 25+ year career as a performing artist **where no counseling or therapy could**—giving me a clear picture of my nervous system states in all circumstances and supporting tools on and off-stage to continue to excel as a performer and advance as a nervous system leader. It's been a **radical freedom** as a sensitive and expressive artist to cross this bridge."

— Amanda Rogers, *Singer-Songwriter*

"The journey of learning about my nervous system has been **life-changing.** MuscleMusic not only reshaped my relationship with performing, but also gave me language to name and understand what I was going through."

— Rocio Cravero, *Singer-Songwriter*

"My experience with the MuscleMusic program has been nothing short of **transformative.** I now feel like I have a **roadmap for moving forward** with my life in all areas, and I can't wait to start performing again! I'm truly grateful for this profound **journey of healing and self-discovery."**

— Violet Stone Gutierrez, *Author, Singer-Songwriter, Filmmaker, Coach*

"Before I learned about the Fox Method, I could not edit my book without dysregulating my nervous system and driving myself into a Freeze State. Ruby's in-depth knowledge of nervous system leadership and her **compassionate coaching has truly been life-changing."**

— Deepshikha Anand, *Writer*

"MuscleMusic not only helped me regulate my own nervous system states while writing my latest novel—it helped me **understand and work with my characters' nervous system states!"**

— Nicole Galland, *Novelist*

SUPERPLAY

YOUR INSTRUMENT IS YOU

A polyvagal-inspired revolution for harnessing **stage fright** *and* **unshaming your nervous system.**

RUBY ROSE FOX

Note to artists and readers: Artistic practices and nervous system protocols evolve over time, and no single technique or recommendation is guaranteed to be universally safe or effective. This volume is intended as a general resource for professionals in the performing arts who seek a trauma-informed approach. The author and publisher cannot ensure the accuracy, effectiveness, or suitability of every recommendation for all circumstances. Readers are encouraged to apply their own professional judgment and consider individual needs when utilizing the content of this work.

Side A: *The Muscle*

Prelude: The Gift of Stage Fright

Polyvagal Foundations

Superplay Theory & Beyond

B Side: *The Music*

*The complete set of tools are available at: www.muscle-music.com

This book would not be possible without:

My partner—and the most incredible mixing artist in Nashville—Colin Sipos.

My editor and one of my favorite artists, Jonathan Russell Clark.

The MuscleMusic Community, who co-created this embodied work born from the lived experiences of real artists.

And the eagle-eyes of Phil Sipos

I want to acknowledge a **personal bias** that I hope you'll keep in mind as you read this book.

It was my grandmother's funeral on a gray day in Queens, NY when a five-foot tall thick-accented Yiddish woman behind me said, "Oh yeah, Ruby? You know, he was on *BROADWAY.*" My head snapped! "She was?" Until then, I'd only known her as a mental patient whose illness left my father an orphan. My brain began to spin as I was just graduating with a BFA in theater.

We all have shame that lives in our families. I remember my Dad's anxious and cowering energy when we would visit Grandma Ruby. He was afraid we wouldn't be able to love her the way he did. I was very connected to my Dad, and unconsciously I was determined to prove him wrong. We could love Ruby, just in a different way.

I knew that after I walked off that graveyard, it was possible that no one would speak her full name again. So, I chose to take on Ruby Rose Fox as my legal name as a reclamation of my grandmother's unconquerable soul. With her name, I knew I could be brave.

Ruby was a first-generation, working-class, Jewish-American poet and actress who endured one of the most anti-Semitic periods in NYC history. She spent much of her life confined in a New Jersey state-run mental institution, struggling with bipolar disorder. I've long believed that, under a different model of care, her life could have been one of freedom and creativity. It's easy to look back on psychiatry from 70 years ago, condemning its savage, unethical practices—from prefrontal lobotomies to patient abuse. Yet it's much harder to critically examine what we could improve today because we can't see it yet. While I am profoundly grateful that friends with severe mental illness now lead meaningful lives thanks to social progress, we must remain vigilant.

When we heal the dysregulation passed down through generations, we help to end a long lineage of trauma. For me, this work is driven by what

I call "regulated urgency"—a deep, steady commitment to ensuring that every artist has a chance at a full, creative life, both on and off the stage.

So, let me be clear: our nervous systems deserve better care when entrusted to therapeutic institutions, and so do artists in the vulnerable process of mental health recovery. If you're a therapist reading this, please know that artists, as a community, are underserved by the pedestalization of their struggles and the dehumanizing myth that suffering produces better art.

Bringing the nervous system into the arts won't be easy—it requires tenacity. But I want you to know that when my clients say, "Ruby, this work has changed my life," that I'm hearing it through a double lens. Ruby's spirit is still shining through, and her presence is flickering through my life, and hopefully by the end of this book, yours too.

Your healing, your life's work, and the way you touch others can be as weird and wild as you are. Do not let the institutions you serve club you into dank submission:

> *…be on the watch.*
> *there are ways out.*
> *there is a light somewhere.*
> *it may not be much light but*
> *it beats the darkness.*
> *be on the watch…*
> *the gods will offer you chances.*
> *know them.*
> *take them.*

-Charles Bukowski

Preface

Welcome to the Fox Method. This is more than just a guide; it's an invitation into the most important relationship you'll ever cultivate in your artistic life—the one with your nervous system. I know you—your depth, your struggles, your hunger for expression. I've walked that path with you, and I respect the courage it takes to keep going, even when anxiety, exhaustion, or trauma seem insurmountable. And, if you are just tenderly coming home to the arts the first time, you are just as welcome.

The Fox Method is built on a simple yet profound truth: your nervous system is your primary instrument, more important than your voice, your body, or your technique. Without it, none of those things can flourish. And yet, how often have we been taught to nurture it? To treat it with the same care we give to our craft? Rarely, if ever, off stage or on. This method was born from that gap—from a deep need to honor and understand the full complexity of our nervous systems, not just as a survival tool but as a finely tuned harmonic system where every state has a purpose.

This method is not focused on trauma healing, though it acknowledges trauma as part of the journey for many of us. Instead, it views the nervous system as a craft that can be honed, again, much like an instrument. Every state you experience—including those traditionally seen as "bad" or dysregulated—is part of the full "musical" spectrum of human experience. There is no 'wrong' state; there is only your body communicating in the language it knows best, the somatic language of survival and safety. What this book offers is a way to work with your nervous system, not against it.

While I've deeply entrenched myself in methods like Polyvagal Theory and Somatic Experiencing, the truth is I've created my own work. I've also only included what either worked for my nervous system and my clients' over the years, to help you navigate the complexities of your nervous system, allowing you to enhance your creativity and performance. Whether you're a performer who can barely get out of bed, a thriving entertainer, or someone caught in the struggle of anxiety, stage fright, or creative exhaustion, this book is for you. It's also for teachers of performance, theater, or music, who can use this work to support their students in ways that go beyond traditional techniques.

I want to particularly dedicate this work to artists living with PTSD or post-traumatic injury (PTI). For too long, artists with dysregulated nervous systems have been sidelined, their challenges either misunderstood or framed as a lack of talent. I want you to know that your dysregulation is not a permanent barrier—it's a temporary disability, one that deserves to be understood, honored, and supported. The Fox Method offers a framework for navigating those challenges, helping you reclaim your full artistic potential. More important than that though, is your full artistic humanity.

If you believe that only certain people belong on stage, that those who can't 'cut it' should step aside for those who can, then this book may not be for you. What sets this method apart is its radical inclusivity. It's designed not only for neurotypical artists but also for those navigating neurodiversity and trauma to stay with their craft and not abandon it to the mangled embrace of shame. This approach offers a groundbreaking opportunity to redefine what it means to be an artist today, celebrating the unique challenges you face rather than merely accommodating them. It's a new field of practice, merging nervous system science with performance, empowering you to harness your body's biology to your advantage on stage.

Drawing from my 30 years of training and performance as a theatrical actress and musician, along with my deep immersion in Polyvagal Theory, I have dedicated myself to understanding how the nervous system shapes our artistic lives. I've coached in universities, non-profits, correctional facilities, and homeless shelters, but I have chosen to remain free from systems of power so that I can speak with truth and integrity about what I see and experience.

This book is my offering to you, born not from a place of pure joy, but from a personal reckoning. After plunging into a career without a method for nervous system regulation, I hit a wall—facing the harsh reality of burnout, anxiety, and trauma. I had to build something new, something that addressed the unique challenges artists face. I saw nervous system patterns and bypasses that no one was talking about. I saw an entire field of practice–the bio-arts–essentially untouched.

I want to be clear: art is not therapy. It can reflect and express our inner worlds, but relying on it as a coping mechanism for decades, without proper mental health support or fostering secure relationships, can lead to a life built on shaky ground. This was the realization I had in my 30s, and it led me to ask some hard questions: Why had my university training failed to address the nervous system? Why were so many fellow artists struggling? These questions led me on a decade-long journey through Eastern mysticism, meditation, psychology, and eventually, to Polyvagal Theory and other somatic approaches.

Polyvagal Theory, developed by Dr. Stephen Porges, explains how our nervous system helps us respond to stress, connect with others, and feel safe. It highlights the vagus nerve's role in moving us between three main states: the "social engagement" state, where we connect with others; the "fight-or-flight" state, when we feel threatened; and the "freeze" state, when we shut down from overwhelm. For artists, understanding these states is essential to managing stage fright, deepening emotional expression, and connecting with audiences.

Polyvagal Theory doesn't pathologize–there is no sin, no moral weight—only biological function. This is incredibly freeing but also potentially dangerous if taken to extremes. The truth is, many artists suffer not from disorders but from the simple byproducts of being human, but they also suffer from severe mental illness as well. We must hold space for both to be true. This book isn't meant to replace therapy, but to complement it, giving both you and your therapist a clearer understanding of how your nervous system intersects with your art.

And that's where we come to the heart of this work: I have wrestled with Polyvagal Theory for so long and made such distinct adjustments to it that the Fox Method has evolved into its own theory. A key element of this evolution is the concept of Superplay, a fourth nervous system state that transcends, includes, and is revelatory to all others—including the defense states. This discovery came to me as an undeniable insight, during a training session with Deb Dana (one of the first therapists to apply Science of Safety to traditional therapy) and this new insight on a fourth state is central to how artists experience creative engagement and states of pretend.

We'll also dive into another crucial realization: the "safe and social" state, while important, isn't the ultimate goal. For artists, play involves risk, role-play, and emotional depth that go far beyond what animals experience in their safe and social state. This book will help you understand that while regulation is vital, so is honoring the complexity and richness of your nervous system's entire range.

Finally, I want to introduce a revolutionary way to think about leadership—both in your artistic life and beyond. The nervous system isn't a simple hierarchy but a **Holarchy**, a system where each state transcends and includes the one before it. This view allows for a more flexible, compassionate approach to leadership and performance, one that fosters true safety and connection without sacrificing creative depth.

My hope is that this book will guide you toward greater nervous system flexibility—not as a way to control or conquer your states, but as an invitation to fall in love with the fierce, beautiful complexity of your biology. Together, we'll explore the full spectrum of your human experience, helping you reclaim both your art and your body.

Though I've had the privilege of teaching this work at Yale, Boston University, Brandeis, and Northeastern, I want you to know that this work is still in its infancy. I approach it with humility and wonder, knowing that it will continue to grow and evolve. My mission is to ensure that every arts training program in America includes at least the basics of The Science of Safety. If this book benefits you, please share it with your alma mater's Dean, so we can build a better future for artists together.

As you move through the "Muscle" sections of this book, you'll learn the foundational science of safety and the architecture of the Fox Method. In the "Music" sections, we'll transform that knowledge into practice, allowing your body to move in harmony with your understanding. Both are essential—without muscle, we're left with tools used for the wrong state and in the wrong order. Without music, we have a head full of information but no lived experience.

Under no circumstances should this work be mistaken for clinical mental health care, nor should it serve as a substitute for any formal mental health institutions. What you'll find here is crafted solely for the art of performance—both onstage and in life—but it is not therapy, nor does it aim to replace it.

Does anyone read prefaces?

Not to my knowledge.

Well, fuck.

The Muscle

Welcome.

I'm so glad you're here.

I've decided to write these chapters as letters because the form of a letter is an intimate one. Still, writing misses the mark on the most basic biological cues of safety; the ability to see a **person's emotional cues on their face**, and **a musical voice** (prosody). I also don't expect you to trust me or my ideas right away. I'd like to earn your trust over a much longer period of time. I imagine that you may have picked up this book because someone did not use their power well, so I will say this: you can disagree, or dissent, and this work will never require you to give up what makes you, you. Thank you for your openness to a subject that is so unbelievably tender: your nervous system.

The first half of this book is the "Muscle." We must build some "Muscle" before we can play "Music." This is the theory, the framework, and the language to play the music of nervous system safety in the arts.

Prelude: The Gift of Stage Fright

Let's cut right to the chase. Your audience can never be "safe."

They are strangers.

If you're seeking love, appreciation, to be seen, held, or wanted by an audience, you are violating the unspoken pact of leadership that comes with taking on benevolent power. This violation is akin to a mother relying on her child for love, validation, and appreciation, instead of giving these freely as the child develops. It's like a teacher needing their students to affirm why they are loved, needed, or intelligent, rather than offering them education. The stage is not the venue to search for the parts of ourselves that were overlooked or not fully nurtured by our caregivers.

Instead, we should seek these aspects in individuals who genuinely know us and can offer love—specifically, not in strangers. Your audience does not provide a secure environment for unconditional care; they are simply individuals looking to adjust their own emotional states. THEY are the kids. YOU are the parent. Recognizing this truth highlights the absurdity of the belief that an audience can heal a performer, a notion that ultimately leads to confusion and disappointment.

The gift of this method is that it forces us to stop seeking love in places it cannot be given and instead embody love and power as a free offering to our audience. It's an invitation to witness our entire nervous system in service of a connection greater than ourselves. We are tasked with channeling the unconditional love of our human biology.

Stage fright is a bit different than a fear of sharks, venomous spiders, or the dark, right? We are wired to be afraid of them for our biological protection. If there is a hot stove, I take my hand off it. If there is a threatening drunk woo-girl coming at me on the Nashville strip, *my body pulls me away*. What about the stage? What is happening?

Well, we are also wired to be scared of people we don't know, especially 100 of them who are not in your "tribe." And, we all vary in terms of how our bodies react. Some of us will have a stress response to a crowd we don't know, others will have a lesser response.

As artist-humans, we live on spectrums because diversity fuels a creative collective's ability to survive. As hunter-gatherers, some individuals thrived in high-stakes pursuits like hunting, using their sharp senses and a well-tuned response to fear to secure resources. Others focused on other resources like tending plants, herbs, or social dynamics, nurturing children or animals, and sustaining the group. We, too, bring our unique nervous system inclinations to the stage, each with a different response to performing for a room of strangers. Some of us might feel energized by the thrill, some are absolutely pummeled by it.

This book is for you, *but this tiny part of it is for me.* I want art that comes from the berry-picker people. It's often profound, revelatory, and I just want more. I think of the neuro-spicy actor who would feel so much more free if they weren't forced to deeply mask their nervous system's diversity. I think of the shy kid forced to sing too soon. Surely, if we can make room for the forceful egos of male directors, we can learn to include those with trauma and neurodiversity in our arts programs.

Firstly, I truly believe many talented poets, writers, and creative geniuses hate performing. They are also the easiest to discard in theatrical or music training, and are told they can't "cut it." And instead of giving them new methods that work for them, we shame them. Then, they go to therapy to work that out and are told that the stage could possibly be a venue to heal them. This, my friends, is not only untrue, it makes them run for the hills even faster.

So let's correct something that therapists often and unknowingly confuse:

Your audience is not safe and they will never be safe for a nervous system that needs to protect itself. They are strangers. Trauma healing doesn't belong on stage, but your body, which may hold trauma, does.

So let's correct something that art, music, and drama teachers often and unknowingly (or knowingly) confuse:

There are not "talented" luminaries that are "meant for the stage," but simply people who have brain predictions which determine bio-chemical safety when faced with strangers. It really doesn't *mean* anything else but that. A performer with no stage fright is less common in our human species because if that brain prediction happened in the face of a bear, we lose a genetic line. If you have stage fright, it means your nervous system is working well! It means if you are under threat you will get a stress response. We *have* to first celebrate this!

Wait, so I'm not broken if I have stage fright? Nope!

Wait, so I'm not broken if I've never had stage fright and suddenly have it as I begin to heal? Definitely not.

Let's break the spell of "charisma." Before we knew that women with a lot to say were not witches, we ascribed a necessary "magic" that explained the unexplainable. I hope to reveal in this book that many terms we use for people who are "charismatic" or "talented" simply have a neurobiology that is tuned in favor of connecting with an audience. The issue is that maturing individually or collectively is never very fun, and surely doesn't feel like magic. It's more fun to think certain people just have some secret sauce instead of understanding that harnessing presence is a *skill that can be taught.* Instead of the incorrect belief that some people are "meant for the stage" or gifted by some pre-ordained art-God, I will show you that when you teach someone's nervous system how to exude presence slowly and at their bodies pace, charisma is for everyone.

Ok, back to the point. Our nervous system is still very much wired to what our species has experienced for the last 200,000 years, and that reality was that standing in front of 100 strangers meant you were in deep shit. It meant you went way too far away from your tribe alone, and that the people in front of you may accept you or kill you. That is why often, if the first 10 seconds go well, a performer can calm down and connect. We know that we have been accepted into this new tribe. Phew!

When I celebrate a nervous system that is working well, it's not to be cute, because not having defense when we need it can be as dangerous as having it. This is why, sometimes, children who do *not* have secure attachments feel totally safe on stage. **Some stage fright is normal** especially for performers who are not constantly performing. This means the art of finding safety on stage is finding safety in a nervous system that is designed to attempt to protect you from a large group of strangers.

But, now we are in a unique evolutionary position. Our bodies don't always know it is safe to be in front of strangers, and yet *we know it is safe*. We are playing a very different game. We are now consciously working with the body to allow us to do something our ancestors would find unthinkable—stand, and lead a group of strange humans you have never met before.

So, if you were hoping for an ultimate cure for stage fright, this is the end of our journey. But, if you stick with me, what is to come is a gift of a lifetime—the gift of stage fright—which is an extremely deep and compassionate relationship to one's nervous system that fuels stage ferocity and peak performance. This is a much better solution than the illusion of total nervous system control, because it gives the ability to guide your nervous system to safety, night after night. Instead of covering up or suppressing your nervous system, I am going to teach you how to reveal it in ways you never thought possible.

Body Fright

When standing vulnerable in front of a group of people we don't know, **what we're really afraid of is our nervous system's expression of pain and activation in our body**. How do I know? If I shot you up with something like morphine, you'd feel very differently about your audience. It's not our audience, but our body's sensations we are afraid of. Since we can't run away from our own bodies, we run away from whatever we see around us. In our case, it might be the stage, marketing our art, or even practicing. As Anya says in the Chekhov play "The Three Sisters," about escaping their misery to move to Moscow, **"Yeah but we would still be us."** So, the things we want to move towards, we end up moving away from. Instead of expanding, we slowly get smaller and smaller. And like Anya's sentiment, we can also wrongfully determine that nothing we are doing externally is helping, so why do anything at all, and we fall into helplessness.

The unconscious or "autonomic" (think automatic) nervous system is tasked with survival, not thriving and adventuring. If we let it run the show, we will have very limited experiences. The reason Anya and her sisters never go to Moscow is because their nervous systems won at protecting them from death, but lost all the opportunity of experiencing anything out of their tiny, limited, domestic prison.

So what *are* we afraid of? You're afraid of two states of being—often called fight/flight and freeze. And you're afraid of them because you were taught to be: in school, in church, in college, at your first job, and sometimes even at home. You're afraid of these normal feelings of defense because they've been collectively judged as sinful, feminine, weak, immature, sinful, wrong, dirty, dangerous, or primitive. And because you fear them, you shame them, and in shaming them, you often express them without loving them.

When it comes to activities that are safe, we don't have stage fright or even life fright; we have **body fright.**

Body fright is natural and takes over animals. For humans, we need a gap between impulse and reaction to survive because our primary mode of survival is cooperation. We now need a gap in between our bodies' reactions and how we move in the world. We are not survival of the fittest, we are survival of the most cooperative. This is why humans with severe body fright don't get along very well with other humans. Unfortunately, this is something that doesn't "come with the box," it must be *taught. [1]

Here's a brief thought experiment: it's almost impossible to judge others once we truly know their story, history, and humanity. Judging becomes so much easier when we lack information about a person. What if your nervous system just needed to be understood?

Now, consider your own feelings of immobilization or fight-or-flight response. These are deeply intriguing biological processes with an evolutionary backstory—not only as part of human species history but also within each of our unique lives. Have you ever taken the time to get to know these responses? In so many myths, monsters are often royalty

---

1. Why? Because all humans are born premature. Our parasympathetic system and social systems are built by our parents, caregivers, and community.

or children in disguise. I hope to show you how the "ugly" parts of our nervous system can transform into something valuable, like gold if we take the time to learn and understand them. In a culture that shames people it doesn't understand, artists (and especially the actors) are uniquely qualified for unshaming their body fright. If you can find empathy for your role as Richard III or Medea, certainly you can learn to have compassion for your nervous system.

The gift of stage fright is that understanding how to work with fear and dysregulation penetrates every realm of life. This turnaround makes your life bigger, not smaller. Sure, there are hack programs that tell you to imagine people in their underwear, breathe, and reframe, but if you're deeply curious or feel like something profound has been missing from your training, the Fox Method might be for you.

Instead of scrambling for love, appreciation, and recognition from an audience of strangers—possibly because you were raised by parents who felt like strangers, and this song and dance feels like home—we will be gently reparenting our nervous systems with a new framework and new tools. We will stop trying to get love from people you don't know and start getting deeply curious about how to love our pain, activation, and mysterious orphaned feelings.

We have a long way to go as we need to start at the beginning of human evolution to reach Superplay, but for now, let's take a look at how stage fright feels and officially begin our journey.

Letter #1: It's Showtime

It's showtime.

You're standing backstage, about to go on. You're prepared. You've even practiced and performed what you're about to perform many times in the past. You look good, the crowd looks good—all you need to do is get out there and show 'em what you've got.

Suddenly, however, a sensation creeps into you as the final seconds pass before your entrance onto the stage, an unsettling feeling of doubt and anxiety and fear: despite all your years of experience and rehearsals, here you are dealing with something that you believed you had gotten over, something that you now associate with beginners.

You have stage fright.

But how could this be? After all, you have every reason to be confident in your abilities. Beyond your dedicated training, you've also performed enough times successfully to know that your skills are not hypothetical. So why are you suddenly nervous? Why do you have the urge to pee and fart at the same time? And why have you lost your faith in your work and experience? You hear yourself say, "What the point? I don't even want to do this."

What is happening?

What's happening is, on one hand, physiological—a complex series of actions involving adrenal glands and cortisol and neurotransmitters—but knowing that isn't going to help you much right now. What's useful to understand is that all those physical things happening at the microscopic level in your body lead to **bigger states of being** that transcend and include all of those smaller realities. The one you're in right now, backstage, is one of three modes that have become relatively common notions. You've probably even heard the terms "safe and social," "fight/flight," and "freeze," which have been in use for a number of decades. But here's a taxonomy that better highlights the type of energy your body is providing:

Connect Mode: This state occurs when our body prioritizes energy to structures, hormones, and functions that facilitate ***connection***, such as the facial muscles for engaging with others. It keeps our heart rate lower aided by the Ventral Vagus nerve, aids in hearing human voices, deactivates the grip of the amygdala, and activates the prefrontal cortex for memory and cognitive functions. This state only functions in its proximity to cues of connection, and a perceived lack of extreme risk (safety). This is run by the Parasympathetic Nervous System (PNS) and acts as a cooling vent or a "brake" for the engine of energy and stress.

*As you are confronted with terms and words you don't know. Please do not worry about not understanding every term. You are not stupid. You are learning. Learning requires mild levels of stress to make the brain neuroplastic. Who gives a f*** what PNS means right now. Let the words wash over you. Let this process be sloppy.

This is the mode you want to be in because you just feel better here, normal, and like yourself. But, this Connect Mode mode isn't how you feel as your mouth dries and your hands shake. You didn't even feel it happening, but for the last 10 minutes you have been in:

Move Mode: This state occurs when our body prioritizes energy to structures, hormones, and functions that support ***movement***, aggression, or fleeing. It increases heart rate, redirects metabolic resources to large muscles, and heightens sensory perception for threat detection. This is run by the Sympathetic Nervous System (SNS) and acts as an engine for movement.

While doubt and uncertainty enter into the equation in Connect Mode, in Move Mode these feelings often no longer safe in your body. This goads you into feeling competitive, into criticizing others, perfectionistic thoughts, and into projecting these negative feelings onto your audience, who you now assume are going to hate you. This is the state of war, and the state in which the body is also at war with itself. Instead of noticing these changes curiously in order to welcome the state, you push the state away. Our body is then trapped, cornered. When we are afraid of our own body, we fall into the arms of our oldest state:

> **Preservation Mode:** This state occurs when our body prioritizes energy to structures, hormones, and functions that support *immobilization* or energy conservation. Sometimes decreases heart rate (bradycardia), heightens sensory perception for threat detection, and activates the amygdala while deactivating the prefrontal cortex. This is run by the Dorsal Vagus (PNS) which is a slow nerve due to its lack of fat for conductivity. This is the emergency brake.

This is you backstage, right now. You're in Preservation Mode. This mode is where your body goes when it doesn't believe there is anything you can do to survive. You're frozen because your body thinks it's in danger, and physiologically speaking, there's no difference between your stage fright and a tiger who has grabbed you by the neck. Your body needs to play dead. In such a state, there's no way you'll be able to perform your best. You've got to do something.

What can you do?

Life Fright

Let's start again.

It's showtime, only this time you're standing at the door to your boss's office, awaiting an annual review. Every year you stand at this door full of nerves and angst, which you especially resent considering that this job isn't even your passion—your true work is out on the road and on stage—so listening to someone comment on and criticize you for a job that you don't even love in more detail than anyone's ever applied to your artistic performances is pretty depressing.

In this situation, you're probably more in Move Mode than Preservation, but during your review an escalation from Move to Preservation is not completely off the table. These kinds of interactions often put you ill at ease, and you've never been able to curb the uncomfortable feelings and physical shaking. You've even sought the advice of therapists, who gave you a box breathing exercise, but it's just not doing much right now. You don't even know at this moment you have the right tools, but for the wrong state. You feel embarrassed that you are failing at work but now you're failing at nervous system regulation too? If you were just smart enough, you could figure this out! But you can't, which makes you feel deeply ashamed and broken. In defense, you notice these breathing techniques absolutely don't *enhance* your performance, let alone take it to new heights. If you are honest, it doesn't work much at all.

The Fox Method:

One last time, but this time *with a new method:*

It's showtime, as you walk in your front door after that job you loathe, and you fluctuate between Move and Preservation. You snap at your partner as they gently try to help you pack for your performance tonight, and watch their nervous system tune to Move Mode. You **"Name and Notice"** your state. Ok, you are in Move Mode. But, you remember you have a new tool called **"Calling Out Your Dog,"** and say, "Hey babe, I'm sorry if I sound cold or rude, I'm dysregulated right now." Unfortunately, your voice *already* triggered your partner's Move Mode and is now also in this state as well. Because of this, their inner ear tunes away from the human voice and can't hear your bid for safety. They retort, "I'm just f***** trying to help you!" The intensity of their voice makes you go numb. Back to Preservation Mode.

But, you have a gig. A big one—time to shift because you deeply care about your performance as a craft and know that your nervous system is your primary instrument and tuning for your audience. Normally, you would throw your body on stage and see what happens, but you want a better outcome. You have learned to become a nervous leader on and off stage.

Since you now know that physiologically your partner can no longer hear well or see connection in your face when they are in Move Mode, you don't snap back like normal, you give them space to retune. You find yourself stunned that you did this because you're a fighter, and while it feels strange to take some space, you have the distance you need to regulate.

Then, you finally remember that to get out of a freeze you have to activate. Since your partner's connection mode is "offline" and can't help you regulate, you go upstairs and gently shake and do some light squats (**The Shake and Surge Tool**) to restore your oxygen to move you out of freezing. Your body doesn't want to do any of this, in fact, it's pulling you, lulling you to collapse to keep your Preservation Mode state going. Your mind kicks in and says, "What's the point of this? I should give up!" Instead of listening to these thoughts you realize these thoughts are a part of your nervous system story (**Nervous System Stories Tool**). You then use the "**Thank You, Ground Control Tool**" to reconnect to the sensations in your body right now. Luckily, The Shake and Surge Tool lifted you up the ladder into Move Mode, you burst into tears which previously would have made you think you were going off the rails, but with a new system you know that this release means your body is *moving towards safety* (Basic Polyvagal Education). This is where you used to get stuck, but now you know you are going in the right direction.

As you drive closer to your gig you feel connected to yourself again as you continue to activate your vagus nerve through the slow breaths (**The Physiological Sigh Tool**) and play a mental game to get excited about the show and stave off any unhelpful rumination (**The It's Totally Possible Tool**). This helps you feel even more in the zone. Sure you feel a bit tender from the wild ride from preservation to connection, but as you get to the theater you find yourself able to lead and communicate with the stage manager and team. Instead of plunging down into dysregulation, you know that instead, you can lift off into letting your entire nervous system play. You also know this wouldn't be possible if you didn't have the tools you have now. If you didn't unfreeze earlier, it would have happened onstage.

This is where the fourth state comes in. Like the other states, this one can't be a permanent state of being, as none of them are equipped to deal with all aspects of life. But when this fourth state is incorporated, your whole nervous system takes whatever energies are available (Connect, Move, Preservation Mode) and begins to play with them in the service of pretend and storytelling.

Here is the fourth state:

> **Pretend Mode/Superplay:** This state occurs when our body prioritizes energy to structures, hormones, and functions that facilitate connection through ***pretend play***. It allows us to suspend disbelief and embody a character, with active superplay involving acting, and Passive Superplay involving activities like watching horror movies or Netflix. It can also support structures of fight/flight and freeze but in the context of overall safety.

Before you say your first line, you take a moment to both connect that Move Mode energy with your character (**The Mississippi Staredown Tool**) and then with the audience. Because you embraced your Move Mode, the whole room gels because they see some sadness that is embraced by signals of safety (**The Start From Where You Are Tool**). The audience's heartbeats sync with yours and you ride peak-performance in the Superplay State. You went from complete immobilization to letting your body play like an instrument. Not only does your audience feel connected, their heart rates sync and they become one big nervous system organism. You take in a moment of the awe that is the human experience.

Invitation

What I hope you noticed was that we use physical and mental tools to play our nervous system like an instrument. This takes practice like any other instrument that is worth mastering.

I hope to show you that your nervous system is not a damaged war memorial but a musical instrument. What if you had tools that work? What if there weren't three states of your nervous system but *four*? What if this fourth (and additional) state, which has so far gone unrecognized by previous contributors, reveals how your performances could be *better* and more safe? And what if, whether you're about to perform for thousands of people or waiting to have a serious one-on-one with a superior, or handling home life—can this method apply to any stressful scenarios? What if you could turn your stage fright into your greatest tool?

You may not want a method, you may wish instead to find a one-stop shop to "cure" yourself of "negative" states of being, but unfortunately, the nervous system is always thrust into role-play. You're not *trying* to be a dog-mom, a teacher, a partner, a performer, a director, or an author—those roles pop out of you like musical harmonics. How do we play our roles well, and in doing so, how do we wield benevolent power in a world full of chaos, inevitable pain, and hard work effectively? This book is a framework, a tool kit, and a practice for life and the stage.

What you will notice is the speed we will move in this book. When you are having a panic attack backstage, we don't have time to sit on a therapy couch for hours and slowly reframe your beliefs. We need to solve for the fact that you need tools to help you have your best night, in a much shorter time frame than anything Freud had in mind. We are solving for nervous system resilience, flexibility, and performance.

It's showtime.

I just want to be seen, appreciated, loved so bad!!!

OK, valid! But, why get this solely from strangers? Maybe it would be better to get this from people who know you? People who can actually love you.

RIP

Well, fuck.

Did your parents feel like strangers?

Yep!

Is it possible you are trying to get the love you never had from strangers because that's all your nervous system understands?

Letter #2: When Life Hands You Avocados...

"And then sweeping up the jokers that he left behind,
You find he did not leave you very much, not even laughter.
Like any dealer he was watching for the card that is so high and wild
He'll never need to deal another."

—*Leonard Cohen, "The Stranger Song"*

Dear Artist,

I thought I would start things off with a story about my own journey as an artist and performer. First, if I am asking you for personal honesty and introspection, I'd better be able to put my money where my mouth is. Second, this story will establish two key concepts for our purposes: **Nervous System Supremacy** and **Co-regulation**. And finally, I hope to show that the ways we've been taught to deal with (or, more aptly, to *not* deal with) our nervous system. So, without further ado, the story of the avocado.

It was a ripe, perfectly delicious avocado, and I should have been hungry. Famished, in fact, because I had just finished performing in the most difficult one-woman show I've ever done. I sang my heart out in a 14-foot gown, for crying out loud. It was a *big* show. The biggest I'd ever conceived, and somehow I'd pulled it off. Why, then, couldn't I bring myself to take a bite? Why did this avocado look like a lifeless turtle shell? Why did I, too, feel like a shell of myself? My body was in revolt.

By this point, in my early-30s, I had invested thousands of dollars and years of my life into self-help books, self-improvement courses, and numerous therapists—you'd think I would have been better prepared to deal with an episode of unexpected Preservation Mode. The reason I was ill-equipped, I discovered, was not that I hadn't learned anything over all that time; it was that what I had been taught didn't help me. I wasn't trying to "regulate" my nervous system. I was trying to *completely overcome it,* as if I could maintain complete supremacy over my states of being. What does this look like? It's the yoga teacher who, despite being clearly annoyed, forces on a saccharine voice to appear "spiritual." It's the countless Christian and Buddhist spaces that, subtly or overtly, suggest that if you're not feeling "the spirit" or calm, you're somehow not "anointed" or "enlightened." It's the toxic positivity in workplaces that avoids addressing or repairing power imbalances. It's a man dismissing another man's emotions by calling him a "pussy." It's the relentless glorification of Connect Mode while scorning all other states.

As I stared at that avocado, unable to relish in its deliciousness let alone my personal triumph in performing my one-woman show, I thought of the Leonard Cohen song quoted at the beginning of this letter. I was searching for "the card that is so high and wild" that I'll never ever need another one. For me that wild card was art, and it was going to buy me out of the hell of dysregulation. I felt like maybe if I gave all my feelings to art, I wouldn't ever have to fully feel gross, dirty, and weak. All feelings that I associated with extreme isolation. I hated feeling them in my body.

I call this **Nervous System Supremacy**, and it's a tempting but ultimately unhealthy ambition. Aiming to only experience Connect Mode so that you never again feel the pain and uncertainty of fear and doubt and self-loathing—this is impossible. What's more: you wouldn't *want* this anyway. As Leonard Cohen says, "It doesn't leave you very much, not even laughter." If you were a business aiming to shame people into buying your spiritual product, this would be an incredibly effective strategy: convince them that two-thirds of their body is inherently disgusting or shameful, and then sell them the solution to "fix" it.

For years, I was a junkie for my craft, and this wasn't just because music is my great passion. Hyper-focusing on my art allowed me to retreat into the Superplay state—the fourth state—which helped me not to deal with stage fright, but with **life fright**. Life fright is just as it sounds: stage fright for the roles of our lives. To be fair, I had good reason to have life fright. With a chronically dysregulated system, it was stressful to show up for the roles of my life not knowing if my body would completely betray me. Hiding in the Superplay mode can relieve the pain and anxiety of this feeling, but if you remain there and neglect the other states, as I did, it can have disastrous results.

For me, this pattern began at the age of seven, when my sister died of cancer, and it didn't end until I was 34, when my life fell apart, which began with a severe freeze that lasted months. The moment I sat staring at that avocado, unable to celebrate what should have been a big success, I fell from the weightlessness of Superplay back to earth. It was a very hard fall this time, as if every bone in my body had broken, and I had to learn to walk again. I was completely undone. Forcing my nervous system into regulation (i.e. Nervous System Supremacy) when it needed to embrace pain and discomfort—caused it to come crashing down from the safety of Superplay. I neglected the full spectrum of my nervous system because I was never taught to value it because I was never taught how to be safe with it.

But, Nervous System Supremacy shows up everywhere, and it especially hides in cultural frameworks:

Growing up as a Christian, in a Christian country, everything that wasn't beautiful, kind, nice, compassionate, and shiny, was "sin." And, even though it was deeply unconscious, I believed these "bad," "lower" feelings needed to be cleaned, scrubbed, and Cloroxed from my body. Dysregulation was the "devil" and regulation was, well, "Jesus"! I was no longer Christian, but the supremacy lived in my body.

As a woman, growing up in a patriarchal country, I learned to preen, pluck, fix, and buy my way out of the ugliness that *was* my body and emotions. The feminine was dirty, emotional and tempting, opposed to the masculine's clean, rational, powerful. I was now a card carrying feminist, but the supremacy lived in my body.

While anyone who can't feel at home in the Connect-Mode state is vulnerable to Nervous System Supremacy, there are aspects of it that are urgent and pernicious to let continue living in our bodies and this is it:

The same language we use to shame marginalized people is the same language we use to shame the nervous system; like lazy, dark, dirty, diseased, stupid, etc. Just as patriarchy has done with whiteness, the culture, including psychologists, did with the nervous system. This is of course disturbing, and hard to unsee once you see this parallel. Immigrants and people of color do not need to be "cleaned" with Christianity, or bleached with whitening creams and neither does your nervous system. Your dysregulation is also not dirty, diseased, or "dark." It sounds absurd to say or write, but this is the cultural waters in which we swim.

Unfortunately, I too had no idea the level at which I believed I could stay out of the "dirty" mess of dysregulation. Instead, I tried fruitlessly to *beat it*, to *win the game*, so to speak. It was a fool's errand. What I needed was a way to manage *all* of the states, to find use in each of them as a means of befriending or regulating all of them. If you've ever felt lost, stuck, or frustrated, I understand because I've been there. I've been there many times, in fact. I am just like my clients; the only difference was I hit a wall so hard I had to find a method to move forward.

I'd like to pause here:

I urge caution in using this phrase within a "woke" lexicon that weaponizes language to shame yourself or others. This term is meant as an invitation to explore collective shame, not as a tool for judgment. As you'll see later in the book, it is our responsibility to steer our own ship. While we may share a collective fear of our defense states, that fear does not grant anyone license to abuse, berate, or harm others who hold differing perspectives or shame their own nervous system.

No one is a "Nervous System Supremacist"; they are simply a temporary victim of a lack of nervous system education. If someone is struggling with the vulnerability of their dysregulation, they deserve more compassion, not less. As a guiding principle, it is a term intended to dismantle hierarchies inside your own nervous system states, not to be used as a weapon.

Back to art:

Art may feel safer than life, but its function is to *reflect* your life, not to biologically support it. You wouldn't build a house on a mirror—you hang them carefully to see yourself. Your Connect Mode is the concrete that creates a strong foundation for Superplay. If you feel like your practice is a pile of broken mirrors, please know it's not your fault, but we do need to sweep up the broken glass and start building a strong foundation for our craft. This means there is no way to "win" the game of escaping human pain and suffering but there is a way to turn around nightmare performances, voice lessons, and have artistic processes that are productive and nurturing. Since there is no way to win, the work of tuning your nervous system never ends. It's an infinite game, whose pleasure is simply that we get to play.

The foundation of a human or homosapien nervous system is the "social engagement system" or the Connect Mode, during which you sense enough safety in your environment for your internal biology to connect with other people. So, the next term to learn on our nervous system journey is ***Co-regulation.*** This just means two nervous systems are vibrationally singing the song of safety to each other, back and forth. Co-regulation is a nervous system dance of equality. Co-regulation is like a human tuning fork. Of course, we also have the opposite, co-dysregulation (not a traditional polyvagal term), which are two nervous systems that can't find safety with each other. In music, we call this dissonance.

I know what you might be thinking, "The core of the nervous system safety is *other people?* Oh barf." I hear you, but stick with me.

The origins of this theory of a nervous system states trace back to the psychologist and neuroscientist Dr. Stephen Porges, who first posited what he called "**polyvagal theory**" (named after the vagus and dorsal vagus nerve), which he also referred to as the "science of safety." In addition to coming up with the idea in the first place, Dr. Porges's most significant contribution was his insight that people can face profound danger but still thrive with enough trusted and secure co-regulators. This means it's not just levels of danger that affected my ability to recover after that performance, it was also how I connected to the people I had around me.

What if my mistake wasn't that I headed toward too much danger, but that I didn't surround myself with enough safety while taking on that danger?

At the time of the avocado incident, I was surrounded by a roommate who made me feel unsafe, my mother's presence was starting to induce extreme anxiety, and a lot of my best friends were starting to "settle down" and naturally have less time for socializing. While I loved our 10-piece band, it was all business, and I hadn't taken the time to deepen our relationships in ways that were nourishing. I had no idea at the time that this lack of co-regulation may have contributed to my nervous system's decision to put me in Preservation Mode (freeze).

Life thrives in community more than it does in isolation. When you're socially isolated from warm secure relationships, it's like being in a house with a shaky foundation—any fun, uninhibited exploration could cause the house to crumble. *Anyone* in a collapsing building will cover their head and immediately stop working, writing, composing, whatever. You are not weak or lazy or unhealthy for prioritizing your safety if this house falls apart. Similarly, during immobilizing nervous system states, your instinctive response is understandably self-preservation, from which it can be very difficult to pull yourself out. Trusted people in your life, your co-regulators, are the best way to get yourself back from danger. Unfortunately, when you are shut down, you aren't exactly attracting socialization, you are repelling it. Luckily, solving for that biological irony is what this book is for.

I'm kicking things off with these two ideas—**Nervous System Supremacy**[2] and **Co-Regulation**—because artists can inadvertently develop two unfortunate habits: first, to seek out cure-all solutions to their nervous system issues, and then, not finding a cure, retreating into the Superplay mode to avoid the pain of reality. Art is a singular enterprise, but life doesn't have to be. I want to begin by asserting two truths I've found in my many years dealing with these issues:

1. If you try to *overcome* your nervous system your life will become smaller and sicker; if you lovingly *manage and unshame* it, your life will expand and heal.

2. If you can, go to the people you love first. *Then*, go to art.

These concepts intertwine. Many artists mistakenly believe that art *is* their regulation, but all they're doing is avoiding the complexities of the other states and the system as a whole. If you treat art like a person you will get more and more lonely. When you are sad, defeated, hopeless, helpless, on the floor with a knife in your back, when you have no love to give, go to the people you love first. Then, go to art. Art isn't made to hold you like people are. It's just made to reflect you, us, and the world.

This of course, can sometimes be helpful but if you are always coping in the Superplay mode and not Connect Mode, the muscle of real connection

---

2. Culturally we embrace more of a nervous system spectrum if they are white, male, and able-bodied. Aggression is "confidence" and direct, present communication is celebrated. Presence that emanates from the Connect-Mode state in women and specifically black women has historically been threatening to systems of power. They have been systematically kicked out of our presence over and over again. This is a kind of nervous system trauma that we must never give up the fight to restore.

We have also erased the ability for men to be transparent about having a "freeze" response or being emotional. To ensure men went to war, PTSD was not included into the DSM. The shame a person must unpack around their nervous system will include their social location. I believe that to shift the violence that is perpetuated from the male body, they too must be included in the ways that Nervous System Supremacy hurts everyone.

gets weak. The Superplay state has no risk, so it's tempting to exile yourself there and even more tempting to view it as healthy. But a balanced self requires fluidity, variation, and near constant change.

The idea that art and performing isn't always safe is not always welcome news, because it means the quick fixes promoted by self-help grifters and cynical corporations aren't the answer. I know this is not what a lot of artists and therapists want to hear. We want to believe the fantasy that art is inherently healing, perfect, beautiful. Art is a great (and maybe the best) coping mechanism but it's still just coping. We want more than coping. **We are social animals.** We need to be held, seen, and loved, by REAL people, not just art. When life hands you avocados, in other words, it doesn't mean that avocados are *all* you have. You deserve to be connected with just because you were born, because you are human.

To play with the Music for this "Muscle" try this Tool:

TOOL 3F: Building Your Minyan

This is nervous system supremacy.

"We have good notes and bad notes."

Gross, dirty, dangerous, feminine, weak, ugly, embarrassing, lower.

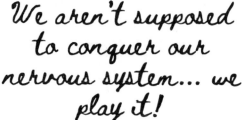

We aren't supposed to conquer our nervous system... we play it!

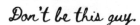

Don't be this guy.

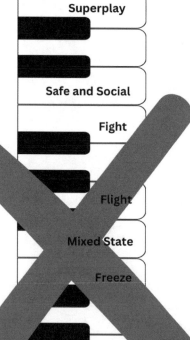

All notes have a purpose!

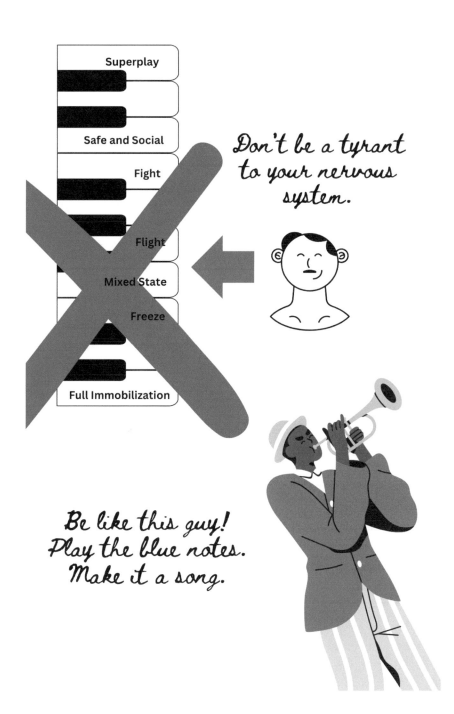

Letter #3: The Astronauts

"I'm feeling very still
And I think my spaceship knows which way to go."

—David Bowie, "Space Oddity"

Dear Artist,

Before we move any further, I feel it's important to orient you in relation to the nervous system, because it's a complex set of ideas involving overlapping states and issues stemming from any number of sources.

There is no "bad" state, no "correct" one, and no ultimate solution that eliminates anything negative or scary. If you are human with a nervous system, you will experience dysregulation inside this flesh rocket until you die.

In the interest of establishing the complicated dynamic between people and their nervous systems, I want to take you through a thought experiment, one we will return to again and again as a way to foster a deeper understanding. Without further ado, I present to you the Astronauts who do, you know—NASA-type shit.

Let's focus on one of these Astronauts. Let's call her Sally (shoutout to her trailblazing namesake, Sally Ride). Sally operates just as the other Astronaut except for one difference. She was born in outer space in a little ship and has parents who haven't explained to her how her ship works. They haven't needed to. So far she's extremely functional and even gets amazing space grades!

But, Sally does not know that Ground Control (our version of NASA) is actually in the driver's seat. In fact, Sally isn't even aware that GC *exists at all*. She functions as if her ship is mainly run by *her*. When the ship is jolted into G force, she thinks, "I did that." When the ship suddenly shuts down and some of her power goes out, she thinks, "Damn, I must have done that too!" Or if the ship is cruising, exploring, and communicating with other ships, she thinks, "Yep! Still me." She's not a narcissist, she just has no clue there's a whole building full of engineers, space doctors, and PHDs back on the ground making all these decisions for her nervous system (I mean, spaceship).

You see, although Ground Control is made up of a lot of people and a series of complex systems working for the welfare of the astronauts, it differs from NASA in some major ways. First of all, GC cannot communicate with Sally directly, it speaks to her through the behavior of the ship. Their instructions are delivered through subtle changes in the ship's behavior, without Sally's awareness. GC merely responds to the situations Sally is in and sends energetic instructions based on that information. GC also has the #1 job of managing the ship's metabolism. When to use fuel and for what, and also it changes the functions of the ship depending on their assessment. Because there is no communication channel, GC can't confer with Sally as to whether she is comfortable with their orders, or even if she agrees that the order is necessary. From their perspective, what she wants doesn't matter because their job is just to keep her and the ship alive and running.

In this metaphor, Ground Control represents something called **Neuroception**, which is the process by which our brain attempts to assess how much risk and safety is present at any given moment *before* we are conscious of that risk. This is bidirectional (afferent and efferent nerves) which means that the ship is sending NASA messages as well. So, when I say "brain," I'm also including the messages this brain gets from outer space. The ship, I mean body, is always looking for safety and danger, and sending signals of safety and danger to other bodies as well. This happens unconsciously, involuntarily, and so lightning quick that it's already in motion before we're even aware anything is happening. Sally gets messages from her neuroception, and then steers the ship.

Neuroception tries to protect us, but it isn't always the best judge. It can misperceive a non-threat for something menacing and send us into hysterics for no legitimate reason. It's a protective force that sends movement to the ship, even if it's not totally sure it's in danger. Think of these ships like a huge creative investment—no one wants to lose one just because they weren't careful enough. We'll explore Neuroception more deeply later, but for now, I just want you to grasp how strange it can be to navigate the space between what we *think* we control in our internal world and what's really happening beneath the surface that shapes those states.

Think of those moments when Sally finds herself working on a creative project that feels off because very subtly her ship is acting up, and she shut that project down. That's what happens when neuroception, the nervous system's radar, makes a mistake. And if Sally's being honest, she'd notice this happening more often as she gets older. For example, the cautious instincts that kept her safe in her younger years are now wearing her down. But if Sally doesn't even realize that Ground Control is quietly steering her, how can she hope to tackle these issues, let alone fix them?

Before Sally can make any real progress, she first has to learn about, and accept, the existence of **Ground Control.** And that's tough, because we all want to believe we're the ones calling the first shots. It's unsettling to admit that there's another force—the nervous system—we have to navigate before we can even think about finding real regulation or making decisions about how to steer the ship. On Earth, accepting that we *are* "Ground Control" is really acknowledging that we're more tied to nature than we ever imagined, and that we have far less free will than we'd like to believe. It can shake your whole sense of self, and it takes time to really grasp. We don't get to choose our nervous system states—they're chosen for us, over and over, without fail. And there's no escaping that truth. We can't clean it up or fix it. Instead, we accept our GC's offering and steer from there.

You might read this chapter in just a minute, but it could take a year of practice before this becomes a real, lived experience in your body. Wait—so it wasn't my fault that my acting teacher pushed me into a freeze state? It wasn't my fault that in my voice lesson, when I didn't feel safe, I shifted into Move Mode and ended up with rigid, judgmental thoughts or stiff muscles in my throat? Exactly. You never choose your states—Ground Control does that for you. Our job is to learn our biology so intimately that we can shift it. Just like a saxophone player can switch keys effortlessly after years of practice, we can train ourselves to understand that we don't choose our nervous system states, but we *can* learn which techniques to use to shift them.

Sally now realizes that just being aware of GC gives her more agency over her Astronaut life. With this in mind, **Sally can say to GC, "Thank you, Ground Control! I'm in the driver's seat now."**

It's showtime.

You're on stage, and suddenly a huge wave of adrenaline hits. Instead of resisting, you say, *Thank you, Ground Control!* This is the first step toward reclaiming your power, both on and off the stage. At this point, you don't need to label how you feel—just notice what's rising up and recognize that the impulse flowing through you isn't your choice.

To play with the "Music" for this "Muscle" try this Tool in the Tool Library in the second half of this book.

TOOL 1F: Thank You, Ground Control

Letter #4: The Phones

"I'm at a payphone, trying to call home, all of my change I spent on you."
—""Payphone" by Maroon 5 ft. Wiz Khalifa

Dear Artist,

"Phylogenetic" refers to how different species or living things are connected through their evolutionary journey, like tracing back a family tree to see where we all came from. Just like an artist might explore the roots and influences of different art styles over time, phylogenetics looks at how living creatures have evolved and branched out from common ancestors. It's about understanding the story of life's creative process, where each new form builds on what came before, much like the evolution of artistic movements.

As we explore the history of how our nervous system states evolved, I'm going to steer us away from calling earlier versions of "us," primitive. They are primitive, but due to the shaming of a culture of white supremacy, it's a knee jerk response to feel like we are above lower states when *we are them.* They are still inside us. They are intimate to us. And I caution you from looking down on these parts of us, as this shame prevents us from seeing how they function to keep us healthy as a whole. Also, I'd like to have some reverence and respect for the fact that when earlier versions of our nervous system states (mentioned in chapter one) evolved, they were the shiny new biological technology of its time.

Please don't get overwhelmed by the word phylogenetic, (I only say that because I did). You know that unique and joyful feeling of seeing pictures of your great-grandparents in black and white? That sense of connection to the past? This is exactly what we're going to do with the nervous system states. So gather 'round. Let's go back in time and see what our states used to look like and where they came from.

In the interest of clarifying the complicated dynamics between **Play/ Connect**, **Move**, and **Preservation** Modes—and how **Superplay** comes into things—I want to briefly talk about the phylogenetic history of nervous systems by talking about phones simply because as a songwriter, there are just some great metaphors, and this one is perfect for the quirks of our nervous systems history.

For the younger folks, we gotta talk about the history of phones...

One of the earliest versions of our current phone was the rotary phone. It had a receiver connected by a cord to a bulky body with a dial. To call someone, you had to spin the dial with your finger, and the phone was plugged into the wall, limiting movement. Calls were local, and the device was shared by the whole house. At the time, this was cutting-edge technology.

Later, landlines emerged with push buttons and features like call waiting, followed by mobile phones. These early mobiles, like the massive one used by Zack Morris in *Saved by the Bell*, allowed people to make calls on the go but were clunky. Over time, cell phones like the Nokia and Blackberry introduced texting, email, and even basic cameras, though they still had limits like complicated international calls.

Then came the smartphone. The iPhone revolutionized everything, combining the best of earlier phones with new features like high-quality cameras, video calling, and social media. Suddenly, phones became tiny computers, essential for navigating modern life. While today's smartphones can do everything their predecessors could, the older phones can't even begin to keep up with modern capabilities.

We are currently in the process of interacting with newer versions of the phone, the oculus, which I imagine will eventually be seamlessly incorporated into our lives without the physical bulk.

Think of these phones as metaphors for the evolution of humanity's nervous system. In our humble beginnings, all that we required was the rotary version of our nervous system, which is the **Preservation Mode**. We were simpler creatures (bony fish, in fact) in a much more straightforward ecosystem. Also, just like the rotary phone the hardware of this is more primitive which includes the dorsal vagal nerve. There is no fat on this nerve so it's a slow signal. If anyone remembers dial up modems, it's that slow. Or, think of how long it takes for Eeyore to respond to Winnie the Pooh. When our nervous system is in this older mode, which includes older biological hardware, it takes a long time to get signals out. Just as it was probably pretty exciting to go from telegram to a rotary phone, when tiny organisms could finally go into fight/flight instead of freeze, this was exciting and new biological technology! We will get into why this state is so hard on humans later, but for now I just want you to take in how primitive this immobilization response is. So when you think of Preservation Mode, which most of us know as "freeze," I want you to remember it's slow and it's also less complex. It does a couple things really well, but if you ask it to do more, you are in trouble.

Also, just like when we feel numb or not like ourselves when shutdown, a rotary phone doesn't give us a full picture of safety. We can hear a voice but unlike later technologies we can't see faces, and the sound wasn't great. That's why when you want to create distortion in Logic Pro (audio software) you can use the "telephone" sounds to create a fuzzy sounding voice! We just get less information in Preservation Mode

The landline and mobile phones are like **Move Mode**, with the landline representing the "fight" (standing your ground and defending your home) and the mobile standing in for "flight," with its portability and personal use. As humans evolved, the need to evade predators and defend their clans became more prevalent, so this state, like the phones, *includes* the aspects of **Preservation Mode** and adds new components. We also got new technology with this mode as well. We now have animals with powerful engines (large hearts), and a chief of fuel (larger brains). This was a huge leap in our evolution. But animals that had this new technology also had the old technology as a backup for extreme danger. So, if these mobile phones got scared, they transformed into a rotary phone to avoid being eaten.

The first smartphones are like **Connect Mode**: they're more complex than their predecessors, they provide us with innumerable uses and include intelligent input from the creators. This new phone came with 1G in the beginning (mammals) which was a big deal, and then 5G (homosapiens and the whole homo crew of early humans), which is the ventral vagus nerve which allows us to cool down that Move Mode energy just enough for some serious connection. If you love cuddly animal videos on Instagram, this is the mode you are looking at. This new fatty and fast nerve allows us to respond quickly, to play, and to connect. And, this Connect Mode spans from small ancient animals collaborating in survival to the enormous complexity of our current modern human civilization. But again, we still have the older phones inside us! So, we also will have our Move Mode, and

Preservation Mode. Unfortunately because we have so many older phones waiting in the wings in our defense, it's more jarring for someone in 2025 to get stuck with a rotary phone. I don't know any phone number by heart except my own. This is the panic we feel when dysregulated, but we don't know how to get back to the future because we have such old hardware and the demands of a smartphone world.

Our newest state, what I call the **Superplay Mode**, is a revelatory extension of new phone technology. This mode is like an oculus because it's the state of pretend. This was when humans not only could use their Connect Mode to get their needs met, they could also pretend to be other humans to explore their own humanity. This also has hardware which advances in the prefrontal cortex. How do I know this? My dog has a Connect Mode, but she can't play Bette Davis. The nervous system now begins to play itself as an instrument just like VR technology adds a completely new dimension of reality to our play. Just like our phone upgrades, our nervous system upgrades are becoming more playful and imaginative.

So when we talk about states of the nervous system, think of the phones as capturing the ways each state has been folded into the next one. In this way the states are not hierarchical, but holarchical as they are in fact linear in the order in which we regulate and dysregulate, like nesting dolls, the latest, most prominent one the big doll encasing all others.

This nesting explains confounding questions about why an actor in Preservation Mode in a difficult acting class might suddenly go into Move Mode before they feel safe again. We reliably move in the order of these nesting dolls and knowing this order and how to steer can be life-changing. This means anyone coming out of freeze is going to not feel immediately safe **and needs to go through Move Mode first.** This is massively important information for any voice or acting instructor helping a student back to safety. As we take each mode one by one, remember that being human is a bit messy because we have so many modes nested inside us.

The problem with trauma is, you can't ask someone to use outdated technology to serve present-day needs long term. So many artists feel they are not talented or hard working enough when they are trying to get a Masters in art when they are a rotary phone. It's hard enough to be the wrong phone for activities you don't care very much about, but it can be even more devastating when we don't have the biological function we need to pursue our dreams. And as artists we are often trying to sing, or act, or play, with technology that simply doesn't support connection, and we blame ourselves for it. We will learn many tools in this book to get to the right phone. I want to leave you with hope that there is a method to switch phones with more control and reliability. Do you see how cruel it would be to shame a music or acting student or tell them they might not be cut out for their craft simply because they are stuck in an older nervous system phone? This shame scares the body and tells it to double/triple down on staying in an older version of our phone.

Let's quickly go back to space. NASA doesn't know what to do when you are in danger, it just sends old programs to handle it. If it worked in the forest for hunter-gatherers, it should keep you alive right? Well that's where we are headed next. Sometimes these older programs are not so helpful.

To play with the Music for this "Muscle" try this Tool:

Tool 3 (P): Shake & Surge

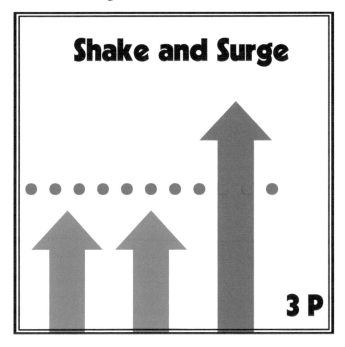

Ps. This tool is the bridge between the rotary phone and the landline (Preservation mode to Move mode). We will cover this later, but notice how each tool leads you up the sequence of phones as they evolved, we are not trying to jump or bypass from a rotary phone to an oculus.

Superplay
150 Thousand Years

Play/Connect Mode
200 Million Years ago

Move-Mode
400 Million Years ago

Preservation-Mode
500 Million Years ago

Letter #5: Houston, We Have a Problem

"I fell in love with the war, and nobody told me it ended."

—Mitski, *"A Pearl"*

Dear Artist,

Now that we have some basic knowledge of the nervous system modes of being, let's address the obvious, and why we are all here. What happens if let's say Ground Control (neuroception), sends our space vehicle a Move Mode response when we need to be exploring our mission, or if it turns off our power right as we are landing on the moon, or what about if it's connective and playful when there is a dangerous ship approaching. Through the lens of, "The Science of Safety," (polyvagal theory), we would call this a "neuroceptive mismatch," but for most people it just feels like shame and stress. On stage, this is "stage fright," or in life let's just call it "life fright." We have these names for neuroceptive mismatches because they are unwanted. No one has haunted-house fright because that fright is expected and welcomed! Most of life's problems are simply a brain prediction we don't prefer. That's why there is so much power in accepting and embracing fright. It's no longer a problem, if we don't shame it or reject it. From there we can redirect it.

Why does the brain get it wrong sometimes? If we are what Fiona Apple calls an "extraordinary machine," why does Ground Control make so many mistakes! Are some of us just Santa's broken toys?

We will establish two really important ideas in this chapter:

Firstly, that your Ground Control can absolutely put you in a state that is not so great for your survival in space, this may include:

Overactive Defense Response in Safe Environments: This occurs when someone cannot calm their defense systems, such as fight, flight, or freeze, even though they are in a safe environment. This can result in hypervigilance and a persistent state of alarm, making it difficult to feel relaxed or connected. One example is stage fright.

Underactive Defense Response in Risky Environments: In contrast, this mismatch can also lead to an inadequate defense response in truly dangerous environments. The person may be dulled to risks and fail to engage appropriate survival mechanisms like fight or flight, leaving them vulnerable to harm.

But that doesn't exactly answer the question of why brain predictions are often wrong. *This is wild, so stick with me…*

Your Ground Control doesn't see the full picture that you see through your space ship's window.

I need to give you a new important detail about "Ground Control" which we now know as your brain's unconscious functioning. This is a brain-twister, but a hugely important detail:

Ground Control makes decisions based on the past, *only sometimes taking in new information.* Researcher Lisa Feldman Barrett refers to this part of our cognition as an airplane's "black box."

For example, let's say, hypothetically, Ground Control *could* look through the screen at the earth. If it has seen the earth many, many times, it takes too much power to run all that electricity, so it creates a *hallucination of earth instead.* Our brains do the same thing. Disturbing, I know. So, the brain quite literally constructs our reality, and takes a small amount of new information in. Why? **Just to conserve processing power.** In the wild, energy is a hugely precious resource and you wouldn't want to waste it on things you have seen before.

Why is this so problematic? Well, because it tends to run past images for Sally and also sends her predictions based on the past. Let's pretend that last year it was pretty rough out in space. Sally actually almost died in an accident with an alien. Ground Control is now overly defensive and tends to put her in Move Mode all the time. Since this wastes a lot of gas, they often have to put her in Preservation Mode quite a lot as well. Lately she's felt like her life is a total rollercoaster. Of course, she can say, "Thank you Ground Control," but until she has new tools to course-correct the ship herself, it's a bit rough out here in space.

Because Ground Control is running a hallucination, they don't see that everything is totally smooth out there and mistake a passing asteroid for Darth Vader. This is what happens to our bodies in an acting class when we know we are safe but our body is screaming, "Run, defend!" The trauma of that bad year in space has changed the predictions that Sally gets every day.

In the arts there are so many kinds of neuroceptive mismatches, I won't be able to cover them all but just remember, this just means the brain predicts a state based on its experience that is no longer advantageous for your survival. Sally's ship is not temporarily "tuned" to danger. Here are some specific examples:

Vishwajeet was cast as an actor in a show he really hates. It's for a bunch of old people in a stuffy town and he has to play a stereotype that makes him feel completely disconnected. Normally, he shames his nervous system states, thinking he caused them. Because of this enmeshment, he can't see that his dysregulation is convincing him that his castmates hate him. When he hits the stage he thinks he should be "regulated," but that is almost never the case. He needs to be in Connect Mode but Ground Control gave him Move Mode instead. Since he rejects this state and hasn't learned to embrace it, his neuroception predicts Preservation Mode.

Amanda is auditioning for a local Shakespeare company and the director wants to meet her later for coffee! She is so excited because she thinks he is going to offer her the role. She is pretty new to theater and also grew up in a small town. She is wide-eyed and a little sheltered but has a huge passion for musical theater and is damn good at it. When she gets to the coffee shop, this director says a bunch of vague and weird things that she doesn't understand, but instead of asking for clarity, her nervous system says, "keep connecting!" She keeps smiling at him hoping he will offer her the role. As they walk out of the shop, he kisses her aggressively, and says, "You got the role." Finally, her body gives her an appropriate signal that she feels shocked and enraged, but she can't seem to get it out! Her system is locked in Connect Mode and she said, "Oh, thank you so much, I can't wait." For days, she can't figure out why or how all of that happened and she is in a real mess. She wanted to be in Move Mode and tell him to "fuck off," but got locked in Connect Mode at that moment. Dr. Porges calls this "appeasement." Also, Ground Control never experiences anything like this before, so it didn't know to give her signals of danger but will do so from now on.

Cam showed up to band practice late. He never means to be but he has ADHD and experiences time-blindness. It's also just embarrassing sometimes so when his bandmate Kim said, "Dude, we only have 30 min left in the space. This really sucks!" The intensity of her voice triggered his body, and he felt some Move Mode energy but was trapped in the room with his bandmates and went into Preservation Mode. He felt numb, cold, and could barely get a word out. Sure, Cam had some serious trauma but has no idea why this might be happening. Suddenly his fingers don't work on his guitar, and he feels like a total failure. He's terrified the band will fire him, but he's also deeply hurt and angry.

There are so many versions of this but my favorite way to remember neuroceptive mismatch is Mitski's song lyric, "I fell in love with the war, but nobody told me it ended."

I want to be clear that **this mismatch is not a disease and your general sensitivities are not a disease. All that said, long-term dysregulation is the source of many, many of the diseases in the DSM (Diagnostic and Statistical Manual of Mental Disorders)** (if you are supported by a therapist or psychiatrist, you can talk to them about the Fox Method). It's a temporary and totally rewirable brain prediction gone wrong. The good news is that by tuning the nervous system back to safety enough times, we can slowly let Ground Control understand that things have changed in outer space. But no one has perfect neuroception, and living with its clunky nature is just part of being human. The real power is knowing that the state your neuroception chose is not and never was your fault.

Finally, if you are a rotary phone and need to be a smartphone, just know that this gap is just a huge pain. It's always so uncomfortable even when we manage to shift (which we will learn how to do in later chapters.) **What I want you to hold is how normal it is to have a neuroceptive mismatch.** Our nervous system is a learning machine and sometimes when it learns the wrong nervous system state prediction for your survival, we need to rewire it by helping it calm or to activate.

Trauma is a kind of long-term neuroceptive mismatch. This means Ground Control decides that when you are reminded of a past danger, your GC sends you to the wrong state. So, it might send you to Connect Mode when you need to run away, or into Preservation Mode when you need to audition for that play you so badly want to be a part of.

If you are my age (beginning to get gray hair or maybe losing some) just know that neuroscience didn't even know that the brain could be this deeply neuroplastic until the early 2000s. Basically, as old as the Backstreet Boys. We didn't have a chance. But we know now. Let's let all that shame drip off us and continue our journey.

When we have a mismatch, the first step is acknowledging that GC has chosen a feeling in our body. Soon we will learn to find your state on the nervous system ladder and even learn to shift states. For now, try the **Thank you, Ground Control Tool** one more time. Even the mismatches were not your fault, but soon we will take the wheel and steer ourselves.

Pause For Poop

When we have a neuroceptive mismatch, we feel like something is wrong. In a way it is! We need to survive and function in one state but our body is responding in a way that is opposite to what we need. In the era of internet psychology, you may be *constantly examining yourself.* When it comes to mysterious emotions, you don't always need to analyze them or figure them out *all the time.* You are not Freud or Jung. You're just Dan from Youngstown, Ohio, whose thoughts are racing about a record release.

I like to think of emotions as poop. Yep, poop. When you poop, it would be wild to pick up your soggy poop and say, "I'm just so nervous. I can't let this poop go until I *know* if there are carrots or broccoli in there! If I let it go, I'll never know WHAT'S IN MY POOP." If any friend saw you, they would say, "Dude, man, let go of the poop!!! Flush it!"

Emotions are meant to be felt and embraced in safety as a daily practice. If you want to analyze, I recommend journaling or bring it to a psychoanalyst. They are specifically trained poop decoders and some are quite good. Just remember that not everything has to be understood, but it does need to be felt. Not only that, our activation and pain (core-affect) need to be attended to.

The "Poop Bit"

When you are emotionally constipated you will be in a lot of pain, a lot of the time. Just know it's safe to not always know "why" and sometimes the "why" can keep us stuck.

Letter #6: "Whole"-archy vs. Hierarchy

Dear Artist,

The history of phones is an incredibly useful way to think of the nervous system, and we will return again and again to those reference points as we move along. But there's just one little thing I wanted to take a beat and elaborate on.

When I first heard the term "hierarchical" in relation to the nervous system, it felt like a contradiction. For a system that's meant to be adaptable and fluid, "hierarchy" sounded rigid, almost oppressive. It immediately brought to mind those dominance hierarchies or managers from my old restaurant jobs breathing down my neck—definitely not the vibe you'd want from your own body.

If the word "hierarchical" gives you a similar visceral reaction, you're not alone. But let's unpack it a bit. There's a writer named Arthur Koestler who sheds some light on this, offering a perspective that might make this idea feel a little less stifling.

In his book "The Ghost in the Machine," Arthur Koestler suggests that "wherever there is life, it must be hierarchically organized." This idea might seem counterintuitive at first, but his point is that complex systems—like our nervous system—can only thrive when simpler, stable systems are there to support and protect them. It's less about dominance and more about building upward from a foundation of support.

I know, this may sound a little abstract, but here's the beautiful part: in nature, anything "higher" on the evolutionary ladder doesn't destroy what came before—it includes it. And in doing so, it transcends. Think of it this way: cells didn't look at atoms and say, "Ew, I need to be special." They included them. Organelles didn't snub cells; they evolved by embracing them. It's a process of inclusion and transcendence, and that's where the magic of growth and complexity happens.

But Koestler doesn't stop there. He digs deeper into what we really mean when we use words like "part" and "whole," terms that seem straightforward until you try to apply them to nature. We tend to think of a "part" as something fragmentary or incomplete, and a "whole" as something that's self-contained, needing no further explanation. But Koestler challenges that by pointing out that, in nature, there are no absolutes in this sense. He writes, "In this absolute sense [they] just do not exist anywhere, either in the domain of living organisms or of social organizations."

What we actually find in nature, he argues, are intermediary structures—what he calls "sub-wholes." These exist on different levels of complexity, and depending on your perspective, they can act like either parts or wholes.

Koestler uses a powerful metaphor here: he describes each part of a hierarchy as being like the Roman god Janus, with two faces looking in opposite directions. One face looks down toward the lower levels and acts as a self-contained whole, while the other face looks upward and functions as a dependent part of something larger.

Frustrated by the lack of terminology to describe this dual nature, Koestler coined the term "holon"—combining the Greek word *holos* (meaning whole) with the suffix "-on," as in proton or neutron, to suggest that these entities are both parts and wholes at once. This idea of holons reminds us that in nature, nothing exists in isolation—it's always both connected and complete, depending on how you view it. Everything is a whole and a part.

Thus we get the word **Holarchy**, which is a better term for our nervous system, as it's a system that houses a series of dual-natured and increasingly complex parts which taken together form an even more complex whole. So when I refer to the structure of the nervous system, this is the word I'll use.

An example of a holarchical structure in the arts can be found in **collaborative theater productions**. In a traditional hierarchical structure, the director often sits at the top, controlling the overall vision, with actors, designers, and crew functioning under strict roles. However, in a **holarchical theater production**, the creative process is decentralized, and every contributor operates as a "holon"—an autonomous whole contributing to and interacting with the larger artistic vision.

This does not mean that there is no order or leadership, but it does mean that each whole is directed towards the larger vision, and is given appropriate levels of power and autonomy. In biology, any part, like a cell, that doesn't want to play in the vision of humaning, is called cancer. That said, it is leadership that makes sure all the cells have what they need to cooperate. Remember this when you negotiate your arts contracts.

Ok, back to the states:

Connect Mode when it "looks down" from the Holarchy is a whole which contains both Move Mode and Preservation Mode. But here's what's really cool. Animals with this state (like humans and my dog) have Move Mode and Preservation Mode for defense states, but when the animal is safe, all of a sudden Move Mode is playful fierce competition and the Preservation Mode can be a chill night with a lover reading and saying nothing. All of a sudden these older energies are repurposed for connection! Every time something takes the lead in a Holarchy, it is truly revelatory. You think, "Damn, I can't believe nature did that! How unexpected."

When Connect Mode "looks up" at the hierarchy, it is just a part of the Superplay state. The Superplay state is now the whole which transcends and includes all states, and the defense states, but this time instead of playing, it's a kind of hyper-play in which the animal starts pretending to be someone or something else in order to explore the human psyche itself. Again, revelatory, no one saw theater or songwriting coming.

As long as we don't mess it up and become extinct, in 200,000 years, I can guarantee there will be **another human state that transcends and includes the others**. Again, this doesn't shame and diminish the other states, it transcends and includes them. It is curious to me whether the Superplay state is itself a solid nervous system state or a transitional state that is still evolving. Either way, it's clearly a new evolutionary development in our Holarchy.

When you think about incredibly successful performers, they don't dominate an audience, they transcend and include them. It's a mistake to say, "that's not a good audience," because the role of the performer is to lead and create a new level of complexity. The audience walks into the room as parts, but when they are led by your nervous system they become a new whole, a kind of **nervous system organism.** This can only happen if the performer doesn't try to dominate an audience by wanting them to be anything else than what they are. But, because this new Superplay mode is new, it is also unstable. Plays and performances are temporary moments of revelation and then the new whole breaks apart and becomes parts again, but leaving as richer, healthier parts.

I love thinking about ancient humans interacting with a state of pretend. I imagine the feeling that a young Greek child must have felt walking home from seeing Antigone through fireflies and dirt roads, just having felt the power of 5,000 other nervous systems all gel as one watching a powerful play under the moon. All I know is that the nervous system is trying to lead us into the direction of unity and connection, not in isolation and violence as it evolves. That force makes me proud to be in this body and trusting of its intelligence.

Finally, if you have been hurt by artistic dominance hierarchies, remember this. They are anti-nature and because of that, tend to self-implode. It is unnatural to dominate the "parts" of any system unless a system or culture is locked in Move Mode. In fact, every Holarchy honors its parts. An unhealthy part that tries to dominate a whole is called, well, cancer. Holarchies are strong and for them to remain stable they must honor and nourish their parts.

Again, remember that when you negotiate your contracts, "Hey! I am a part. But, boy do I care about the whole. For me to play this part well, I'm going to need a lot more money. And, I can promise you, if I'm a well-taken-care-of "part," your play is going to go very, very well.

When you ask yourself, should I take this gig? Should I do this show? Ask yourself if your nervous system will be well cared for by those in power. Don't be afraid to ask this question to the people you are in deference to. No leader is even close to perfect, but there are leaders who want to protect your autonomy, choice, and ability to lead your own Holarchy (your body).

Later in the book, this framework will also guide us to become fantastic nervous system leaders on and off stage, but for now, let's learn about the states, so that when we say "Thank You, Ground Control," we have more specificity.

Finally, I'll leave you with the Tuning Fork Tool. When you lead a Holarchy you are on a mission (a show, a zoom meeting, a rehearsal) which you must keep in line, but you also are responsible for respecting the autonomy of every part/person in the room to whom you lead. Also, because your nervous system is the leader, everyone will tune to your nervous system. So try this tool.

To play the Music for this "Muscle" try this Tool:

Tool 1L: "I am the tuning fork."

Holarchy

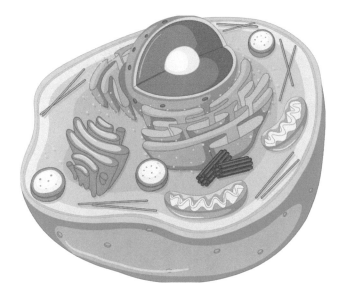

A cell
doesn't say, "Ewe, gross,
mitochondria--
it transcends and includes.

Don't shame your parts!

Dominance Heirarchy

Lessens, diminishes, and exploits the "parts" in its care.

The States:

"We Are Ugly

But We Have

The Music"

- Leonard Cohen to Janis Joplin

Nervous System Harmonics

In music, harmonics are the natural overtones produced when an instrument is played. These overtones blend with the fundamental note, giving each instrument its distinctive timbre or tone color.

For instance, when you play a note on a violin, piano, or even with your voice, **you're not hearing just a single pure frequency, but a combination of the fundamental frequency and its harmonics.** These harmonics are what make a violin sound different from a piano, even when playing the same note. They add richness, depth, and complexity to the sound.

In music, when you play a "C" note, harmonics—also known as overtones—are naturally produced. These are higher-frequency sounds that vibrate in harmony with the fundamental note (the "C"). Each harmonic has a specific relationship with the fundamental pitch and forms part of the harmonic series.

Here are the first few harmonics of a fundamental "C" note:

1. **1st Harmonic (Fundamental):** C (the base note you're playing)
2. **2nd Harmonic:** C (one octave above the fundamental)
3. **3rd Harmonic:** G (a perfect fifth above the 2nd harmonic)
4. **4th Harmonic:** C (two octaves above the fundamental)
5. **5th Harmonic:** E (a major third above the 4th harmonic)
6. **6th Harmonic:** G (a perfect fifth above the 4th harmonic)
7. **7th Harmonic:** B♭
8. **8th Harmonic:** C (three octaves above the fundamental)

The first few harmonics (2nd, 3rd, 4th) are strong and clearly heard, contributing to the character of the "C" note. As you go higher in the harmonic series, the notes become more complex and softer, adding subtlety to the tone.

Nervous system harmonics is the idea that each nervous system state has common physical and mental features that appear with the state.

For example: Us vs. Them thinking, perfectionism, obsession, and black-and-white thinking are harmonics of the Move Mode "tonic."

The psychological, biological, neurochemical changes that come with the shifting into defense states are not "fixable." They come with dysregulation the same way harmonics come with a "tonic" or root note. Trying to erase them instead of getting curious about what our nervous system needs to anchor to safety is a twisted path. Embrace your harmonics as a means to determine which nervous system state you are currently in.

Sally is going to feel the harmonics of the ship before she realizes what state she is in. Unlike in music, we hear our nervous system harmonics first. They are clues to lead us to where we are on our nervous system GPS. We will learn our harmonics first and *then* learn how to find our nervous system on a map!

Every single note has many other
notes that pop out of it called
Harmonics...little weird but it's
true.
Here are some harmonics of move-
mode...

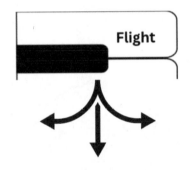

Black and white thinking,
dilated pupils,
increased heart rate
Us vs. them thinking
"My Audience Hates Me!!!"

We are music. Our nervous system
is tooooo.

Brownie
sugar
water
flour
chocolate
baking soda

Preservation-mode
numb
dissociated
low heart rate
high cortisol

Musical Note C:
1st Harmonic (Fundamental): C
(the base note you're playing)
2nd Harmonic: C
3rd Harmonic: G
4th Harmonic: C

Letter #7: Nervous System States, In Focus: Preservation Mode

"Like bringing a knife to a gunfight."

—Norma Jean, *"Creating Something Out of Nothing, Only to Destroy It"*

Dear Artist,

As we've established, understanding the nervous system states is vital for self-regulation, especially for working artists. Unfortunately, information about our biology is missing from the arts, as if performance was somehow an extraterrestrial pursuit. But artists' physiologies are no different than anyone else's. In fact, it is more important that artists are more acquainted with their states, as their primary instrument is their nervous system. So with this in mind, let's take a little time to go through the three already established modes (Polyvagal modes) before we get into the fourth one (the Fox Method).

Let's start by defining what creates a nervous system state, or what we call a "mode." Imagine baking a brownie—it requires ingredients like flour, sugar, water, oil, and chocolate. When all these ingredients come together in the right way, we get the finished product: a brownie. Similarly, a nervous system state (or mode) is made up of various behavioral ingredients. When enough of these ingredients combine, we label the state—such as "Preservation Mode" or "Move Mode." Without the ingredients, there's no state, just like there's no brownie without its key components. Some states share similar ingredients, but it's the quantity and type that determine the specific state. That's why we use these behavioral shifts (the ingredients) to help map our nervous system and understand what mode we're in.

For artists, instead of thinking of baking, here's another metaphor: the ingredients of a state are like musical harmonics that naturally accompany each state. Just as tiny harmonic notes emerge from a root or tonic note, behavioral shifts "pop out" of a nervous system state.

Let's start with a very old harmonic series or for the bakers a very ancient recipe for survival. You may know this as "freeze," but we will use new language to direct your mind to what exactly the state is pulling the body towards:

Preservation Mode, although we've envisioned it metaphorically as the rudimentary rotary phone, is probably the least understood nervous system defense state. In evolutionary terms, it's quite simple: when an animal senses danger, their body freezes or hides. In the wild, many predators' senses rely on movement or sound, so an immobilization (paralytic) response was an effective enough trait to last through natural selection. The muscles harden to ensure the predator can't get to its vital organs, and natural painkillers (analgesics) are released to ensure that if there is a struggle, the animal won't feel the attack. In fact, freezing often made organisms and animals invisible to their predators, so at the time (600 million years ago) this was some super snazzy nervous system hardware, definitely worth waiting at the phone store for.

We are not ancient creatures. Our Preservation Mode is wrapped in the nesting dolls of all our modes. So, we don't become bony fish when dysregulated, but that's where the function evolved from. Yet, your body can still lock you into Preservation Mode when faced with modern "dangers"—like auditions, networking, or the overwhelming challenge of trying something new. These threats aren't like predators that eventually leave, allowing us to return to safety. Instead, they take the form of abstract pressures—stress, grief, taxes, and countless other psychological burdens— that can show up anywhere, anytime, and linger for as long as they want. While we won't dive into the details here, it's important to know that we can retrain our internal environments to hold sensations that might have once sent us into freeze mode. We may not be able to rid ourselves of all the tigers, but we can make the tigers in our minds feel at home.

Rather than seeing this kind of Preservation Mode as a normal part of the experience of being human, many people—particularly artists— blame themselves for freezing. Before I read the work of Dr. Porges and others, I just assumed the nervous system was either stressed or not—an either/or functionality that seemed out of my control. Once I discovered that there were *three* states (before, obviously, I discovered the *fourth*), I immediately grasped what was happening to me at the time. I had lost interest in performing, I wasn't just severely depressed, I basically shut down completely. It felt like an insurmountable obstacle, as if my weaknesses had allowed my stagnation to take over; as if I weren't strong enough to pull myself out of it.

What was actually happening, though, was my body's perfectly natural physiological response to feeling unsafe, but the biological consequences were not obvious to me, uninitiated and with no nervous system education from my university. If the brain (which extends itself deep into the body through nerves) believes it's in peril, it will utilize a kind of security detail to protect itself. Like some over-protective superhero, the body will swoop in to save the day even when there isn't a day to be saved. Our minds, however, aren't always prepared for the change and assume the body has acted appropriately, thus we are prone to think that this mode is part of who we are—that, essentially, we're overly sensitive or unable to handle challenges—instead of a bodily mistake (a neuroceptive mismatch).

For a moment, though, let's imagine an actual emergency, a situation in which we are in real, animal-kingdom-style danger. Even though Preservation Mode was the first one established by evolution, it is, for us, the *last-ditch* effort to protect ourselves. This is why if you look at our nervous system card for Preservation Mode at the end of this chapter, there is no "lower" card than freeze. In the animal kingdom, for an animal in freeze there is only one lower state and that is death. We begin with the most recently formed state and move down the ladder to the older ones. As we are moved through our nervous system states, we are, in a sense, traveling backward in time to our ancestors who had *only* this mode for survival. We've developed much more complex states—which we will get into in the next chapters—that we depend on first, but if danger persists and the other states prove ineffective, our final gambit is a complete shutdown.

In non-literal situations, the fact that Preservation Mode is the last step creates problems because once we're frozen, there aren't any steps after that physiologically. It feels not like merely another mode of the nervous system but somehow like our default setting, as if the other modes acted as ornamentation to our true, less effective self underneath. What's worse is that while we remain in this state, anything we come across can seem unsafe to us—think of a person who survives a bloody war finding it difficult to trust people in the aftermath. Or, the inverse occurs: you allow into your life people or behaviors that are disastrous to you, because you're unable to distinguish between safe and harmful which is another byproduct of this state. For actors reading this book, I hope this brings up many characters you may have played in a Preservation Mode state.

Although much of the specific neurology of the nervous system is still not wholly understood, there are some physiological insights here worth pausing on. Preservation Mode is also known in Polyvagal Theory (PVT) as "dorsal vagal" state, so named because of the "vagus nerve," the one thought to be responsible for the "cooling down" of the heart rate and stress systems, and its location, "dorsal," referring to the back of the ventral nerve. This is proposed in PVT as a kind of "emergency brake" of the nervous system. Scientists are still duking it out over the details of this nerve, but one thing that is certain is that during the freeze state, energy flow to the prefrontal cortex is significantly lessened, which means that Preservation Mode actively prevents us from accessing our skills and abilities. If you find yourself psychologically paralyzed before a performance, even a regiment of thousands of hours of practice won't save you, because you won't be able to pull from that training. Similarly, in a non-performance situation, you also won't have as much access to your histories with people, all of your hard-earned wisdom almost gone from your head in those moments. This means, though, that the part of you that is "revealed" while in this mode isn't the real you, but merely you without many of the aspects that make you you. You are *less* you when in this state, not *more*.

I just want to pause for a moment. Even if we are "less" ourselves, it's so important not to judge or shame this physiological phenomenon in our bodies. Do we want to regulate a lot of the time? Yes! Is this a normal part of being human? Yes.

Preservation Mode is simple to simpler organisms and is frankly less cruel to them, but when thrust into the complexities of human existence, it becomes very much *not* simple. A rotary phone can only call other phones, nothing more, so if it were suddenly the only device you possessed in 2026, you would probably struggle to maneuver your way through life. In 1950 this phone was celebrated, but giving a kid this phone instead of an iPhone in 2026 is a cruel, grueling punishment. In the same way, the freeze state is insufficient to cope with our Connect Mode problems. Lucky for us, evolution wasn't merely finished.

Also the freeze state is a spectrum which includes various levels of activation and deactivation. Some in freeze can have bradycardia, which means that their heart rate drops dangerously low. Or, alternatively, there is something called "functional freeze" in PVT, which is a significant amount of sympathetic-dominant energy. And also shutdown, which makes a person feel like the gas and brake of the car is on at the same time. You are revving but you just seem to spin your engine.

Finally, let's check in with Sally. She has a dream of doing "A Midsummer Night's Dream" on the moon, but an alien came by the other day and sent her ship a message that she was too big to be an actress. Despite this alien being known for its truly reprehensible behavior, NASA heard the whole thing go down. NASA shuts down her ship. The lights and power dim so low, it's almost impossible to do space-shopping, or even do her nervous system course she's been so excited about. The harder she tries, the more shutdown the ship seems to feel. Luckily, Sally now knows this is not her fault. But, it's still such a pain. She starts noticing her Preservation Mode harmonics:

I said that the nervous system is music, but the Preservation Mode can be one frightening song. I don't know anyone who enjoys it.

In the Preservation Mode, just as harmonics add complexity to a single note, there are various layers of experience that emerge, each contributing to how the freeze state manifests in behavior and sensation. Let's map it out using the structure of musical harmonics:

Basic Preservation Mode Harmonics

1. **Fundamental (C note): The Core Freeze Response**
   The fundamental tone represents the most basic freeze response: immobility or shutdown. This is the body's primal survival mechanism, characterized by minimal responsiveness (energy conservation) and immobilization. Just like the fundamental tone in music grounds all the higher harmonics, this core freeze response underpins everything else. The body is saving energy in collapse.

In the arts: For a dancer, this can feel like being stuck in place, unable to begin or flow with the movement, even when you know the choreography.

2. **1st Harmonic (C an octave above) : Physical Tension**

    The first overtone might represent muscle rigidity. Even though the body is still, there's often tension or stiffness, almost like holding still requires effort. In freeze, the nervous system is still engaged, but movement is suppressed, similar to the higher energy found in the first harmonic compared to the fundamental note.
    In the arts: A singer experiencing this might feel their neck, jaw, or diaphragm lock up, making it difficult to produce sound or access vocal flexibility. In singers, this is often called Muscle Tension Dysphonia (MTD).

3. **2nd Harmonic (G): Numbness or Dissociation**

    The second harmonic could symbolize numbness or dissociation. Just as a harmonic drifts further from the core tone, the freeze state often involves emotional or sensory disconnection, as though you're not fully present in your body or environment.
    In the arts: An actor might feel like they're "watching themselves" perform from a distance, unable to fully connect with the character or the audience.

4. **3rd Harmonic (C, two octaves up): Slowed Cognition**

    This harmonic might reflect slowed or foggy thinking. In the freeze state, thoughts become sluggish, as though everything is moving in slow motion. It's a higher harmonic because it's more removed from the body's core freeze mechanism but still deeply tied to it.
    In the arts: A performer may struggle to recall lyrics or lines they've practiced endlessly, feeling like the words slip away in the moment they're needed most.

5. **4th Harmonic (E, the major third): Hyper-Awareness or "Deer in Headlights"**

    The next harmonic could represent hyper-awareness. While the body is immobilized, there may be an exaggerated sensitivity to external threats, as if every tiny movement or sound could be a danger.

In the arts: A musician might become overly focused on the faces of the audience or bandmates, looking for judgment or criticism, instead of staying present with the music.

6. **5th Harmonic (G): Emotional Shutdown, Depersonalization**

   The harmonic represents emotional blunting. Just like this harmonic adds complexity to the note, emotional shutdown adds another layer to the freeze state. While still and hyper-aware, the emotional experience can feel muted or detached.

   In the arts: An actor might find it difficult to access the depth of emotion needed for a powerful scene, feeling strangely detached from the emotions they're supposed to express.

7. **6th Harmonic (B♭) : Shallow Breathing or Reduced Heart Rate**

   The next harmonic can signify physiological shutdown—slowed breathing, reduced heart rate, or a lack of energy. These are the physical markers of the freeze response, similar to how this harmonic deviates from pure consonance, showing the altered physical state during freeze.

   In the arts: A performer may feel too exhausted to even show up to rehearsal or push through the final act of a show, weighed down by an invisible force. This shallow breathing creates numbness.

8. **7th Harmonic (C, three octaves above) : Adaptive Holding**

   The final harmonic could represent the adaptive function of the freeze response. Just as the high harmonic ties back to the fundamental note, freeze serves a protective purpose by conserving energy or avoiding danger. It's not an ideal long-term state, but it's adaptive in the moment.

   In the arts: This could manifest as a performer instinctively shutting down during a high-stress audition or show, a protective response to preserve their energy and emotions under pressure. This is a VERY tired performer who feels like everything is heavy and hard even if it's quite easy or simple. You are just getting by.

Mapping the Freeze Harmonics:

In this metaphor, each layer of the freeze response "pops out" like a harmonic from the fundamental note, shaping how the freeze state feels physically, emotionally, and cognitively. The different "harmonics" are the subtle variations in the freeze state that blend together to create the overall experience, from numbness to hyper-awareness, slowed thinking to shallow breathing.

The goal, just as in music, would be to understand and recognize these harmonics to shift out of the freeze state when it is no longer adaptive—similar to modulating from one key to another in a musical composition.

Here is a list of all possible freeze harmonics:

External Preservation Mode Harmonics

1. **Physical Immobility:** The person might suddenly become very still or rigid, unable to move or take action, even when movement is necessary.

2. **Decreased Breathing:** Breathing may become shallow, slow, or even seem to stop momentarily. Oxygen deprivation is a key factor in the issues that come with freeze, and many of them are similar to a foot or leg that falls asleep.

3. **Muscle Tension:** The body may become tense, with muscles tightening, especially in the face, neck, shoulders, or jaw.

4. **Feeling Detached or Numb:** A sense of disconnection from one's surroundings, body, or emotions. The person may feel like they are watching themselves from outside their body.

5. **Inability to Speak:** The person may find it difficult or impossible to speak, or their voice may become very quiet or monotone.

6. **Dazed or "Zoned Out" Look:** The person may have a blank or glazed-over expression, appearing lost in thought or disconnected from the present moment.

7. **Loss of Awareness of Time:** There may be a sense of time slowing down or speeding up, or a complete loss of awareness of time passing.

8. **Feeling Overwhelmed or Stuck:** The person may feel trapped or unable to make decisions, even if the situation is not physically confining.

9. **Cold Extremities:** Blood flow may be redirected to vital organs, leaving hands and feet cold.

10. **Startle Response:** The person might be overly sensitive to sudden stimuli, reacting with an exaggerated startle.

Internal Preservation Mode Harmonics

11. **Dissociation**: During a freeze response, individuals may experience dissociation, which can range from feeling disconnected from their surroundings or their body to having an "out-of-body" experience. This can include a sense of detachment from emotions or a feeling that the world around them is unreal (derealization).

12. **Immobility and Paralysis**: Psychologically, the freeze response is characterized by a profound sense of being stuck or unable to act. The person may feel mentally paralyzed, unable to make decisions or take action, even though they are aware of the need to do so.

13. **Emotional Numbing**: Individuals may experience a blunting of emotions, where they feel emotionally flat or numb. This numbing is a defense mechanism that helps the person avoid the emotional pain associated with the situation.

14. **Heightened Awareness and Hypervigilance**: Paradoxically, while the body is immobile, the mind can become hyper-aware of the environment. The person may feel acutely aware of details in their surroundings, yet unable to respond to them.

15. **Helplessness**: The freeze response often brings a profound sense of helplessness. The person may feel that there is no escape or no way to alter the situation, leading to a feeling of being trapped.

16. **Overwhelming Fear or Panic**: Despite the external appearance of calmness or stillness, the person may be experiencing intense fear or panic internally. This fear is often accompanied by an inability to express or process it in the moment.

17. **Mental Fog or Confusion**: The freeze response can lead to a state of mental confusion or fogginess. The person may have difficulty thinking clearly, processing information, or recalling details of the event afterward.

18. **Memory Impairment**: During a freeze response, memory encoding can be affected. This may result in fragmented or incomplete memories of the event, or in some cases, the individual may have difficulty recalling the event entirely (trauma-induced amnesia).

19. **Avoidance**: Following a freeze response, individuals may develop avoidance behaviors, steering clear of situations, people, or places that remind them of the triggering event, as these can bring back the feelings of helplessness or fear experienced during the freeze.

20. **Internal Conflict**: There can be a significant internal conflict between the desire to flee or fight and the inability to act, leading to frustration, self-blame, or guilt after the event has passed.

It's Showtime!

I was right out of college auditioning for The Actor Shakespeare Project's "Othello" and I got called back. This is big because even though they may not pick you, it means you were good enough to be considered. They gave the other actor and me a second to go through some basic communication as there was some violence in the scene, and we quickly decided that he would push me to my knees. I had taken stage combat, and felt totally comfortable to have him lead my body safely to the ground. But that's not what ended up happening. Unfortunately, the other actor was too "in the moment" and actually slammed my knees to the ground. My script fell out of my hands and I went into **a rotary phone**. I felt immediate **dissociation** like I was watching what was happening, I was so numb **I didn't know where my body was in space**, **I lost all ability to speak,** and I wish I could tell you what happened next because all I can remember is hearing the director say, "Thank you." In the theater, this means we are done here. I felt so much shame that it took me days to tell my roommates what happened. When I reached out to tell the theater company what happened, I just got total denial of my experience, which shamed me further. While I did do two other productions after that, my body fought me. It just didn't like theater anymore, it wasn't fun and it wasn't safe. My Ground Control also learned that if you are harmed and tell your truth, no one will believe you. This made it impossible to continue. I felt so lost, shamed, and frightened.

Luckily I was surrounded by **co-regulation** and artists who encouraged me to pick up the guitar, and I started singing, which helped me find my voice again. I would later integrate theater back into my music career, but I never went back. If I had tools, a nervous system education, and a system to come out of freeze, my outcomes would have contained much less suffering.

The hardest part about freeze is that because the prefrontal cortex is diminished, you can't remember all the details. You think, "Did that even happen? Did I make it up? Why didn't I say something?" You are left with a blur that never comes into focus, until it does, until you finally go into Move Mode.

The Secret Backdoor of Superplay

Well, I wasn't totally transparent. Preservation Mode *is* at the bottom of the ladder in PVT, but it's not in the Fox Method. There is in fact a frightening basement to the nervous system and that is to go into pretend play in order to regulate a traumatized nervous system. When children are very, very unsafe, you will often see them play-pretend from Preservation Mode. **But this is not from safe and grounded safety but a place of deep dissociation and delusion.** This explains Ophelia from "Hamlet" or Laura from "The Glass Menagerie." As I share some examples of characters in freeze, notice how many of them also fall into a delusion of pretend. In these character descriptions below you will see the nervous system ladder twisted into a circle, much like a snake eating its tail. I call this the "Superplay Back Door." This is the fire escape of the Preservation Mode state. When those in a freeze state face pain too intense for freeze to numb, they cope by turning to delusion. This isn't pretend play rooted in safety; it's pretend play driven by extreme duress and terror.

Examples of Theatrical **Characters in Freeze:**

1. Ophelia in *Hamlet* by William Shakespeare

Ophelia's gradual mental decline can be seen as a response to the overwhelming emotional turmoil and trauma she experiences, including the death of her father and Hamlet's rejection. At various points, she exhibits signs of emotional withdrawal, detachment, and helplessness— classic freeze-state symptoms. Her descent into madness can be viewed as the final collapse of her ability to cope as she leans into pretend play (Delusional Freeze/Superplay).

2. Willy Loman in *Death of a Salesman* by Arthur Miller

Willy exhibits behaviors that could be seen as a freeze response, particularly in the way he retreats into memories of his past and becomes trapped in delusions about his and his family's success. His inability to confront reality and make active changes to his circumstances suggests a type of emotional paralysis. (Delusional Superplay.)

3. Blanche DuBois in *A Streetcar Named Desire* by Tennessee Williams

Blanche's fragile mental state and retreat into fantasy and illusion are hallmarks of someone overwhelmed by trauma. Her inability to deal with reality, especially when faced with rejection and humiliation by Stanley and others, could be interpreted as a prolonged freeze response. She withdraws into her memories and delusions, unable to confront the harshness of her present circumstances (Delusional Superplay.)

4. Laura Wingfield in *The Glass Menagerie* by Tennessee Williams

Laura is a deeply introverted and socially anxious character, who often withdraws into the safety of her glass figurines and avoids the outside world. Her tendency to isolate herself and her difficulty engaging with others, especially in moments of stress, could suggest a freeze state. Her emotional paralysis is evident when she faces real-life pressures, such as meeting Jim, the gentleman caller (Delusional Superplay.)

5. Nina in *The Seagull* by Anton Chekhov

In "The Seagull," Nina suffers immense emotional trauma over the course of the play, particularly due to her failed acting career and destructive relationship with Trigorin. By the end, she appears numb, emotionally frozen, and detached from the person she once was. Her disillusionment and retreat into survival mode reflect a freeze response to overwhelming disappointment and heartbreak.

Examples of **Song Characters in Freeze:**

1. "Breathe Me" by Sia
This song portrays someone trapped in a state of emotional paralysis and isolation, pleading for help. The character feels broken and frozen by their pain, unsure how to break free from their emotional distress.

2. "Hurt" by Nine Inch Nails (also covered by Johnny Cash)
The character in "Hurt" is emotionally frozen, numb to feelings and detached from the world. The lyrics capture the sense of being stuck in deep despair, unable to escape the pain.

Under the Hood:
In the freeze state, according to Polyvagal Theory, the body enters a state of immobilization driven by the dorsal vagal complex, part of the parasympathetic nervous system. This is a survival response to overwhelming danger, where the body essentially shuts down to conserve energy and protect itself. Physiologically, heart rate and respiration slow dramatically, and there may be a feeling of numbness or dissociation. Blood flow decreases, and the body may feel cold or weak. This state, often referred to

as "shutdown," is an adaptive response to extreme stress or perceived threat, prioritizing survival over action. With slowed respiration, we have an issue of oxygenation, which will later be the key to activating out of this state.

*This is the most difficult state to read about. Please take a pause, take a walk, a shower, or co-regulate after reading this chapter. Many tender things may come up. This is one of those moments I wish we were together, or that I could pop out of this book and offer a hug. Most of us felt the most abandoned in this state. If those feelings are coming up, remember they are like kids who need your care and attention. Don't push them away. Be with them as much as your nervous system will allow.

Dorsal Pathway Dominant

The Mobilized Freeze State

3.

Paralyzed between
Flight / Freeze, Stuck,
Frozen, Dissociation

The immobilized Freeze State

2.

Numb, Flat, Passive
Fawn / Appeasing.

1.

"Collapsed," Withdrawn,
Self-Preservation, Struggle
to do anything.

MORE **Ability to feel** LESS

Hey. I'd like to return my nervous system harmonics.

I can't do that. They come with the box. I gave them to you so you would know what state you're in! This is how you know to shift.

But, I don't like them.
Plus, my therapist says
I can stop my black and
white thinking. Can I
try to...

THEY COME
WITH THE
BOX.
*slaps forehead

Is there a manual?

I ate it.

Letter #8: Nervous System States, In Focus: Move Mode

"His palms are sweaty,
knees weak, arms are heavy,
there's vomit on his sweater already,
mom's spaghetti."

—*Eminem, "Lose Yourself"*

Dear Artist,

I don't need to explain the Move Mode state to many artists. A whole new term for this experience is called "stage fright," as if stage fright is a physiological experience that is unique in its properties. Luckily, it's not. The way it changes a human physiology is the exact same way it changes for tennis players, lawyers, or any other performing profession.

Before we go into a bit of history about this state, I just want to remind you that this state often just feels like a big pulse, a large wave of electricity or energy that fills our body. If any of this feels complicated, just come back to this description when you think of Move Mode.

You've probably heard the phrase "fight or flight" before, which is a handy rhyme to somewhat capture our autonomic responses, but it's a woefully incomplete term. I wanted to briefly discuss the origins of that phrase and the person who coined it, as it underscores the complexity of our nervous systems and the slow progress we've made in understanding them.

Walter Bradford Cannon was a Harvard physiologist in the early 20th century, a scientist with a knack, in the words of Bill Bryson, for convincing people "to do rash and uncomfortable things in the name of science." But Cannon was also willing to put himself through peril for his experiments. During World War I, he volunteered to serve with the Army Expeditionary Force and eventually worked on the front lines. His purpose was to study the nature of shock, a condition many soldiers evinced during and after battle. Along with his colleagues, Cannon discovered that the blood of shocked soldiers was highly acidic, meaning that acidosis occurred in response to the initial cause. Our bodies, in other words, experience intense and potentially dangerous physiological changes as a result of trauma. Although Cannon had essentially recognized and defined what we now know as post-traumatic stress disorder (PTSD), his work wouldn't be fully appreciated until many decades later.

Additionally, Cannon gave us two very relevant terms for our purposes. The first is *homeostasis,* the self-regulating processes in our bodies, a mostly biological concept. The other is *fight or flight,* the phrase commonly associated with what I call *Move Mode.* Cannon's contribution to our understanding of the self is the way his ideas contradicted the status quo. As the physician and biologist Siddharth Mukherjee puts it: "For generations before [Claude] Bernard and Cannon, physiologists had described animals as assemblages of machines, sums of dynamic parts." Now the emphasis lay on "the maintenance of fixity" rather than on continuous action.

As we noted in the chapter on structures, a state of stability is required for more complex systems to develop. In a similar way, our bodies need homeostasis in order for us to live and grow. As Carl Zimmer points out, "homeostasis is not a physical thing to be weighed or poked. It is not a particular assembly of atoms forming a molecule like DNA or proteins. It's instead a principle you can find throughout the living world, acting on many levels at once." Homeostasis is easily disrupted by external or abstract stimuli, meaning animals and cells and cultures all must work to maintain them. The body—or the atoms or the society—can't do it entirely by itself.

To be clear, for a human being, whose brain depends on a "safe and social state" according to PVT, to survive in a very social environment, Move Mode is out of homeostasis. It's a temporary imbalance in our metabolic system. I also need to mention that due to artists' professions, there is quite a lot of homeostatic imbalance.

Cannon's "fight or flight" construct became so well known it did a disservice to Move Mode's complexity. Cannon created a binary in which our psychologies and our physiologies are reduced to an either/or, but the general insight underneath the simplification is important. When thrust into dangerous situations, it is perfectly reasonable for your body to prep you to either run (flee) or stand your ground (fight). Our ancestors didn't have too many choices beyond those, so a straightforward command to either flee or stay served its purpose. Now, though, in our age of evolutionary anachronism, when we enter Move Mode, it often isn't because we're in *literal* danger, but rather that we're triggered by a source associated with things that either have put us in danger in the past, or by threats to our mental well-being. Sometimes, an initial cause of Move Mode can be so intense that the victim can't seem to bring themselves out of it for a long time—we call this trauma. This of course isn't the event, it's how the nervous system reacted to the event. The body no longer believes its homeostatic set point can help you survive and retunes its entire system of balance to danger itself. Someone stuck in Move Mode longer term can come in all kinds of degrees of severity, with PTSD and trauma on one end of the spectrum, and the more common kinds of stress and anxiety and fear we experience with relative regularity. These iterations can all have drawbacks, because the only times a severe Move Mode is necessary in an *emergency* situation is when your safety is actually threatened, which is a rarer occurrence than the other examples. When the Connect Mode evolved it took Move Mode with it and simply gave it more energy to socialize, play, compete, to feel irritation in the creation process, or to even a pulse of energy on stage to help us focus and play.

Also noted in the structure section is the metaphorical shape of Preservation and Move Modes: **Preservation is a mode housed *within* Move Mode.** This is why the fight-or-flight construct is incomplete, as someone facing peril could just as easily freeze in response to it and thus put them into even more danger. I use the term Move Mode because at its most effective; this state encourages us to move—but not just in the run-or-battle sense. Instead, Move Mode includes our ability to differentiate between predator and prey, and allows us not just to avoid predators but also to chase down prey.

Most significantly, though, is that Move Mode also deals with our levels of excitement and stimulation (our bodies metabolic energy budget), which leads us to the next state, Connect Mode. Because just as Preservation is contained within Move, so too are both Move and Preservation contained within Connect Mode, the next largest doll in our matryoshka. But the final point before we move on is this: Preservation and Move Modes are meant to be **temporary states of being.** If you get stuck in either of these modes, ordinary life will become much more arduous. They are not *bad* states (there's no such thing), but an extended duration of them causes all kinds of problems.

Later under the umbrella of Connect and Superplay Mode, we will see that this energy no longer lives in our body as defense but transforms into connective functions like healthy competition, joy, exhalation, or the fire that lights up Lady Macbeth. This energy adds that extra charge that makes your heart pump when listening to your favorite punk bands.

So, when we talk about Move Mode, please keep in mind we are talking about a series of biological changes that specifically relate to the body's defense. We are not referring to all the movement that happens under the umbrella of regulation.

Let's use Sally as an example, to demonstrate how we know if the body is truly in Move Mode and is not merely in an energetic form of Connect Mode:

Imagine Sally is floating in space when she spots a strange alien from the corner of her eye. NASA is about to send Sally a surge of G-force energy to help her either attack or escape. But as you'll see in the Move Mode harmonics, there's much more happening than just an energy boost. Yes, her heart rate will speed up, but many other changes occur within her ship. These changes are what make the difference. This energy transforms her ship into something resembling a Mad Max vehicle. It alters how she thinks, and all of the energy in the ship moves toward separation rather than connection.

NASA can also send energy to the Connect Mode, as we'll explore soon. This energy is geared towards learning or connection, which may require NASA to use some of its energy budget. However, it's nowhere near the amount needed to launch Sally's ship into Move Mode.

Just like when we think of Preservation Mode as the emergency brake (parasympathetic), I want you to think of Move Mode as the gas in your human car. Your Ground Control can whip out its metabolic credit card and start going broke, but what you will feel is energy. Likely, an unforgettable amount of it. If you remember, we don't control this. We only control how we deal with the energy that hits our body and do our best to tend to it.

But, we aren't there yet. First, you need to learn how to spot when you are even in this mode.

Before I go through the Move Mode Harmonics, I need to map out two distinct changes that affect performers and musicians the most.

1. The first thing to remember in this state is that **happy faces look neutral and neutral faces look threatening.** If you are stressed and your audience looks unhappy, they are probably just fine.

2. **The inner ear shifts to ear high and low sounds better.** This will dull the center EQ of human hearing. If you are stressed and suddenly you can't hear your voice in the monitors, it may be that your brain is beginning to prefer the bass notes.

Let's map the Move Mode nervous system states using the harmonic series metaphor, much like we did with Preservation Mode. The Move Mode response, part of the sympathetic nervous system (SNS), is activated in response to perceived danger, preparing the body for action. As with Preservation Mode, different "harmonics" of Move Mode represent layers of physical, emotional, and cognitive responses. Here's how we can break it down:

Basic Move Mode Harmonics

1. **Fundamental (C note): Core Fight/Flight Response**
   The fundamental tone represents the body's immediate fight/flight reaction—a surge of energy primed for confrontation or escape. Heart rate rises, muscles tighten, and adrenaline floods the system. For an artist, this could manifest as stage fright or a sudden feeling of overwhelm in front of an audience. This raw survival energy may kickstart movement, but it can also make the body feel like it's on the edge of a cliff, poised for battle or retreat.

2. **1st Harmonic (C, one octave up): Increased Breathing**
   The first harmonic corresponds to the physical escalation: rapid heart rate and breathing. While this state fuels the body for action, it can also leave artists gasping for breath mid-performance, struggling to maintain vocal or instrumental control. A wind

instrumentalist might find their breath control suddenly faltering, or a dancer may lose coordination as their heart races faster than they can regulate. This harmonic becomes an unsteady heartbeat within the artist, disrupting rhythm and flow.

3. **2nd Harmonic (G): Muscular Tension and Readiness**

The second harmonic symbolizes muscular tension, where the body stiffens in preparation for action. For artists, this tension can be both an asset and a hurdle. A cellist, for example, might grip their bow too tightly, causing the sound to become harsh and uncontrolled. A painter may find their hand shaking as they attempt to add delicate detail. This automatic muscle tension, while useful in true emergencies, can impede the fluidity and precision required for creative work, turning the natural harmony into forced movement.

4. **3rd Harmonic (C, two octaves up): Narrowed Focus and Tunnel Vision**

This harmonic represents tunnel vision—a state where the mind focuses intensely on a perceived threat, tuning out everything else. Artists experiencing this may find their creative process or performance thrown off course by an obsession with a mistake or audience reaction. Imagine an actor on stage, so fixated on a forgotten line that they lose track of the entire scene's flow. The narrow focus, while helpful for survival, strips away the peripheral awareness needed to stay connected to the larger artistic vision.

5. **4th Harmonic (E): Hypervigilance**

The fourth harmonic reflects hypervigilance—an exaggerated sensitivity to any sign of danger. For an artist, this can lead to over-criticism of their own work or hyper-awareness of audience feedback. A performer might feel every cough or fidget in the audience as a judgment, amplifying self-doubt. A visual artist might endlessly revise a piece, unable to feel satisfied, as they perceive flaws no one else would notice. This heightened sensitivity creates a sharpness, but it can also erode confidence and spontaneity, turning creation into a battle against invisible threats.

6. **5th Harmonic (G): Emotional Intensity (Fear/Anger)**

   The fifth harmonic represents emotional intensity—fear that drives escape or anger that drives confrontation. In creative settings, fear can manifest as an urge to abandon a project midway, a sense that failure is imminent. Anger may show up as frustration with oneself or collaborators, causing interpersonal tension in a band, a cast, or a creative team. Just as this harmonic adds emotional color to sound, it can color an artist's experience in overpowering ways, pushing them to react impulsively or give up altogether.

7. **6th Harmonic (B♭): Cognitive Overload or Impulsivity**

   The sixth harmonic represents cognitive overload, where higher-level thinking shuts down and impulsivity takes over. For an artist, this might manifest as poor decision-making under stress—forgetting lines, playing the wrong chord, or making an impulsive artistic choice that feels "off" but happens too fast to correct. Like a dissonant B♭ in the harmonic series, these rushed decisions can create jagged, unpredictable moments in a performance, where the artist is reacting more than creating.

8. **7th Harmonic (C, three octaves above): Short-term Survival Focus**

   The seventh harmonic symbolizes a singular focus on immediate survival. In this state, the nervous system prioritizes short-term success—like finishing the song or getting through a scene—over the bigger picture. An artist might feel as if they're racing just to reach the end, rather than enjoying or fully inhabiting the creative moment. It's the singer who powers through a song without connecting emotionally, or the actor who rushes their lines. This short-term focus can leave artists feeling disconnected from their craft, as though they're merely surviving rather than creating.

External Move Mode Harmonics

1. **Increased Heart Rate:** The heart beats faster to pump more blood to the muscles, providing them with oxygen and energy needed for quick action.

2. **Rapid Breathing** (Hyperventilation): Breathing becomes quicker and shallower to increase oxygen intake, which is necessary for sustained physical exertion.

3. **Dilated Pupils:** Pupils expand to allow more light into the eyes, improving vision and awareness of the surroundings.

4. **Sweating:** The body begins to sweat to cool itself down, preventing overheating during intense physical activity.

5. **Tense Muscles:** Muscles become tense, preparing the body to spring into action. This tension can lead to trembling or shaking.

6. **Pale or Flushed Skin:** Blood is redirected from the skin to the muscles and vital organs, which can result in the skin appearing pale. Alternatively, some people may experience a rush of blood to the skin, causing them to flush.

7. **Dry Mouth:** Saliva production decreases, leading to a dry mouth. This is because digestion is deprioritized in favor of more immediate survival functions.

8. **Butterflies in the Stomach (Gastrointestinal Discomfort):** Blood flow to the digestive system is reduced, causing sensations like nausea, stomach churning, or "butterflies."

9. **Heightened Senses**: Sensory perception becomes more acute, with heightened awareness of sounds, sights, and smells, allowing for quicker reactions to potential dangers.

10. **Adrenaline Surge:** The adrenal glands release adrenaline (epinephrine), which increases energy availability and sharpens focus, contributing to the overall readiness for action.

11. **Clenched Jaw or Fists:** In preparation for fight, individuals may clench their jaw or fists, a sign of readiness to engage physically.

12. **Shaking or Trembling:** The rush of adrenaline and the rapid mobilization of energy can cause trembling or shaking in the limbs or throughout the body.

13. **Tunnel Vision:** Focus narrows, concentrating on the threat at hand, sometimes at the expense of peripheral awareness.

14. **Increased Blood Pressure:** Blood pressure rises as the heart works harder to circulate blood, ensuring that muscles and vital organs receive adequate oxygen.

15. **Decreased Pain Sensitivity**: Pain perception may be reduced, allowing the individual to continue functioning despite potential injuries.

Internal Move Mode Harmonics

16. **Heightened Anxiety or Fear:** The individual may experience intense anxiety or fear, which drives the need to take immediate action. This can include a sense of impending doom or the urgent need to escape a situation.

17. **Hypervigilance:** There is an increased state of alertness, where the person is constantly scanning the environment for potential threats. This can lead to a heightened sensitivity to stimuli and a difficulty in relaxing.

18. **Irritability and Anger:** In fight mode, the individual may become more irritable, aggressive, or prone to anger as they prepare to confront the threat. This can manifest as impatience or a short temper.

19. **Racing Thoughts:** The mind may become flooded with rapid, often disorganized thoughts as it tries to assess the situation and determine the best course of action. This can lead to difficulty concentrating or making decisions.

20. **Tunnel Vision (Narrowed Focus):** The person may become extremely focused on the perceived threat, to the exclusion of everything else. This narrowed focus can make it difficult to think about or engage with anything unrelated to the immediate situation.

21. **Impulsivity:** In Move Mode, individuals might act quickly and impulsively, sometimes without fully considering the consequences of their actions. This is driven by the need for immediate action to address the threat.

22. **Feeling Overwhelmed:** The sheer intensity of the emotions and thoughts during this state can lead to a feeling of being overwhelmed, where the person may struggle to process the situation or feel that it is too much to handle.

23. **Sense of Urgency:** There is a strong sense of urgency or pressure to act quickly. This can lead to hasty decisions or actions, often aimed at resolving the perceived threat as rapidly as possible.

24. **Difficulty Sleeping (Insomnia):** The heightened state of arousal can make it difficult for the individual to relax or sleep. The mind may continue to race, replaying scenarios or worrying about potential dangers.

25. **Reduced Ability to Think Rationally**: The fight-or-flight response can diminish the ability to think logically or rationally. The brain prioritizes quick, survival-oriented decisions over more complex or reflective thinking.

26. **Difficulty in Verbal Communication:** During this heightened state, some individuals may find it challenging to articulate their thoughts clearly or may become more abrupt in their speech as they focus on the immediate threat.

27. **Increased Sense of Empowerment or Invincibility:** In some cases, particularly in the fight response, individuals may feel a surge of confidence or even a sense of invincibility, believing they are fully capable of overcoming the threat.

28. **Sense of Detachment from Emotions:** While some may feel heightened emotions, others might experience a form of emotional detachment, focusing solely on the practical aspects of survival rather than their feelings.

29. **Perceived Time Distortion:** Time may seem to slow down (allowing the person to react to the threat more efficiently) or speed up (creating a sense of urgency).

Examples of Theatrical **Characters in** Move Mode**:**

1. Medea in *Medea* by Euripides (Fight)
Medea responds to betrayal with a fierce fight response. When her husband, Jason, leaves her for another woman, Medea takes violent action, plotting and executing a plan of revenge, including the murder of their own children.

3. Jean Valjean in *Les Misérables* by Victor Hugo (stage adaptation) (Flight)
Jean Valjean spends much of his life in a flight response, constantly running from the law, particularly from Inspector Javert. His years in hiding and evading capture illustrate the flight response, driven by fear of returning to prison.

4. Coriolanus in *Coriolanus* by William Shakespeare (Fight)
Coriolanus reacts aggressively to perceived threats to his honor and authority. His inability to handle criticism and his quickness to confront enemies—whether the Roman citizens or political adversaries—exemplify the fight response.

5. Troy Maxson in *Fences* by August Wilson (Fight)
Troy consistently displays a fight response in his relationships with his family, especially in his conflicts with his son, Cory. His aggressive, domineering behavior is a way to maintain control and assert authority in the face of personal and societal challenges.

Examples of Songs with **Characters in Move Mode:**

1. "Eye of the Tiger" by Survivor (Fight)
This classic anthem is all about the fight response, with the character pushing through adversity, ready to "fight" for survival and success. The lyrics focus on resilience, determination, and staying aggressive in the face of challenges.

2. "I Will Survive" by Gloria Gaynor (Flight and Fight)

The character in this song starts in a flight response, escaping an unhealthy relationship, but soon transforms into a fight mentality, standing strong and reclaiming power and independence. The song is a defiant declaration of survival and personal strength.

3. "Running Up That Hill" by Kate Bush (Flight)

The character in this song seems to be trying to escape the pain of love and life's challenges. The flight response is reflected in the metaphor of running away or trying to make a deal to switch places and avoid the emotional burden.

Under The Hood:

In the fight-or-flight state, according to PVT, the sympathetic nervous system is activated in response to perceived danger. This state prepares the body for action, either to confront the threat (fight) or to escape it (flight). Physiologically, the heart rate and breathing increase, muscles tense, and blood flow is redirected to vital areas like the limbs to support quick movement. The body releases adrenaline and cortisol, heightening alertness and focus. Digestion slows, and other non-essential functions are put on hold as the body prioritizes immediate survival.

The "Scared As All Hell" Harmonic Series.

Fundamental: High arousal, mobilization.
1st Harmonic: Increased heart rate and breathing.
2nd Harmonic: Muscular tension, physical readiness.
3rd Harmonic: Tunnel vision, narrowed focus.
4th Harmonic: Hypervigilance.
5th Harmonic: Emotional intensity (fear or anger).
6th Harmonic: Cognitive overload or impulsivity.
7th Harmonic: Short-term survival focus.

It's a song you little twit!

Immoral, bad, mean, SHAME

Sympathetic Dominant

6.

Significant Anxiousness,
Fear, Worry, Irritability.
(Functioning)

FIGHT

5.

Action-oriented fear, over-
working, overwhelming anger,
crawling out of the skin,
mobilized panic, uncontrollable
fidgeting,
racing thoughts,
Angry Fawn -people-pleasing
but internally angry.

FLIGHT

4.

Wanting to Escape,
Terrified, Frightened,
Overwhelmed,
Mobilized to Flee,
Pleasing others with
one foot out the door,

Letter #9: Nervous System States, In Focus: Connect Mode

"Something always brings me back to you. It never takes too long."

—Sara Bareilles, "Gravity"

Dear Artist,

Remember our artist friend, Major Sally? She lived the life of a creator, diving deep into her art without fully realizing the presence of Ground Control—the unseen force influencing her creative flow. This "Ground Control" was her neuroception, that subtle, often overlooked system constantly scanning for danger and risk, which was affecting her ability to perform at her best. This is a key idea we'll revisit often. It connects to the newest development in human evolution, the Connect Mode—our first step on the nervous system ladder, yet an expansive, all-encompassing stage in our creative evolution. **This is the "first" step for humans, because if a human thinks it can survive by connecting it will choose that first.** When that bid for safety doesn't work, it shifts to our defense states mentioned earlier.

Like the smartphone to modern life, it's a vital tool that shapes everything we do. This is an important idea we'll return to many times, and here it relates to the most recent nervous system state to emerge in humanity's evolution and the first step on our *hierarchy* (ladder) but an all-encompassing later stage in our *holarchy* (smartphone)—and that is the **Connect Mode**.

The previous two letters addressed parts of our anatomy and physiology that were vital to the survival of our species throughout the hundreds of thousands of years of our evolution. Preservation and Move Modes kept our ancestors alive, and with each passing generation those instincts deepened themselves into our natures. But what happens when survival becomes less precarious and more predictable? Can the nervous system states of past species address the needs of a time of relative leisure, creativity, and civility?

Obviously not, right? This new stage of evolution (social connection) requires something slower, more methodical, and linear in a way Preservation Mode and Move Mode don't usually allow for. You can't think critically or invent productively or create expressively if you believe you're in danger. But that's not why animals biologically expressed a brand new state of connection and cooperation. It happened because they were **better able to survive by teaming up.** Survival of the fittest was still in place, but being fit didn't mean you were the biggest, scariest monkey anymore, It meant you were the most caring and cooperative. In fact, the more we teamed up, the more stable our Holarchies (environments) became. To the point that they are now so stable we suffer from too much food, fun, and boredom. And, the electrical evolutionary upgrade that ensued is why we spend hours on tik tok watching dogs, hedgehogs, and horses lick each other's faces. We even get a feeling of connection from *watching* connection. Humans have an enormously advanced version of Connect Mode (the safe and social state (PVT)), but it's important to remember this state is still rooted in survival. We are still using this state to survive together.

Now, if this makes it sound as if Connect Mode were the *best* state, or the *safest* state, or the *final* state, let me clarify: Connect is full of risk and uncomfortable feelings—after all, it's the one mode we most interact with in our social lives, which is just as complicated and perilous as the others. It's risky because if there is a chance we can connect, we can also disconnect, which means danger to our human nervous systems.

Let's compare a mammal like my dog Yuna and myself as we both have a Connect Mode. Mammals with a Connect Mode have less sensitivity to our human signals to connect. While my dog understands some of my facial expressions (Connect Mode hardware) and words (particularly "walk"), if I look a tiny bit "off" to my partner, he notices and checks in with me. He may not say it explicitly, but he means, "Hey, do you not feel safe?"

My dog Yuna isn't less advanced; her Connect Mode has simply adapted to a different environment. Her ability to connect with other dogs through smell, for example, is 10,000 to 100,000 times more sensitive than ours. As you observe different animals, remember not to mistake differences for a measure of species intelligence.

Humans developed a wildly intricate system of abstract tools called language to not only warn each other of oncoming danger, but to connect. We would later create an equally intricate system of belief that would glue certain co-regulatory groups of people together. Also, something to note here is that having and using language is a vital part of keeping humans in Connect Mode. For example, having a nervous system vocabulary allows us to stay more regulated with it, because the Connect Mode and human language evolved together. That is why even simply giving artists a language for their nervous system massively helps them feel more curious about their lived experience.

Connect also still needs access to Preservation and Move Modes, for both the external and internal emergencies that inevitably befall us. Remember, this more recent state is slower and more social, so some kind of unconscious safeguard must function within it so that we can focus our energies and intellects on denser stuff.

Enter back **neuroception**! Think of it as a habitual remnant from thousands of years of well-honed survival. Rational thinking isn't quick enough. Neuroception is just the right speed; the speed of survival. It acts within 1/100th of a second to recognize either cues of safety or danger in your mental, physical, or bodily environment. It triggers what it thinks is the most appropriate nervous system state to respond with. And by compartmentalizing this job to this elusive Ground Control, we're able to go places with our minds and imaginations that defy mere evolutionary need—and step into something deeper, more beautiful, and more mysterious than we could have without it. In other words, Ground Control works so that Sally can explore space.

The word "connect" has a positive connotation. It's true that this mode helps us make friends and make art—but this is also the state in which "play" is just as much about playfulness as it is about taking on a social role. And "connect" implies only the tie between two separate things and not necessarily a symbiosis or enmeshment. As we'll see, Connect Mode, as our primary mode of living, **needs co-regulation and care just as much as the others, if not more so.** And as we'll also see, although returning to the relative safety of Connect is usually the aim of most nervous system therapies, there are other paths to regulation and renewal. A big part of my advocacy with artists is showing them that this state is the concrete of the art-house they build and we must keep it strong and flexible.

But wait, what is one of the main components that drive neuroception to put a human in this mode? There are three major factors; the first is that there is a reasonable level of safety in one's body (lack of pain), environment (lack of danger), and mind (lack of danger in our imagination). Secondly, a person's tolerance for risk. This is really wonderful news because we can work with risk. If I'm pushing myself too hard, I can pull back and find my ability to stay in this Connect Mode. Remember, co-regulation? The more co-regulators, the more I can take on risk that would be intolerable without it.

Co-regulation, or what Deb Dana would call a "ventral (meaning ventral vagal) anchor," is game changing for someone with high, hard goals. When I first started this book, I felt so much dysregulation. I was on the verge of tears and I told my editor Jonathan, "Well, I'm dyslexic, so I just have no idea how to lay out ideas the way other people can." He took a long calm breath and said, "Ruby, you just sound like a beginner with writing, I felt the same way." Jonathan was like a cool, calm writing spaceship that was tuning mine so I could stay connected and playful even if Ground Control was saying, "Panic!" He helped me keep my smartphone, well, "smart!"

Due to his experience, my limiting belief peeled off with no resistance and I was open to the idea that it was safe to learn. This is the magic of healthy co-regulation. We live in a self-help world but this mode can't be kept healthy by yourself. It evolved explicitly to be in connection with others, with nature, and with animals.

What's some of the "hardware" involved in this state? The big thing to remember is that the vagus nerve (called the "wanderer" as it is attached to almost every organ in the body) is like a **bicycle brake** for the whole body. If this brake is pushed down, it inhibits our sympathetic system (Move Mode) from pummeling into our system like a freight train. As you breathe out, you slow down this brake, but ultimately it is your brain's assessment of safety and risk that will decide whether it gives you a slow, calm ride or if it releases and you speed down the hill.

So, remember how I said Ground Control makes all the decisions? Well, it still does, but one of the conscious ways we can slow down our system is to push on our vagal brake. How do we do that? Two short inhales, and one very long exhale. As Sally rides the brake she slows the ship that has perhaps just received way too much gas from GC. Why can we do this with our breath? The vagal brake presses down and slows our bike down when we exert very long exhales.

The other hardware I want singers and actors to remember is that the striated muscles of the face, the throat, the soft palate, the neck–as well as the wetness in your mouth–are all part of the Connect Mode state. So, if you are having trouble, our protocol in MuscleMusic is to find a safe and social state, and then practice! The hardware that lights up when this state is active is literally the hardware of human language and verbal connection. For some artistic professions like opera, a Move Mode state is catastrophic to the functioning of the vocal instrument. What's wild to me is that for decades we have been shaming artists for dysregulation instead of educating them and giving them useful tools to keep their smartphones smart!

Finally, something to remember is that language, or what actors call "voice work," evolved with the Connect Mode state. When humans lose the ability to speak, they dysregulate.

Let's apply the harmonic metaphor to the safe and social nervous system state, which is tied to the ventral vagal complex of the parasympathetic nervous system. In this state, the body is relaxed, connection with others feels possible, and the system operates in a balanced and regulated way. Just like in the other states, we'll explore the "harmonics" that emerge from the core feeling of safety and social engagement.

Basic Connect Mode Harmonics:

1. Fundamental (C note): Core Safe and Social Response
The fundamental tone represents the core feeling of safety and connection. In this state, we feel calm, grounded, and open to engaging with others. The body is in a state of homeostasis, with a balanced heart rate, steady breathing, and overall ease. This is the foundation of the safe and social state, like the fundamental note grounding a harmonic series.

2. First Harmonic: Relaxed Breathing and Heart Rate
The first harmonic (C, one octave up) represents a state where breathing is slow, rhythmic, and the heart rate is steady—like the foundational note

that sets the tone. This is the physiological baseline of calm, a state where artists like Yo-Yo Ma might be when performing a deeply serene piece. Their breathing and heart rate support a flow state, allowing the music to come through effortlessly. This harmonic reflects the artist's ability to stay grounded and attuned to their surroundings, just like a steady rhythm holds a composition together.

3. Second Harmonic: Open Facial Expressions and Eye Contact

The second harmonic (G) corresponds to open, relaxed facial expressions and easy eye contact, signaling connection and safety. When performers like Dolly Parton engage their audience, they do so with subtle but powerful expressions and moments of eye contact that create a deep emotional bond. This harmonic adds warmth and depth, much like eye contact and a smile build trust and rapport during a performance or collaborative moment in rehearsal.

4. Third Harmonic: Clear, Calm Communication

The third harmonic (C, two octaves up) represents a state of clear, calm communication. Artists in this state, like Kendrick Lamar during a spoken word performance, use their voice with intentionality. The tone is steady, the pace is natural, and they have the presence to listen as much as they speak or play. This harmonic highlights how feeling safe allows for ease in both self-expression and connection, enabling artists to deliver their message powerfully and confidently.

5. Fourth Harmonic: Curiosity and Playfulness

The fourth harmonic (E, major third) symbolizes curiosity and playfulness. Think of Robin Williams during an improv session—his nervous system is grounded in safety, yet alive with spontaneous, playful energy. This harmonic invites exploration and experimentation, whether it's a musician riffing on stage or a painter adding whimsical flourishes to their work. The sense of joy and freedom infuses their creativity, enriching both the process and the result.

6. Fifth Harmonic: Emotional Flexibility

The fifth harmonic (G) reflects emotional flexibility—the ability to move between different emotional states with grace. Artists like Björk embody this harmonic, shifting from intense emotion to light-heartedness within a single song or performance. In this state, an artist can embrace the full spectrum of emotions without being overwhelmed, allowing their nervous system to remain balanced, resilient, and in harmony with their creative flow.

7. Sixth Harmonic: Creativity and Collaboration

The sixth harmonic (B♭) represents creativity and collaboration. When artists feel safe and connected, they are more open to working with others in creative, generative ways. A band like Radiohead, known for their innovative soundscapes, exemplifies this harmonic. Their collaboration is built on a foundation of trust, and their creativity flourishes as each member contributes something unique to the whole. This harmonic resonates with the collaborative spirit that drives innovation in the arts.

8. Seventh Harmonic: Empathy And Emotional Flexibility

The seventh harmonic (C three octaves above) signifies compassion and empathy. Artists like Nina Simone, whose music was infused with a deep sense of empathy for social justice, embody this state. When artists are grounded in a safe and regulated nervous system, they can connect with the emotions of others on a profound level, using their art to reflect and amplify collective experiences. This highest harmonic shows how safety fosters a deep emotional resonance, making art a vessel for compassion and shared understanding. I also want to emphasize that emotions like sadness, anger, and even fear can be communicated effectively in this state, provided there is sufficient vagal tone. This is exemplified in the oratory of Martin Luther King Jr., who masterfully used the full palette of human emotion in his highly regulated speeches. Passion, after all, does not inherently equate to dysregulation.

External Connect Mode Harmonic

1. **Regulated Heart Rate:** The heart rate is typically slower and steady, reflecting a state of relaxation and calm. The variability in heart rate, known as heart rate variability (HRV), tends to be higher, which is associated with greater adaptability and emotional regulation.

2. **Normal Breathing Patterns:** Breathing is deep, slow, and regular, promoting relaxation and optimal oxygenation of the body. The diaphragm is fully engaged, allowing for effective gas exchange and reducing the need for rapid, shallow breaths.

3. **Facial Expressions and Tone of Voice:** The facial muscles are relaxed, allowing for a range of positive expressions. The tone of voice is warm, melodic, and inviting, often referred to as "prosody." These cues facilitate social bonding and communication.

4. **Relaxed Muscles:** The muscles throughout the body are somewhat relaxed, and without extra tension. This relaxation supports ease of movement and contributes to a sense of physical comfort. *This said, we are not overly relaxed, but our muscles have the appropriate tone for the expression or connection that is required.*

5. **Optimal Digestion:** The digestive system functions efficiently, as blood flow is directed towards the stomach and intestines, promoting healthy digestion and nutrient absorption. This state is often referred to as "rest and digest."

6. **Immune System Functioning:** The immune system is more balanced and functions optimally in this state, supporting overall health and the body's ability to fight off illness.

7. **Energy Conservation:** The body conserves energy rather than expending it on the stress response, leading to a general feeling of well-being and physical ease.

8. **Appropriate Pupil Constriction:** Pupils are normally constricted, allowing for comfortable vision in normal lighting conditions and signaling a state of relaxation and safety.

9. **Healthy Sexual and Reproductive Function:** The safe and social state supports healthy sexual function and reproductive health, as the body is not in a state of survival but rather in a state that promotes procreation and connection.

10. **Balanced Hormone Levels:** Stress hormones like cortisol and adrenaline are at homeostatic levels, while hormones that promote

well-being, such as oxytocin (often called the "bonding hormone") and serotonin, are prominent.

11. **Stable Blood Pressure:** Blood pressure is typically lower and stable, reflecting a state of relaxation and reduced physical arousal.

12. **Healthy Sleep Patterns:** The body is able to enter deep, restorative sleep, with regular sleep cycles. This is crucial for overall health and emotional regulation.

13. **Attunement to Others:** In this state, individuals are more attuned to the emotional and social cues of others, promoting empathy, compassion, and effective communication. This attunement is supported by the engagement of the parasympathetic nervous system.

14. **Increased Salivation:** Saliva production is normal or increased, supporting digestion and oral health, as the body is in a state conducive to eating and processing food.

Internal Connect Mode Harmonics

15. **Clear Thinking:** The person is able to think clearly, process information, and make decisions with ease. They are not overwhelmed by anxiety or stress, allowing for rational and flexible thought processes.

16. **Focus and Attention:** They can maintain focus on tasks or conversations without being easily distracted by intrusive or anxious thoughts. They are present in the moment and able to engage with what is happening around them.

17. **Open-Mindedness**: The person is open to new ideas and perspectives. They are less defensive and more willing to listen, learn, and consider other points of view.

18. **Positive Social Engagement:** They are able to engage in meaningful, reciprocal social interactions. They feel comfortable making eye contact, reading social cues, and communicating effectively. There is a sense of ease in connecting with others.

19. **Problem-Solving:** In the safe and social state, a person is more creative and resourceful in solving problems. Their cognitive flexibility allows them to approach challenges with a constructive mindset rather than feeling stuck or overwhelmed.

20. **Curiosity and Exploration:** The person feels safe enough to explore new ideas, environments, or relationships. They are curious about the world and open to discovering new things without fear of threat or harm.

21. **Empathy and Compassion:** Cognitive empathy and compassion are strong in this state. The person can understand others' emotions and perspectives, and they are capable of responding with care and kindness.

22. **Sense of Safety and Trust:** They have a baseline feeling of safety and trust in their environment and relationships. This trust allows them to lower their guard and engage with others in a vulnerable, authentic way.

23. **Balanced Perspective:** The person can see situations from a balanced perspective, neither overly optimistic or pessimistic. They are able to evaluate events without being driven by fear or anxiety.

24. **Reflective Thinking:** They have the cognitive space to reflect on past experiences and learn from them, rather than being stuck in reactive thinking patterns. This helps with personal growth and making better decisions in the future.

25. **Flexible Boundaries:** The person is able to maintain healthy boundaries in social interactions, knowing when to say 'yes' or 'no' based on their own needs and comfort levels, without feeling overwhelmed or shut down.

The "Actually It's All Gonna Be Ok" Harmonic Series

Fundamental: Core sense of safety and connection.
1st Harmonic: Regulated breathing and heart rate.
2nd Harmonic: Open facial expressions and eye contact.
3rd Harmonic: Clear and calm communication.
4th Harmonic: Curiosity and playfulness.
5th Harmonic: Emotional flexibility.
6th Harmonic: Creativity and collaboration.
7th Harmonic: Compassion and empathy.

ugh, Go home.

Wicked boring dude.

Examples of Songs with **Characters in Connect Mode:**

1. "What a Wonderful World" by Louis Armstrong

The character in this song expresses a deep sense of peace, joy, and connection with the world around them. The lyrics highlight the beauty of nature and human interaction, reflecting a profound sense of safety and social engagement.

2. "Lean on Me" by Bill Withers

In this song, the character offers and seeks support from friends, fostering a strong sense of connection and community. The willingness to lean on others during difficult times shows a deep trust and engagement, characteristic of the safe and social state.

Under The Hood:

When the body detects safety and enters the **safe and social state**, the **ventral vagal complex** of the parasympathetic nervous system is activated, creating a sense of calm and connection. This part of the nervous system, rooted in the **vagus nerve**, down-regulates the body's stress response, leading to slower heart rate, regulated breathing, and relaxed muscles. The brain interprets cues from the environment—such as soothing voices, facial expressions, or safe surroundings—as signs of safety, allowing the body to shift from defense to social engagement mode. **Neurotransmitters** like **oxytocin**, **serotonin**, and **dopamine** are released, promoting feelings of trust, connection, and well-being. Blood flow is directed toward areas responsible for digestion, healing, and higher cognitive functioning, such as communication, empathy, and creativity. In this state, the body's resources are no longer consumed by survival instincts but are instead devoted to building relationships, fostering learning, and promoting physical and emotional restoration. This harmonious state, regulated by the ventral vagal system, allows for optimal social engagement and overall well-being.

Letter # 10: Houston, We Have a Problem With Preservation Mode

Dear Artist,

Let's take it back to the basics: imagine you're using a rotary phone—one of those old-school, one-function devices. That's kind of like being in **Preservation Mode.** It's simple and efficient when you're in survival mode, where there's no room for complexity or nuance. But what if you needed to send an email or process a payment with that same rotary phone? Impossible, right? You'd need a modern device to handle those tasks.

Problem #1: Preservation Mode limits our ability to connect and perform as it evolved for a very different purpose.

Now think of your nervous system like that rotary phone. When you're in a basic state, like Preservation Mode, it's built to get you through an emergency, but it's not designed for anything more complex—like performing on stage, where you need nuance, emotional depth, and precise control. That's why, when you're hit with this outdated "rotary phone" nervous-system state in the middle of a performance, it can feel like panic. You're trying to perform with a tool that's not equipped for the job.

Before stepping on stage, you might find yourself in a situation that isn't literally life-threatening, but your emotions are so intense that your nervous system reacts as if it were. You freeze—not because the threat is real, but because your nervous system can't tell the difference between emotional overwhelm and actual danger. It automatically kicks into whatever mode it thinks is necessary for survival.

The challenge with Preservation Mode is that it often locks us into inaction when what we really need is movement—whether that's a physical response or mental clarity. And once you're stuck in that mode, it feels almost impossible to break out, making it even harder to regulate yourself and shift into a more adaptive state. That's where the real struggle lies—getting yourself unstuck when your nervous system is convinced you can't.

Let me paint you a picture. Laura is a professional writer who's been approached by a wealthy entrepreneur for a ghostwriting project. The thought of asking for what she needs—whether it's payment, time, or clarity—makes her feel incredibly unsafe, triggering a sense of panic. She knows she has to ask, but the fear grips her, and she freezes. Suddenly, she feels numb, disconnected, unworthy. She goes to use her mouth and nothing comes out.

If she had a "smartphone" version of her nervous system, she could easily call up a friend and ask for advice on how to negotiate. But that doesn't even cross her mind. Why? As she holds her breath, her dorsal vagus nerve kicks in, slowing down her heart rate to keep her immobilized, but in doing so, her body redirects oxygen away from the parts of her brain that handle problem-solving and decision-making. Her mind goes blank like her creative and cognitive circuits are offline. Her brain prediction has redirected its metabolic resources (her energy) towards shutting the system down for protection.

For performers and artists, spending too much time in Preservation Mode—whether triggered by a major emotional event or over an extended period—can have lasting effects. Dr. Stephen Porges explains that when this happens, "the social engagement system and ability to down-regulate defensive systems are compromised," which is what we see in conditions like PTSD.

While it's no big deal to experience a brief Preservation Mode response, staying in that state for too long can become harmful. For adults, it impacts our ability to connect, express, and create, but for a young, developing brain, it can be catastrophic. When stuck in this mode, the very tools we need as artists—our emotional range, creativity, and ability to engage—become stifled.

The instructions for this protocol are this. The stage is not a place to work Preservation Mode or heal PTSD. In fact, it's one of the worst places to do that and can reinforce signals of danger that keep a nervous system set point to a deeper immobilization.

I'm deeply skeptical of the trauma-industrial complex due to the perilous history of their experimentations on women and Indigenous communities. **Even with that in mind, I would go to a therapist first before trying to work out my trauma on stage.**

I've had countless conversations with brilliant artists who feared that healing their trauma might diminish their genius or weaken the power of their art. There's no simple answer to this, but I've observed that great art is often created *after* periods of intense depression, not *during*, as the physiological toll of depression can be deeply punishing or immobilizing. This may also be a decision you want to make based on your resources. I don't have $100-500k lying around to support my body should my immune, reproductive, or digestive systems begin to express disease due to chronic immobilization and stress. I can't afford **not** to put my body first.

Problem #2: It's difficult to advocate for a physiological system that has been ignored, suppressed, and shamed.

The impact of Preservation Mode is so profound that you might wonder why artists, teachers, and even therapists are only just learning about it now. In the therapy world, I often point out that PTSD—essentially when Preservation Mode becomes a disorder—wasn't even officially recognized in the DSM (the manual for diagnosing mental illness) until the early 1980s. Why? Because, historically, the military needed men to feel like they were weak if they didn't want to go to war or if they froze under pressure. Acknowledging "freeze" as a real, valid response would have threatened national security, making it harder to recruit soldiers during drafts. If society had fully understood PTSD back then, it would have exposed the reality that war not only destroys lives but also deeply damages the brain and nervous system. And, you know, the government would then have to support veterans.

Think about it: PTSD is only as old as I am—and I've only got a few gray hairs! This might explain why your acting or music teachers may not know how to help you when you freeze on stage. For years, Preservation Mode responses have been shamed, and countless people have gone without the support or treatment they needed. As artists, this means we're often left struggling alone with nervous system states we haven't been taught to navigate.

Problem #3: Preservation Mode can be confused with tiredness, glucose crashes, and dopamine lows.

With only a few decades of focused research, the nuances of Preservation Mode are still often misunderstood—especially in the arts. The "freeze" response occurs when the nervous system is triggered by a perceived threat. While there's ongoing debate about the exact physiological mechanisms (most agree the dorsal vagus is involved, but I'll leave those debates to the neuroscientists), what we do know is that it's marked by numbness and dissociation.

From the outside, this Preservation Mode response can look similar to other nervous system states, but it's actually very different and requires a completely different approach. This is why, as artists, we sometimes misinterpret what's happening in our bodies or apply the wrong tools to address Preservation Mode. With artists, using the wrong tool with the wrong state feels like shame. Using the right tool for the right issue is freedom. Understanding Preservation Mode for what it really is can help us tailor our methods of self-regulation and avoid feeling trapped in the moment.

I often question clients when they say they are in Preservation Mode. It's not because I don't believe them, it's because I want to make sure we are really talking about the most severe of human physiological defense states (in relation to the arts) and not something else. So, if you are not sure if you are in Preservation Mode, here are some more questions to consider:

Is it a dopamine low?
Dopamine, often called the "feel-good hormone," plays a major role in our moods. If we have more dopamine than our homeostatic level we feel pleasure, if we are neutral we don't feel much, and if it drops we experience a "dip" or what is known as a "dopamine low." When dopamine levels are high, you can feel euphoric, focused, and energized—imagine a performer soaking in thunderous applause after a career-defining show or an athlete standing on the podium with a gold medal. But this high comes with a catch: it's often followed by a crash, as the body works to bring dopamine levels back to homeostasis.

This is why some of our greatest successes are immediately followed by feelings of emptiness or letdown. And it's not just the big moments—this cycle happens in smaller ways too, especially in today's world, where constant demands and stimuli put pressure on our dopamine system. As artists, understanding this dynamic can help us navigate the emotional ups and downs that come with our craft.

Outwardly, someone in a dopamine dip and someone in Preservation Mode might look similar—both might seem despondent, lethargic, fatigued, and still. But the ways to address each state are very different. As we'll explore in more detail later, the most effective way to move out of Preservation Mode is through Activation—a technique that restores energy and movement through your nervous system, guiding you back toward Connect Mode.

However, this approach wouldn't work for a dopamine dip. In that case, the best thing you can do is rest and ride out the low until your brain naturally restores its balance. When dealing with a dopamine dip, you don't need to re-energize or restore blood flow to the brain. Instead, you need to either embrace discomfort (like a cold shower or acupuncture) or, even better, simply rest and allow your brain to recalibrate through recovery. We will address "the how" to manage this later, but for now, I just need to put this on your space radar.

Is it mild anxiety over the stresses of socialization?
This brings me to another common mistake therapists make. If you give someone a hammer, they'll see everything as a nail. Similarly, if you give someone Polyvagal Theory, they start seeing everything as "freeze." I recently had the privilege of talking with a brilliant woman and painter who was confused about whether she was stuck in a Preservation Mode. She said, "I mean, talking in this Zoom felt hard and awkward, and I was worried about what people thought of me."

When we dug into her sensations, it turned out she wasn't in Preservation Mode at all—she was actually in an agitated Connect Mode, just feeling the normal awkwardness that comes with human interaction. She felt like this social navigation should always be fun or enjoyable and if it wasn't, there was something wrong with her. In this case, we don't need to use Preservation Mode shifting protocols. Instead, we need to unshame that very human experience and use Connect Mode protocols.

Is it fatigue?

Another common mistake when it comes to Preservation Mode is confusing tiredness with freeze. In our culture, rest is often shamed. There's little space for it, and many of us feel we can't afford to make time for it. As a result, we've forgotten how to simply surrender to and unshame the normal sensations that come with being truly tired.

When we're exhausted, we don't need to activate or restore blood flow to the brain like we do in a Preservation Mode state. We just need to rest. As artists, honoring the need for rest is crucial to sustaining our creativity and energy, rather than pushing through fatigue as though it's a problem to fix.

Is it an insulin crash?

Finally, the last mistake is insulin spikes and crashes. Anytime we eat too much sugar, we force our insulin to swoop in and save our body from high blood-glucose levels, and then we crash. This can cause lethargy, sleepiness, and brain fog. When we spike insulin we do not need to employ Preservation Mode protocols like light movement (to activate to restore energy to the brain), we need significant muscle contraction to aid glucose absorption. This will require better food choices. There is of course crossover between dopamine and insulin. *Please refer to the reference library for further study.*

So what is the Preservation Mode exactly?

Overall when you think about Preservation Mode the first thing you should connect it with is slight **oxygen deprivation.** The image I want you to spotlight in your brain around this mode is a numb limb. When we go numb, we need to restore oxygen to our body slowly and carefully. In the clinical world they call this **titration**. The real world calls this taking your damn time. You would never feel a numb leg and then get right on it. You would pat it, shake it, feel it, rub the muscle. We do the same when we are frozen.

Fish don't get PTSD (while underwater) because they don't have oxygen-hungry brains (like we do) that are quickly starved of oxygen when they are in Preservation Mode. Boney fish and reptiles helped invent Preservation Mode, so it doesn't come with as many glitches in the system.

Remember when you put a rubber band around your finger as a kid and it turned blue? Your body will never turn blue in Preservation Mode, but you will notice when you lose your lyrics or sense of self (dissociation). If we could tolerate holding our breath for 20 minutes like our amphibian or fish friends underwater, the trauma therapy industry would be wiped out overnight. Hold this thought because we will revisit this reality when we get to how to shift into Move Mode and towards safety.

Preservation Mode is the oldest state of our nervous system, but it is also in some ways the most powerful, as it reaches back to our primordial selves to a far recess of physiology. It can save our lives, but it can also cut us off from the parts of society and culture that are equally as important to our growth and happiness.

Just like a short visit under water is fine, a long one is lethal for human functioning and often why trauma survivors say, "I feel like I'm drowning and no one can hear me scream for help." I hear you, friend, and I'm hoping the tools in this book become a new life-preserver for you the next time you are in a Preservation Mode.

Later in the shifting chapter, I will give you tons of ideas of what you can do to get out of Preservation Mode, but in this chapter, I simply want you to build awareness that tiredness, dopamine lows, and glucose crashes are also the cause of very similar feelings.

The problem with this mode is that it starves us of oxygen and can't serve us when we need to do almost anything requiring careful thought or connection. And also, it can be confused with so many other issues. Here is a quick offering to help you navigate but please know we will be diving deeper–especially with dopamine–later in the book, if you are left with questions.

The "4 Question Quick Check"

Question 1: Did something significant or jarring overwhelm my body budget recently, and do I notice numbness or dissociation?

Question 2: Did I just experience something *unusually* exciting, pleasurable or novel (new to you)?

Question 3: Have you physically or mentally been working hard? Have you felt overstimulated at work or home?

Question 4: Did you just consume a lot of sugar or simple carbohydrates without combining them with vegetables, proteins, or fats?

Q1: If the answer is "yes", you might be in freeze mode.
Q2: If the answer is "yes", you might be in a dopamine dip.
Q3: If the answer is "yes", you're likely just tired.
Q4: If the answer is "yes", you're likely just experiencing an insulin crash.

Killer Harmonics: My Freeze (Preservation Mode) Stories
There's another major challenge with Preservation Mode that we often overlook: the internal "harmonics" of this state—the ways it changes our thoughts and perceptions. The problem is that these harmonics can sometimes be deadly or harmful. In Preservation Mode, your nervous system is essentially trying to keep you "horizontal," playing dead to protect you. It numbs your body, preparing you for a worst-case scenario, like being caught by a predator. This state is deeply wired into us from hundreds of thousands of years of evolution, when freezing was a survival tactic. The truth is, this was the state animals often went into as they were nearing death.

For artists, this can be dangerous. If we stay in freeze for too long, our thoughts can convince us that we don't belong, that we should give up, or even that we should leave this planet. But these thoughts are just the physiological effects of the nervous system trying to immobilize us, not reality.

In later chapters, we'll dive into how to move out of this state. But for now, I want to introduce you to a concept you may not be familiar with: **your Preservation Mode "story."** We all have stories and narratives that pop up when we're triggered into a survival state—whether it's the Connect, Move, or Preservation Mode. These stories, often called anticipatory stress or rumination, seem to have a life of their own. It's like playing a game of mental whack-a-mole.

Imagine a rabbit caught by a predator. It freezes, hoping the predator will lose interest. Now, if that rabbit unfroze too early, trying to "stay positive," it would likely get eaten. Similarly, the longer our defensive state and story stay active, the better our chances of survival—at least according to our nervous system. So if I start thinking, "I'm a terrible artist, I should just give up," am I likely to take positive action? No. I'll stay stuck in that freeze, because my nervous system's priority is not thriving, it's survival.

This is why, when we're not in actual danger, it's important not to overanalyze these thoughts. Instead, we should use tools to shift out of that state, because often, our thoughts are what keep us stuck in Preservation Mode.

Here's an assignment for you: either now or next time you feel like you are in Preservation Mode, write down five Preservation Mode stories you tell yourself in this state. Once you have done that, identify three to five Preservation Mode stories that directly relate to your art. Examples of mine are, "Why even try" or "This is stupid."

Why is this important?

Because it helps you avoid what Lisa Feldman Barrett calls **"affective realism"**—the trap of believing that the way we feel in our nervous system state is the only objective reality. In that mindset, you don't just have a nervous system state—you *are* your nervous system state.

In Preservation Mode, your thoughts become amplified, due to the body's lack of feeling. If you can catch one, you can start to say, "Wait, that's my freeze state talking." Your freeze stories can act as clues, helping you become a kind of Sherlock Holmes, using those stories to identify the state you are in.

There's one key exception that doesn't apply to Move or Connect Modes: in Preservation Mode, due to a lack of energy to the neocortex, you might go completely mentally blank. Having no story—feeling like you're nowhere, or like you're watching yourself from across the room—is also part of your Preservation Mode "narrative"---well, anti-narrative. When you feel empty or blank, the absence of a story becomes its own clue, helping you identify where you are on the nervous system ladder. In this case, Preservation Mode.

One final note: This is only appropriate for those who can see their thoughts as objects, not subjects. **For very young children, who *are* their thoughts, this wouldn't be suitable. Similarly, it wouldn't be appropriate for someone who is developmentally delayed or severely traumatized, where separating thoughts from self isn't possible.** This should never be forced on anyone. That said, when something that once felt subjective becomes objective, it's a sign that we are growing and maturing.

Reflections of Preservation Mode

- If you are in freeze for a prolonged period of time, seek mental health support from a trauma-informed therapist or practitioner.

- If you are feeling low, try to determine the cause of your feeling so you can pick the right protocol for shifting. If the protocol doesn't work, you are not doing anything wrong. You just need a tool that works for you.

- If you are in Preservation Mode, you are not broken. If our bodies can go into this mode, they can find their way out.

- If you hear your Preservation Mode story tell you that you shouldn't be here anymore, please remember that it's just the story's attempt to keep us protected, it's not a legit instruction.

SHADES OF BLUE

Preservation Mode is a song of neurobiology that lives on a color palette with various shades. These variations of Preservation Mode can be experienced offstage in our personal lives, and onstage as a palette for expression in theatrical performance.

Offstage, outside of the protection of play, this Preservation Mode state spectrum lures and seduces a human being to stay in the state as long as possible.

*Let these songs wake you up from the sleep of your dysregulation and **do not follow them as instructions.** Unlike at the top of the ladder, these "freeze" songs are more like Odysseus' cruel sirens.*

*As you can see from your **nervous system cards (#1-3),** the Preservation Mode is a spectrum of experience that contains different levels of activation.*

Black and Blue

#1. Black and Blue: Is the "song" of death. It's the song that asks an animal to stay still as it passes on to the other realm (the rainbow bridge). The numbness is nature's design to prevent unusually cruel and painful death. This is not a song we ever want to believe or listen to. This song requires help from a mental health professional or one's community. Its pull can be hard, humiliating, and terrifying. Artists may find themselves here after experiences of deep distress, of overreaching or abusive leaders or directors, or even from intimacy onstage gone wrong. Do not follow the instructions of this song.

If this state was a literal song:

- **"Gloomy Sunday" (originally composed by Rezső Seress)** – Often called the "Hungarian Suicide Song," this classic has a melancholic tone and has been rumored to influence despair in listeners. The song became infamous for its dark, haunting lyrics about sorrow and longing for death, though different versions exist, some more hopeful than others.
- **"Adam's Song" by Blink-182** – Written from the perspective of someone contemplating suicide, this song dives into feelings of isolation and despair. However, it ultimately ends on a more hopeful note, suggesting that things can get better.

- **"Hurt" by Nine Inch Nails (and the Johnny Cash cover)** – Both versions of this song deal with deep pain and self-destruction. While the lyrics express profound sadness, it's more of a reflection on the emotional fallout of life's struggles rather than an encouragement of death.

Grey Blue

#2. Grey Blue: This is often called "functional freeze," and is as old as Richard Burton's work on melancholia, "The Anatomy of Melancholy," and extensively by the therapeutic community, including PVT. In humans, this state is about staying as small and out of the way as possible to avoid being harmed by a potential threat. There is more sympathetic activation (energy) here than in the "black and blue" freeze state but is still very collapsed. When masked by the appearance of the safe and social state, it can look quite normal from the outside which is why it's referred to as "functional." This is an exhausting song to live every day.

As you'll sense from the songs listed below, there is a feeling of vertigo and disconnection, stemming from the loss of connection with our cognitive structures—and therefore, with ourselves. This version of Preservation Mode has a greater sense of exhaustion and lowness than our next flavor of Preservation Mode.

- **"Motion Sickness" by Phoebe Bridgers**
  Phoebe Bridgers captures the feeling of being overwhelmed but unable to fully express it in this song. The idea of "motion sickness" metaphorically describes the internal turbulence beneath a calm surface, echoing the Grey Blue state where sympathetic activation is present, but the person appears functional on the outside.

- **"Mad World" by Gary Jules (cover of Tears for Fears)**
  This song is a haunting reflection on the quiet, numbing sadness of life. The lyrics "I find it kind of funny, I find it kind of sad, the dreams in which I'm dying are the best I've ever had" suggest someone operating in a state of functional despair, emotionally detached yet moving through life in a surreal haze.

- **"Everything in Its Right Place" by Radiohead**
  This song explores the tension between maintaining order and control externally while feeling off-balance and disconnected internally. The repetitive, trance-like melody mirrors the sensation of functional freeze, where a person is operating, but something vital feels missing or numbed.

Bright Blue

#3. Bright Blue: For this state imagine an unstable blue star about to explore into heat. This state is the dorsal vagal shutdown but also contains a lot of activated energy. You could think about this as a part of the Preservation Mode spectrum or as an extension of the bottom of the Move Mode spectrum since this state contains both energies. **Imagine you are in a car and the gas and the brake are fully engaged.** You are revving hot but you aren't going anywhere. This state feels a bit like Sisyphus trying to go hard to bring a boulder up a mountain just to fall back down.

- **"Running Up That Hill" by Kate Bush**
  This song conveys a sense of pushing forward but being held back simultaneously, with its driving rhythm and emotional intensity. The feeling of wanting to escape or change something, but being trapped, mirrors the Bright Blue state's tension.
- **"Unfinished Sympathy" by Massive Attack**
  With its powerful, pulsating energy combined with an undercurrent of emotional pain and longing, this track captures the sensation of

emotional tension without resolution, much like the gas and brake dynamic of the Bright Blue state.

- **"Help I'm Alive" by Metric**
  This song embodies the internal struggle of feeling like you're about to "explode" from the inside, while remaining outwardly still. The pulsating beat and lyrics about the heart pounding and feeling on the edge match the dual forces of activation and shutdown in the Bright Blue state.

"I can't feel my face when I'm with you."

But literally. I'm frozen.

Letter # 11: The Potential Problems of Move Mode

Dear Artist,

The other night the battery in my smoke alarm finally croaked and began emitting those irritating beeps at 3am. Before I was fully awake, my heart raced, my pulse quickened, and my body launched into **Move Mode**. After my groggy perception caught up with my neuroception, I understood the situation and curbed the escalation toward a genuine panic.

Problem #1: The predictive brain is trigger-happy when it comes to Move Mode.

Neuroception—the Ground Control from our Astronaut chapter—intends to match the environment of your body to the environment of the world around you as quickly as possible. And it is very good at its job, but it also regularly overreacts, as in the smoke alarm beep in the middle of the night. **My body would much prefer to overreact and potentially waste metabolic energy than risk being burned alive.** An acceptable compromise, on the whole, but one that would become less so if I lost or damaged my conscious self's ability to recognize the confusion and regulate my nervous system accordingly. Otherwise I would have ended up standing outside my not-burning house in my underwear panicking.

The point is, just like **Preservation Mode**, Move Mode is activated by our neuroception in scenarios when it is uncalled for, ineffective, or otherwise unproductive, perhaps even dangerous. Like I said in an earlier chapter, Ground Control can't fully see what's happening out the spaceship's window. It needs to make choices fast to ensure the ship's survival.

Of course, for our ancestors, Move Mode was a fiercely vital adaptation for thousands of years. Because real threats can still occur in our lives that demand Move Mode's rapid decision-making and instinctual awareness, we obviously still need to keep it exercised and at the ready. This is a delicate, difficult balancing act. This is the work of **Regulation**. What many people don't know is that without slowing down the heart rate (with the help of the vagus nerve), our heart rates would naturally run over 100 bpm. So when the vagal brake is released (just like a bicycle brake down a hill), energy comes pouring into the system. It's always at the ready! This is the mechanism that allows for that intensely fast response. The tiger is always waiting in our body to pounce, and thank goodness it was built this way, otherwise our species would not have survived. So, here we are with a very obvious issue. When we don't feel safe, we are flooded very quickly with an excess of energy. While this is actually a metabolic jolt to the system of cortisol leading to more glucose for our muscle, we often experience it as deep shame when it's one of the most common experiences we have as humans.

When our ancient forebears began cooperating and operating as tribes, the development of social and cultural capabilities within our nervous systems became not only necessary to give us enough time away from peril so that we stop seeing others as a constant threat, but it also soon became evolutionarily advantageous for our species. As Dr. Stephen Porges puts it, our "survival became dependent on satisfying a need to interact for nursing and for other forms of social interactions and group behaviors linked to obtaining food, reproducing, playing, and supporting general safety needs." We are, in effect, "able to turn off defense systems." But, Porges continues, "to balance the needs of social interaction with the needs of safety, it is necessary to know when to turn the defenses off and when to turn the defenses back on."

Researcher Lisa Feldman Barrett, PhD, has come up with some massively helpful language around this "pulse" of metabolic energy into the body. She calls the energy our brains think will help our body survive, our **"body budget."** When this budget is out of control or our bodies are "spending" metabolic "money" (energy) we can't afford, I call it a "body-budget leak." We are leaking valuable, energetic resources. So when we are stressed, this is equivalent to being at a store and then your brain whips out your Mastercard and spends your entire credit limit.

Problem #2: Stress is viral in groups.

If I gave you a pill with adrenaline in it, you might assume it's going to amp you up, make you aggressive, or even angry. But adrenaline does more than that. It's an **amplifying hormone**. Imagine a group of gazelles all surprised at the same time. Adrenaline is meant to make you "catch" the emotion of another person around you. Thanks to Schachter and Singer's study at Minnesota University in 1962, it turns out if you give someone adrenaline in a waiting room with a friendly person, you will feel more friendly. If you are in a waiting room with someone aggressive, you will get angry. This is really wild because, in this case, adrenaline could help an audience feel more invested in the drama of the play or make two actors feel more emotionally connected. In this case, we might want to ride out adrenaline instead of shutting it down. And, you may want to be aware of this if your director is sad, as you are more likely to "catch" that feeling if you have more adrenaline in your body.

Just as a little bit of adrenaline can be good and natural and appropriate to an exciting situation, too much can make that same scenario frightening and uncomfortable. So too must we tread the fine line between too little fear and too much.

This is also why casts of the play Macbeth can become unbelievably superstitious. You are putting stressful language through your body every day, and in an adrenaline-fueled environment, it's easy to catch it and think it's yours. Let this biological reality sink in as you recall the collective dysregulation that may have occurred in rehearsals, acting classes, or even backstage.

Problem #3: Move Mode is culturally applauded.

It's often easy to function within a social environment entirely in Move Mode, even when you might outwardly project Connect Mode. I certainly did this in my twenties, when survival and success were so socially and emotionally intertwined that I'm not sure I ever fully left Move Mode during those years. In many artistic communities, Move Mode is celebrated as the best way to live. Think of George Clooney's corporate guru in the movie *Up in the Air*, who conducts seminars at business conferences promoting ideas like "moving is living" and "the slower we move, the faster we die." Our culture incentivizes incessant movement, a constant hum of unsatisfied ambition that is just as obstructive to our individual progress as not developing the much more effective social skills and possessing only Move Mode is to our progress as a species.

But there is nuance here, don't forget that the Connect Mode sucks up this state and reframes Move Mode as play and healthy competition. This energy within regulation is really, really good for us. The friction of movement is crucial to the success of any musician, artist, or entrepreneur. This adrenaline might easily be confused with stress and shut down. Within the warm embrace of Connect Mode, this energy is very powerful and sustainable without detrimental health effects. Basically, the difference between stress that kills you and stress that fuels you (hormesis) can be a small distance, but that distance may be the difference between longevity and burnout.

It is our nervous system's ability to temporarily *quiet* or background our neuroception that allows for Connect Mode. Which is another way of saying that it is only when we feel safe enough to let our guard down that social engagement is possible. Which is another way of saying that Clooney's guru is wrong; *moving* is not living. Safety is.

Problem #4: A small amount of Move Mode is necessary for creativity.

A certain amount of stress or body budget is one of the first steps of Herbert Benson's famous "flow cycle." If we shut down irritation, we shut down creativity. This is a huge pitfall to be wary of in the arts. We don't need to fix this feeling, we just need to unshame it.

My Fight/Flight (Move Mode) Stories

Talk about whack-a-mole: our Move Mode stories become much faster and more rambunctious in this state. Just when you think you've stuffed all your raging thoughts away, they pop up over and over. For many people, alcohol or drugs feel like the only way to drown out this mental vortex of panic. Rumination can be excruciating in this state because of the ferocity of defense.

While the stories we hear in Preservation Mode may sound like, "Pfft, what's the point of living?" and have a certain distance from us like a haunted echo, our Move Mode stories are often urgent, and they feel *super,*

super real. In terms of "affective realism" the feeling like our thoughts and feelings *are* us. They *have* to be in this state. Nature's job is to protect us at all cost. This means we have a little less free will in Move Mode than in Connect Mode.

When we dysregulate our thoughts become polarized with black and white, us and them, good or bad thinking. This is not something to "fix," it's something to unshame. This kind of thinking is baked into the system and it's going to be very hard to separate the flour from the sugar once the cake is baked. But, we can **unshame and notice** perfectionistic, extreme, judgmental, territorial, or just mean thoughts. When I am really angry but also in Move Mode, boy, am I a lean, mean nervous-system machine. I call this "Mob Wife Mode." Does this mean I'm a bad person? No, it means **my thoughts are trying to prolong a nervous system response that is trying to keep my body alive for as long as humanly possible.** So, while I may feel mad or want to say something mean, the key is to hear my Move Mode story, identify my state, and regulate (find safety for my nervous system) before I respond.

If I judged every thought I had in Move Mode, I would hate myself! It is such a relief to know it's safe to feel rage in my body without hurting anyone. Before PVT, I would judge the mental "harmonics" of Move Mode, aka the biological and behavioral changes that accompany the fight/flight response. They are normal. Everyone says things they don't mean or that, if expressed out loud, might feel embarrassing or childish. These Move Mode harmonics are designed to help us recognize the state we're in so we can address the underlying issue at its root, rather than attempting to erase the natural structural qualities of our biology. In many ways, Cognitive Behavioral Therapy (CBT) aligns with this concept by focusing on identifying patterns within Move Mode harmonics. However, it often falls short by overlooking the body's fundamental need for safety as an integral part of the process. For some it's life changing, and for others it bypasses their need to identify the core needs of Move Mode.

Before I have you look at your Move Mode stories let's borrow some of the Move Mode Harmonics of CBT as they can be helpful to understand what kind of stories might pop up if you are in this state:

All-or-Nothing Thinking: Viewing situations in black-and-white terms (e.g., "If I am not cast, I'm a total failure").

Catastrophizing: Assuming the worst possible outcome (e.g., "If I mess up this audition, I'll lose this part").

Overgeneralization: Drawing broad conclusions from a single event (e.g., "They didn't cast me last season, so I'll always fail").

Mental Filtering: Focusing only on the negatives while ignoring positives.

Discounting Positives: Dismissing positive feedback or experiences (e.g., "They said they loved my audition but didn't cast me. I was clearly terrible").

Emotional Reasoning: Believing emotions reflect reality (e.g., "I feel unworthy, so I must be a horrible actor").

Labeling: Assigning a negative label to oneself or others (e.g., "I'm a bad actor").

Mind Reading: Assuming you know what others are thinking (e.g., "They think I'm too ugly for this part").

Fortune-Telling: Predicting future failure or disaster without evidence.

Personalization: Blaming oneself for events beyond their control.

Again, I love that my brain does this harmonic dance to keep me safe! I love that I don't have to clean it up. I do need to see when thoughts of this nature arise. You are not broken. This is your nervous system's mental structure. Knowing this makes me feel so free.

So, your assignment is to identify three to five Move Mode stories (stories you tell about yourself or your artform in Move Mode). Mine are, "Boston doesn't support the arts and is just here to leave us as shriveled, dry artists," or "She probably got that opportunity because she's rich!" or "I will never have enough money, time, or freedom!" None of them are totally true, but boy do they feel true when I'm in Move Mode's mental web of intense harmonics.

What are yours?

Reflections of Move Mode

- If you are in Move Mode and you need to move to defend yourself from a deadly attack or crisis, your nervous system is working well.

- If you are in Move Mode for a prolonged period of time, seek mental health support from a trauma-informed therapist or practitioner.

- If you are feeling anxious, check your surroundings and leaders as they may be affecting your nervous system through the power of adrenaline.

- Move Mode is the cultural norm. It is also deadly if prolonged.

SHADES OF RED

Move Mode is a song of neurobiology that lives on a color palette with various shades. These variations of Move Mode can be experienced offstage in our personal lives, and onstage as a palette for expression in theatrical performance.

Offstage, outside of the protection of play, this state spectrum lures and seduces a human being to stay in the state as long as possible. They are like spells that should never be believed unless your life is at urgent risk. The songs of Move are asking you to move towards or away! Look at your nervous system cards. Let these songs wake you up from the sleep of your dysregulation and do not follow them as instructions.

*As you can see from your **nervous system cards (#4-6),** the Move Mode is a spectrum of experience that contains different levels of activation.*

Deep Red

#4. Deep Red: Is the "song" flight. This is the song that moves our bodies out of danger. It's the song of "run!" It's the chase scene, it's the deep need to not be where you are right now. It's the impulse to ghost, it's the dysregulated "Irish goodbye," it's the song of the prey.

- **"Hunted" by Kesha**
  Kesha's song directly tackles the feeling of being hunted, with lyrics describing a desperate attempt to flee from danger. It's all about survival and the feeling of being prey in a threatening situation.

- **"Running With the Wolves" by AURORA**
  This song explores the wild, primal urge to escape, feeling hunted, and the need to run with urgency. The ethereal yet intense energy captures that animalistic flight response.

- **"Survival" by Muse**
  Muse's dramatic song channels the raw emotion of survival, with the feeling of being chased or on the verge of danger. The lyrics and

music exude the intensity of running for your life, much like prey escaping a predator.

Bright Red

#5. Bright Red: This is the song of attack. This is the song of dysregulated perseverance. This is the dance of the lone wolf. This song is telling you your life's in danger and it's time to save it right now. This is the call to blood, the call to war, this is the song of emergency.

The **Bright Red** state, representing the "fight" response, is charged with urgency, survival, and a raw, aggressive energy. It's the call to act immediately, fueled by danger and the instinct to protect or persevere at all cost. Songs that match this state often carry intense, driving energy and a sense of confrontation, aggression, or emergency.

Here are some songs that resonate with the **Bright Red** state:

- **"Killing in the Name" by Rage Against the Machine**
  This song is pure fight energy, full of rebellion, anger, and defiance. Its powerful, relentless rhythm and aggressive lyrics embody the call to fight back and persevere against oppression—perfect for the Bright Red state.

- **"Sabotage" by Beastie Boys**
  With its fast pace and high-energy beat, "Sabotage" captures the feeling of urgency and anger that comes with needing to act now. The sense of frustration and rebellion aligns with the instinct to fight in the Bright Red state.
- **"Welcome to the Jungle" by Guns N' Roses**
  This classic rock anthem is full of aggression and intensity, with its theme of survival in a dangerous, chaotic world. The driving force of the song embodies the energy of attack and survival under threat.

Orange

#6. Orange: This is the song of fighting not other people but for connection and for your dreams. It marks the transition out of dysregulation and the return to balance and safety. Singing this song is like calling out for a lifeboat to rescue you and bring you back to the shores of safety and stability. It's the song of perseverance, of holding on and reaching for hope, as you fight to reconnect with yourself, others, and your aspirations.

- **"Stay" by Rihanna (feat. Mikky Ekko)**
  This emotionally raw ballad is about vulnerability and the plea to hold onto connection, even when things feel uncertain. The repeated refrain of "Stay" begs for emotional closeness, making it a perfect fit for a song about fighting for connection.

- **"Fight Song" by Rachel Platten**
  This track is an empowering anthem of self-perseverance, a declaration of strength to keep fighting for one's self and dreams. It speaks to a regulated fight, where the battle is fought with hope and resilience, rather than desperation or chaos.

- **"Hold On" by Alabama Shakes**
  This song is a perfect fit for the Orange state—it's about holding on and fighting through tough times, but with a sense of emotional balance and groundedness. It reflects perseverance and the strength to keep pushing forward.

Letter # 12: The Potential Problems of Connect Mode

In many ways, Connect Mode is the riskiest nervous system state. This may sound counterintuitive, since it is the state in which we feel the safest. Indeed, we can only enter such a state if our neuroception (our Ground Control) feels our safety is ensured enough to not activate our ancient guards. So while we are at our most relaxed and unfearful, we are actually at our most vulnerable to our own dysregulatory defense states.

Why does this word, "vulnerability" come up when we feel risk in Connect Mode? We don't have the analgesic effects (our natural painkillers) we get in defense so we feel it all. The total emotional spectrum (core-affect) which ranges from pain to pleasure to calm to excitement. So if you felt flooded with emotion when you were healing and entering into Connect Mode, this is why.

When climbers come down from mountains completely frozen, they often beg rescue teams not to warm them up because it's so deeply painful to unfreeze. This is a powerful metaphor for how frightening the feeling of safety can be for people who are just coming back "home" for the first time in a long time. Furthermore, any musician familiar with acoustic instruments knows that unboxing a newly delivered cold guitar in a warm house can be hard on the wood. It's best to bring it into the house without opening it right away so the guitar can acclimate to the indoor temperature naturally without shock. Therapists call this process, "titration." We must be very gentle as we return to the Connect Mode state after long periods of dysregulation.

Problem #1: Socialization is risky.

But there's also another reason this Connect Mode is risky. It is often called "the safe and social state," yet there's nothing entirely safe about being social. Even the closest families, partners, and friends experience disconnection and require repair. No relationship remains permanently connected; in fact, relationships deepen precisely because of their cycles of instability and reconnection. When I can't experience anger in Connect Mode and feel it in Move Mode, I don't feel much risk, but when I'm apologizing for something I said or did in that state—when I'm coming from a place of connection— that's when it feels risky and scary. Many people avoid this altogether.

As I mentioned, we can only enter Connect Mode when our neuroception deems us safe enough, but that doesn't mean the Ground Control crew has taken the day off. On the contrary, just as our safest state is also our socially riskiest, Ground Control remains highly alert even when it appears least active. Cues of danger in our environments signal our neuroception, working tirelessly to bring things back down to Earth. In contrast, while the Connect Mode spectrum is officially less activated (and less metabolically demanding), it comes with a new layer of anticipatory alertness and acute anxieties. For example, social awkwardness, the worry of offending or saying the wrong thing, and the mild activation from being misunderstood are fresh concerns for Ground Control to monitor.

To employ another of our extended metaphors, it's kind of like the way we interact with our smartphones. We'll scroll on them incessantly without a notification bringing us to them, and this "leisurely" activity, we can all attest to, is not in any real sense relaxing or refreshing. This amazing new technology, like the development in humans of increasingly complex nervous system states, provides us with many new avenues for growth and betterment, but it carries with it just as many pitfalls.

Problem #2: It's full of weird, awkward, or uncomfortable feelings.

Another pitfall is that the Connect Mode is the best mode in which to operate or is the state to which many therapeutic maps are directed. Like all the modes, we cannot live in Connect only. **We cannot remain in any of the states for too long a period of time.** This pedestalization of the Connect causes shame in people who don't find this state fun at all. I asked a group of sixty Yale MFA Art students if any of them just *loved* social interaction and only one raised their hand. Connection is not something we have to love or something that comes easy. It can be like fitness. The more you try to make weightlifting pain-free the more psychologically shameful it is. but if you can walk into the gym and say, "You don't have to like this." You are setting yourself up for a much better workout. Socializing can be the same. Personally, I think The Polyvagal Institute has put way too much effort into selling "play" to make the safe and social state more fun, instead of unshaming just how terribly awkward it is for most people. That said, I can't blame a group of trauma therapists for feeling drawn towards something a bit... lighter. And, they are right, animals are more playful in this state. **But, Connect Mode is still a survival state for humans.** Every actor who has done an Oscar Wilde-esc British comedy knows that there can be some serious teeth behind a Connect Mode conversation over "tea and sandwiches." And, it's not enlightenment either. It's *only* an oasis for people who have finally found safety after finding themselves locked in the defense states.

Problem #3: This state is always shifting due to the roles we are playing.

The other problem with this paradigm, though, is that it suggests that Connect is the state in which "who we really are" is allowed to exist— and this has some truth to it. But in a way that complicates its reductive nature. In Connect, we are not necessarily "being ourselves"; rather, we are *performing* our "selves," in the many Roles we take on throughout our day. Sometimes we're Friend, Employee, Partner, Stranger, Daughter, Subject, and so on—and each one reflects (or, perhaps, refracts) one of our "true selves" by revealing our feelings toward a given person or situation by the role we take on in their presence. Which you is really the real you, anyway? The one completely at ease with your best friend or lover? Or the one who tenses up at work and never feels like you fit in there? Why do we always act as if the truest parts of our identities are the ones buried deep beneath our numerous guises and affectations, when we spend more time in those roles than we do out of them? Should we measure it in Hours?

My point isn't that the Roles better represent you than the so-called "true self" underneath. My point is that no one part represents your whole. Every part is worthy of our time and attention; each part, then, is its own whole. Each part, in other words, is you. It is your performance and integrity that give you a sense that "you" performed well, and therefore contributes to a larger "self-esteem."

Problem #4: Connect Mode confronts us with our ability to hold power benevolently.

The final problem with Connect Mode is that this mode thrusts us into relationships and roles, which immediately brings up two words artists hate: power dynamics. We often just don't want to think about what power means, how to hold it well, how to be led well, and how to repair with someone if there has been disconnection or harm. While we will cover this nuanced topic in a future chapter, I hope you can see just how not perfect, calming, joyful, or fun this state is, even though all those things could certainly be included in its enormous spectrum.

In Connect Mode, your stories are not always going to be "positive." Connection is unbelievably risky and will always be. So while you think your Connect Mode stories might be: "People love me and I am loved!!!" They probably aren't.

Again, Polyvagal Theory was first translated by therapists who work with trauma patients who are often locked in Preservation and Move Modes. So, for their clients, Connect Mode feels like a complete oasis from the nervous system hell they are experiencing. This experience is real, but the feeling that Connect Mode is weightless is only in contrast to how awful it feels to have chronic dysregulation due to trauma, chronic illness, or extreme neurodivergence like those with autism.

My Connect Mode Stories

Your assignment is to identify three to five Connect Mode stories. Once you have done that, identify three to five Connect Mode stories that directly relate to your art. Mine are, "Gah! I'm not sure I want to go out and socialize but I probably should," or, "I'm making progress with this song," or, "This feels hard and scary but I bet it will be ok."

What are yours?

Reflections of Connect Mode

- If you are in Connect Mode and you need to connect with other people, you are regulated.

- Connect Mode is a really wonderful state but can also contain anger, fear, and sadness under the hold of safety and vagal tone.

- Connect Mode is often the hardest state for artists to navigate due to their lack of experience by defaulting to Superplay in crisis. It's normal for Connect Mode to be hard or awkward.

- Connect Mode contains a lot of risk. This is why we often dysregulate.

SHADES OF GREEN

Connect Mode is a song of neurobiology that lives on a color palette with various shades. These variations of Connect Mode can be experienced offstage in our personal lives, and onstage as a palette for expression in theatrical performance.

*As you can see from your **nervous system cards (#7-10)**, the Move Mode is a spectrum of experience that contains different levels of activation.*

YELLOW

#7. **Yellow**: This is the song of bringing ideas together. It's the song of mild frustration, the process of learning something new. It's the song of social awkwardness, those odd rehearsals, and uncomfortable dinner parties. It's when two or more people—or ideas—are trying to connect, but things aren't quite clicking the way you expected. This song, if embraced, helps us enter a flow state, guiding us through the rough patches. It's also the song of neuroplasticity, a key part of learning and artistic practice, as it opens the door to growth and adaptation.

If this state were a literal song:

- **"Unwritten" by Natasha Bedingfield**
  This song reflects the feeling of stepping into the unknown, with a sense of mild frustration and excitement about learning, trying new things, and the creative process.
- **"Weird Fishes/Arpeggi" by Radiohead**
  With its layers and complexity, this song reflects the feeling of moving through creative tension and awkwardness. It's about

navigating confusion and frustration, ultimately leading to something more fluid and connected.

- **"This Must Be the Place (Naive Melody)" by Talking Heads**
This song is about finding connection in a simple, almost awkward way. It embodies the feeling of navigating weird social interactions and growing into something more comfortable and meaningful.
- **Almost anything written by Sondre Lerche**
Check out his records, you will thank me!

NEON GREEN

#8. Neon Green: This is the song that balances excitement with regulation. It's the high-energy, electric pulse that keeps us engaged and activated without tipping into overwhelm. Think of the vibrant, controlled intensity of Serena and Venus Williams on the tennis court. Or the boundless, yet perfectly timed energy of Robin Williams onstage. Neon Green is all about the thrill of pushing limits, while maintaining just enough control to keep things fun and dynamic.

This state is the epitome of regulated stress—where the pressure is high, but the joy of the challenge keeps us coming back for more. It's playful, wild, and exhilarating. While this song may be expensive in terms of dopamine, requiring a lot of mental and emotional fuel to maintain, we crave it. There's something addictive about the rush it gives us, that moment of flow where everything clicks and the energy feels both intense and sustainable. It's the state of peak performance, where excitement and purpose align. Despite the cost, we love returning to it again and again, chasing that perfect balance of joy and effort.

- **"Uptown Funk" by Mark Ronson feat. Bruno Mars**
  This song is pure, infectious energy with a perfect blend of excitement and control. It's fun, wild, and irresistibly upbeat–with a groove that keeps you engaged and wanting more.
- **"Happy" by Pharrell Williams**
  Pharrell's anthem of joy is a perfect match for Neon Green—a full-on positivity party with a hook-filled rhythm that keeps you moving and smiling.

Forest Green

#9. **Forest Green:** This is the song of **balanced energy**—the song of being fully present while maintaining a deep connection with yourself and others. In this state, there's a playful spirit, but with a wide dynamic range that allows for subtlety and flow. It's not about pushing to extremes. It's about embracing the beauty of the in-between.

This song is all about **exploration, curiosity, and play**—but without the overwhelming intensity. It's the dance of creative flow, where you can experiment, take risks, and explore new ideas–all while staying grounded and in control. It's lively, fun, and spontaneous, yet there's a steadiness beneath it that allows you to navigate each moment with ease and confidence.

Here, you're free to **improvise**, to push the edges of your creativity, but always with a sense of balance. It's about leaning into the joy of discovery, exploring new possibilities, and embracing the excitement of the unknown–without tipping over into chaos or stress. It's light, but rich with potential—energetic, but perfectly measured.

- **"Good as Hell" by Lizzo**
  This song radiates self-assured, balanced energy while encouraging fun and connection. It's about feeling good, taking care of yourself, and staying grounded while embracing play and joy.
- **"Electric Feel" by MGMT**
  This song has a lively, fun energy that feels playful but still very steady. It's upbeat and exciting but not too chaotic—perfect for leaning into discovery with a sense of ease.

Mint Green

#9. Mint Green: This is the song of **balanced energy, presence, and connection**, a harmonious blend of **ventral and dorsal energy**. It carries the lightness of exploration and curiosity while maintaining a grounded sense of stability. Playful yet steady, this song allows you to experiment and try new things without the pressure of intensity or overwhelm. It's the sweet spot between excitement and calm, where you feel both energized and anchored.

In this state, there's room for a wide dynamic range—you can be spontaneous, creative, and open, without tipping into dysregulation. The ventral energy keeps you connected and engaged with the world, while the dorsal energy provides just enough containment to keep you feeling safe and rooted. It's the dance of balanced play, where the joy of discovery and learning is supported by a sense of inner calm and control.

This song is about **gentle perseverance and exploration**, the fun of trying something new or stepping into the unknown while still feeling connected to yourself and others. It's that perfect balance where you can stretch beyond your comfort zone, knowing that you have the energy to return to safety whenever needed.

- **"Put Your Records On" by Corinne Bailey Rae**
  This laid-back, uplifting song captures the essence of gentle exploration and staying present. It's playful and carefree, encouraging listeners to enjoy life while staying connected to the moment.
- **"Dreams" by Fleetwood Mac**
  This song has a flowing, light energy, perfectly capturing the balance between introspection and playfulness. Its steady rhythm and soothing melody give it an air of calm exploration.
- **Almost anything written by Andy Shauf**
  Check out his records, you will thank me!

We are nervous system music

Interlude:

Your Nervous System GPS: Find Your Location

Now that we have established that there are four major states, it's time to locate your nervous system on a map. It's often called a ladder, as it's helpful to see it as a linear structure. However, remember that each state transcends and includes the "technology" that came before. While it's often referred to as a "hierarchy," it's not. It's Holarchy or "whole-archy." This just means, again, that every "new" state **transcends and includes the states before**. Higher states are not "better," the "higher" states are only easier for humans to connect with, if and only if, they need to be connected for survival.

I say this because the second you look at the nervous system cards in this book you may see a ladder and numbers and want to Win The Game of The Nervous System! Don't make that mistake. And, if you do, laugh it off and remind yourself there is no winning the nervous system. The name of the game is flexibility, not supremacy over bad or "lower" states of being. Wouldn't it be awful if the point of Mozart's symphonies were to play them as fast as possible? The nervous system ladder is much more like music.

What is the point of a map? Well, it's very similar to a GPS system. When we get stuck and need to shift our state, we can't drive to New York if we don't know where we are located. A nervous system map lets you know what state you are in, not just to show you what advantages or limitations you may be experiencing, but which protocols you may want to choose to move closer to safety.

So, let's track your nervous system for the first time. Since we haven't yet learned each state in depth, I just want you to make a guess and, as we go deeper, make corrections. Go to your nervous system cards in the index and make a guess to which mode your Ground Control has predicted. **If you have the MuscleMusic app* you can track your state in the tracking section.**

This is the first step towards taking control of your spaceship. Before we can say, "Thank you Ground Control, I'll take it from here!" we need to know and name what exactly Ground Control has predicted for our spaceship!

*To sign up for the MuscleMusic app please go to the Apple Store and it's also included in our Certification program.

Letter #13: Roles, Risk, and Play

Dear Artist,

I hope you're starting to grasp that our nervous system states, chosen by the fine-tuned radar of our neuroception, aren't just different "moods" or shades of feeling, but powerful energies we'll soon learn to harness when we tap into Superplay. But before we get ahead of ourselves, we need to take a breath and examine what play looks like in the context of Connect Mode. In this letter we will explore even further why this state often feels so complicated and even heavy at times.

Dr. Stephen Porges frames play in its simplest, most primal form—something even my dog, Yuna, instinctively knows how to do. It's that pure, present connection, rooted in trust and ease. For her, it's not about rules or roles; it's about existing in a shared moment, fully engaged.

But we're not dogs, are we? We're humans, and with that comes a much more intricate kind of play. Once we're in Connect Mode, a different kind of creativity kicks in—one that involves complex role-playing, imagination, and the deeper narratives we weave. It's a level of play unique to our species, and it's here where things start to get really interesting.

Roles

In Connect Mode, we slip into different roles—like the Artist, the Performer, the Collaborator, the Mentor—not unlike characters we take on in the various stages of our creative lives. But these aren't the scripted roles we prepare for on stage or in the studio; they're the fluid identities we embody across different spaces and relationships. In a rehearsal, you might be the director's right hand. While in a gallery opening, you shift to the role of the observer. These roles, shaped by context, weave together the full scope of who we are.

As we discussed with Holarchy, no role holds more value than another, as they are embraced as a group, all included under the umbrella of self. Every version of ourselves—the one who thrives in front of an audience and the one who stumbles through a rough draft—contributes to the whole. Even in those moments when a role feels misaligned or out of place, it's still part of the creative self we bring into the world. Each shift, each role, whether it feels like a natural fit or not, helps compose the larger narrative of our lives as artists.

What's more significant, though, is that in this safe and social state, we're not particularly skilled at quickly shifting between roles or blending multiple personas at once. This is why performers sometimes feel unsettled when their different creative worlds overlap—like when a director, a fellow actor, and a musician friend all show up at the same opening night afterparty. It's not that we think these people won't get along. Rather that the roles we inhabit in each context don't mesh smoothly.

The version of ourselves that's sharp and focused in a rehearsal room might not know how to interact with the laid-back, free-flowing energy we embody when jamming with fellow musicians. Trying to shift from one to the other—or worse, trying to juggle both at the same time—creates a kind of friction. These roles in isolation feel natural, but when they collide in the same space, the tension between them becomes palpable. It's not the people that clash; it's the dissonance of switching between who we are in each world that leaves us uneasy.

And the reason these are awkward for us goes beyond the contrast in our roles. What gives it **stakes (a term often used in theater training)** are the potential consequences for our actual lives. You could reveal to your friends just how deferential you are to authority figures. Or you could show your partner how mean and gossipy you become when surrounded by your work buddies. Or someone from one group could talk to you when you're in the role of another group—in this case you might sound completely unfamiliar to them. The effects of these clashes are honestly beside the point. The real issue is our instinctual desire to protect the boundaries between each scene, as we're unconsciously aware of both the necessity of code-switching *and* the discomfiting implications it has on our identities. Who am I if I can take on so many different roles? Am I phony when

I'm in certain roles? Or does the mere fact that they're all *roles* make my disingenuousness unassailable? Am I ever truly *myself*? Or is it all an act?

All of which is to say that I have named this state the Connect Mode and not the "safe and social" state—as it's been referred to for two decades in PVT—because in many senses it is not wholly safe. When we violate the rules of our roles, it can disrupt the social system predicated on that role.

Risk

Risk is an inherent part of Connect, ranging from minor (like casual social interactions or time alone) to extreme, like the risk of death. What matters isn't the outcome, but how we perceive those risks. Just as Ground Control sometimes triggers emergency protocols for false alarms, we too stay unconsciously alert to potential consequences in Connect.

Risk keeps us in check, preventing us from doing whatever we want whenever we want. Society uses shame as a powerful tool, more effective than legal punishments. But while shame helps maintain social order, it can interfere with our nervous system regulation. The societal benefits of shame shrink as we move from collective norms toward individual well-being— what works for the group often harms the individual. Finding the balance between societal expectations and personal authenticity in the complex world of Connect is tricky, but transformative. Ultimately, the frustration we feel in Connect Mode comes from the fact that it's still a survival state— just a highly nuanced one, layered with complex role-play.

Finally, two additional factors influence performing artists in the Connect Mode state when it comes to risk. First, the nervous system perceives wasting energy as risky. It resists activities—like auditions—that it doesn't anticipate will succeed. After all, the nervous system's primary job is to protect our energy and ensure it's used effectively. Second, the brain's risk assessment during an audition can be significantly affected by financial needs. If a person depends on the opportunity to meet basic needs, like affording food, their perception of risk will differ dramatically from someone who doesn't share that urgency.

Performing Roles Well

The biggest stress of Connect Mode is that we need the right energy for the right role. If I need to have big neon green energy (an eight on the nervous system ladder) but can't get myself out of mint green energy (a 10 on the ladder), *I feel off.* I need to shift. I need to find the role. Or, I need to unshame the gap between where I am and where I need to be. Connect Mode is just awkward when we don't have the right feeling for the right activity. This awkwardness is normal and easily pathologized.

Play

There are endless ways artists can "play." Dr. Stephen Porges frames play as something that "requires social interaction." That's not to say solitary play—a painter lost in their canvas, a musician deep in practice—isn't meaningful. But the social aspect of play serves as "neural exercise," helping us co-regulate our emotional and behavioral states.

When artists collaborate—whether it's an improv troupe, a band, or a creative workshop—they're not just reacting to lines or notes. They're responding to the emotions beneath them. Your scene partner isn't mad at you; they're playing the role, channeling the antagonist you're building together. This kind of play trains us to recognize emotional signals and improvise with them.

What makes Connect Mode more complex is that we're not pretending but truly connecting. Ketchup isn't blood—it's blood and that is risky. Even in the artistic realm, play carries vulnerability. When you think of risk in Connect Mode, think of gravity on earth. It's real, palpable, and we can't escape it. Total freedom from that risk? That's something we only encounter in Superplay—the space where true creative liberation begins. And with that, I think it's time to dive into that next level, so without further ado...

Superplay

11.

Role-play/Pretend
(All states
move into play)

The only non-survival state.

Letter #14: Superplay & The Three Astronauts

Dear Artist,

Here we are. The big idea. I know it's taken a little bit to get here, but all of the previous letters were necessary to ready us for The Fourth State of the Nervous System. You had to grasp the foundational ideas before we could dive into my contribution to a new, extended version of PVT: **Superplay Mode.**

Lift off! Remember when I mentioned how heavy Connect Mode can feel? Superplay is the one state we consciously choose to enter—and it's also the one that can feel completely weightless. It's our only pathway into nervous system space, so it's no surprise that we zoom towards it when the weight of Connect Mode becomes too much to bear.

Superplay is the fourth and newest evolutionary state for the homosapien species, and it likely started whenever a tribal leader put on a mask and said, "I am NOW the god of_____." **It is the state of advanced pretend.** For early human primates (we don't know if other hominoids were capable of Superplay but it's possible) there were no professional actors or singer-songwriters that separated their identities from roles. If you were channeling the God of War, ...look out. Superplay at that time was not pretend, it was thought of as real. There was no "theater" or "cultural critique" and it likely took a long time before some brave human was like, "Wow, we made all these Gods up!" And, this distance was only possible with human development, which can only mean that our minds developed too.

Anthropologists believe that the origins of acting date back tens of thousands of years, emerging from early human rituals, storytelling, and mimicry. In prehistoric societies, people likely took on roles during spiritual or communal rituals, imitating deities, animals, or forces of nature. This kind of performance, rooted in ritual and communication, helped early humans share stories and convey cultural knowledge, often through gestures and vocalization.

Thanks to the lineage of developmental theories (Kohlberg to Integral Theory), we know that humans in the magic/mystic realm of development didn't play roles. When they put on masks they *were gods,* or channeled gods. This early version of Superplay was likely very utilitarian, in that these "Gods" could lead and help people feel there may be human control when there wasn't. This must have been thrilling at the time because your Pharaoh was a living God. This delusion still exists in countries unwilling to develop or be influenced to change, like North Korea.

While formalized theater as we know it began in ancient Greece around the sixth century BCE, evidence of performative behavior can be found in much earlier art, such as cave paintings from 17,000 years ago. These images, along with early storytelling traditions, suggest that acting evolved from a natural human inclination to mimic, represent, and narrate within social and ritual contexts.

How can I stake a claim that this Superplay mode is a brand new state on the former Polyvagal ladder? Superplay is an advanced level of masking that can **only be done by human beings.** All mammals have a Connect Mode, but none of them have the ability to play Medea, Willie Loman, Hedda Gabber, or the God of Rain. Humans can try on masks and feel the cascade of nervous system resonance down our bodies and then go home and have a hot tea by the fire. A hedge hog and even a chimp can't do that. They don't pretend in the advanced ways we do.

Big pause for clarity. None of this means we are "better." Humans are simply highly adapted to their environments. My dog's sense of smell is objectively superior to mine, but in my environment that amount of smell would ruin my life. Bacteria can live in space, some animals can regrow limbs, and some can fly. All that said, I can play Hamlet and that's a really cool Superplay power but that doesn't make me "superior." Got it?

When our nervous systems are relieved of the weight of real "self" they can feel what it might be like to be someone completely different. I will never forget the first mask workshop we had in college. When my fellow classmates wore a mask, they could do things with their bodies that they could never do even in character. It was life-changing to watch. Their Connect Modes were being run by a force of weightless play. My professor,

Sarah Hickler, said she was once working with an old man with severe arthritis who could dance with freedom and joy with a mask on. I don't want to get "woo" about it, but I will say that the nervous system gains a heightened sense of relief from risk and an infusion of "super" play while wearing the mask of pretend. This is a key understanding for coaches who want to make their clients feel safer. Masks create safety.

Superplay in humans is natural and is also connected to their survival strategy. Since the Connect Mode is anything but risk-free, it's important that children learn how to socially interact in ways that feel safe. Otherwise, social interaction would be too overwhelming. You see, unlike in other animals, our culture and its rules and moral code are tied to our survival. So instead, you will see children naturally going into Superplay, "You play the teacher, and I'll play the baby bear!" This is how children and siblings learn about the adult world of play before they are ready. The Superplay state is a temporary holding zone of safety for human primates to experiment risk-free before they get into the adult sandbox.

So, in short, Superplay occurs when you engage in playing a character or consciously pretending. Therefore, Kim Jong Un is not Superplaying. He is in the worst kind of nervous system delusion, which is the backdoor of Preservation Mode, Superplay Delusion. Thus, a king who is just a king who believes he is a God, or an Alien. We see this in severely traumatized children, so it's no surprise we see it in dictators.

Superplay is the extended use of imaginative constructs—essentially it represents the core of the creative act. But the most important aspect of Superplay is that there is **very little risk for your character.** The Superplay state transcends and includes all the other states, but again, **not only includes regulation, it includes dysregulation.** *Whoa.* Wait, we can hold dysregulation in regulation? Yes. Any actor can attest. That is a revelatory shift for what our nervous systems are capable of. I dare you to say to a friend, "Oh I just learned about this thing called Superplay and watch them light up." We are drawn to this experience like flies to a light. This is our version of flying.

Let me be clear, Superplay is not like the deceitful role-play we see in sociopathic behavior. Deception violates the rules of the safe and social state that requires a person to enter a role honestly. To Superplay, there must be transparency, or else it may fall into the category of performance art (another nervous system can of worms).

Why *would* the Polyvagal Institute overlook something this obvious? Well firstly, they are focused on trauma, and Dr. Porges' crown jewel is the crucial understanding of the dorsal vagal/freeze pathway. So they prioritize Preservation Mode and getting traumatized populations out of it. When the Polyvagal Institute considers advanced levels of play, they *sometimes* fetishize it as the experience of the desired fantasy of the Connect Mode, intimating that if we were just regulated enough this state would feel like Superplay. I'm not saying that the Connect Mode can't include fun and joy, but as we established in previous chapters, it's no oasis. So, I come to this party not to dismantle PVT, a revelatory theory in its own right, but to transcend and include the Theory into a new theory that includes Superplay.

The addition of Superplay is at the very top of the nervous system Holarchy because it fully transcends and includes all other states. Superplay is revelatory (surprising in its uniqueness), and it changes the brain and hormonal cascade. It is also a temporary Holarchy. We feel this specialness and temporal nature when we go to a concert or play. We know that for *one night only* we will have both a very special collective and individual experience with our nervous system.

Let's go back to the idea of a Holarchy, which is that anything "above" in a Holarchy doesn't diminish its parts, it celebrates them but includes them in something bigger. Superplay embraces every state below it, but with more distinction and acceptance. In Superplay, a villain's dysregulation is not shamed, it's explored. In Superplay freeze is not trauma, it's feeling one's character. Rage is a color. Jealous love is a wondrous curiosity. All of a sudden the rotary phone, the landline, and the smartphone are all dancing in one show. **All of the "songs" we explored in the previous chapters become paint for a canvas of human exploration.** There is so much cruel nervous system "music" that plays from the Preservation and Move modes—and as we know even Connect Mode can be difficult. It's such a relief to have a state of being that feels, well, lighter.

While Sally may go to space to explore the outer reaches of the universe's mysteries, we Superplay to understand the depth of what it means to be human. That way, when we come back to the Connect Mode state we know more about ourselves and our species. And, we are a particularly mean species. There is a reason the Neanderthals, Homo erectus, Homo habilis and so many more didn't survive and I agree with author Yuval Noah Harari that it wasn't because we are particularly nice. Superplay Mode likely evolved as a developmental aid in growing and maturing children, but it's also clear we are a species with a knack for violence. This Superplay Mode helps adults develop compassion that mirrors a need for humanity that may not "come with the box." Superplay is not therapy, it's a mirror. We need this state to be a kinder, more loving, more compassionate group of people. This, I believe, is the important work and role of artists in society.

But here is an important point. Everything "above" in Holarchy is unstable. There will always be more cells (lower) than bodies (higher). There will always be more bacteria (lower) than organs (higher). So pretend play (higher) is a temporary Holarchy that is in service of opening humanity up to the confusing complexity of the Connect Mode (lower), but it's not meant to last too long. So, just a reminder, Superplay is not an achievement we want to stay in as long as possible, but just one of many human experiences.

Connect Mode must also be massively secure and safe as a base to Superplay from, otherwise we get pathological Superplay. For example, you would never keep a production of King Lear going if you were being bombed. And when children don't feel safe they scream, "TIME Ouuuuuuuuuuuuut!" I call this the **time-out effect.** And we don't need to be taught the time-out effect, we naturally stop pretending when we are in danger. It's a safety reflex strongest in children, who have sensitive and flexible nervous systems. This is why when someone continues to Superplay in danger, I refer to this as **pathological or delusional Superplay.**

Now, we said that each successive technological development in phones metaphorically represents the Holarchical structure of the nervous system—each new iteration both expands upon and contains the uses of the previous generations. Let's explore that notion in more depth here. Superplay is like an oculus. What makes it so incredible is that you have amazing experiences that may change you forever, but you don't have a full grasp on your surroundings. It would be very unwise to put on an oculus in a very dangerous neighborhood, on a slippery road, or in the woods. You need your survival states to be sharp and focused. **Superplay is the first**

non-survival state, it's an exploratory state, much like dreaming, but with greater lucidity.

But, just because you are in Superplay doesn't mean you can check out of survival completely. If you are an actor in a live show, and an audience member pulls out a gun, it would be pathological to cling to the state. For artists, there is always a craftsperson (actor/singer) who has their eye on survival. We have to have this to have safe play. So to be clear, part of you should always be in Connect Mode (otherwise this play would be psychosis). First and foremost, we must contend with our nervous system; next, we consider the role of the practitioner (actor, singer, clown, comedian); and finally, the pretend role (Hamlet, Juliet).

We also have **Active** and **Passive Superplay.** Active Superplay is when you consciously take on a role and let that role play your nervous system like an instrument. Passive Superplay is when we surrender our nervous system to a show and let the character's story passively wash over us. Here too, our nervous system feels a wave of activity we would have never felt in "real life." So, **Active Superplay** would be playing a role in a movie, and **Passive Superplay** would be watching a movie. Globally, Passive Superplay is much more popular than Active Superplay. We've turned active role-play into a profession which many adults never touch. Active Superplayers send their nervous system on a ride of imaginary circumstance. Part of our nervous system knows it's not real, but another part doesn't. If we didn't have this dual awareness we wouldn't have Netflix because it would be too scary or not scary enough! Also, if the part of us that felt it was too real was too sensitive, we would be too overwhelmed by movies and television. I personally experience this with horror movies.

Heading back to outer space, even in real life, Astronauts experience something known as the **Overview Effect,** which is a rewiring of their perspectives on the world, humanity, and existence. The astrophysicist Heino Falcke describes it this way:

"After the cosmonaut Yuri Gagarin became the first in 1961, more than 550 people have been in space. Almost all have reported that their amazement at the sublime fragility of the Earth left a deep impression on them, **and left them profoundly changed as**

individuals. The experience of gazing upon the entire globe seems akin to an **ecstatic state.**"

Superplay, at its best, allows us to see ourselves anew, to reconsider our base assumptions, and to divorce ourselves from the limitations of our singular identity. While the Overview Effect-like profundity of Superplay can alter our perspective of all aspects of our lives, so too can it bring us harm. Here's a concept that's tricky to wrap your head around: although it's true that while in Superplay Mode, a person relinquishes a lot of risk, it's also true that the act of moving into Superplay Mode is itself a risk. Just like real astronauts, who transcend Earth's gravity to venture into realms beyond human limits, they face higher radiation levels in space, risking gastrointestinal cancer and other health issues during extended stays. There are actually "space doctors" who specialize in this field. For our (artistic) nervous systems, a prolonged residence in Superplay can weaken our ability to handle the heaviness of the Connect Mode experience. Also, just like it's a risk to leave your friends and family to go to space, when we make art we are often not paying our bills, maintaining our health, or focused on securing resources for our survival. Unfortunately, the general psychiatric community is not trained to see the pitfalls of the risks of Superplay and end up fetishizing it instead. We need our own version of "space doctors." So many artists fall in love with Superplay and leave their Connect Mode reality in shambles. And, even worse, culturally this is celebrated in the Starving Artist stereotype.

Superplay, then, is meant to be a temporary reprieve from, and illumination of, our Connect Mode world, not to ultimately escape it. Someone planning on going to space with no intention of returning is the kind of behavior we see in people with psychosis. This is also why many actors find young Method Acting obnoxious at best and dangerous at worst. Method actors forget that we are playing pretend and often end up hurting themselves. If you grew up in a dangerous environment or are prone to self-harming, severe Method Acting might feel quite normal.

Also, Superplay must separate risk from reality in order to provide us with the necessary freedom to explore, express, and expand uninhibited and unburdened. But it shouldn't be sought simply for the relief from those burdens, although clearly that's a component of its use. Superplay is not a

Spa. In fact, I wish more actors would just let themselves go to a real spa and stop pretending that Superplay is their sole method of self-care. It's tiring, exhausting, exhilarating, and requires recovery, just like space.

Speaking of, back to Sally in space...

Let's return to our Astronauts. Remember Sally? Well, she took a nervous system course and now knows that Ground Control (neuroception) exists. Since she found out, she listens to Ground Control's predictions but has begun taking the wheel and getting out of Preservation Mode much more lately. This has made Ground Control much more flexible and happy too.

But, something new came up. Because Sally is in Connect Mode more often now, she and Ground Control got bored! One night she called and said, "Hey guys, I know I'm in space, but what if we did a production of A Midsummer Night's Dream? I've always wanted to play Helena! But, if I'm going to do this I'm going to need you guys to play along and **give me the energy that she needs, not what I need.**" At first, Ground Control was skeptical. Is this safe? Can we keep her alive and let her play like this?

So, Ground Control came up with a brilliant plan. They decided that 20 percent of them would always focus on keeping her alive in space. But 80 percent would devote themselves to giving the right ship-energy (nervous system states) to play Helena! But, if for any reason they felt that the play was interfering with survival, they would have to shut the production down immediately. And then, Shakespeare in the Park...I mean the Dark...was born!

But Ground Control didn't think through all of this. How could they? They've never had a spaceship ask to be a character before! Superplay is more than the Mode; it's also a Practice. So, here's what happened and what happens to many artists.

To do this we need two more astronauts. Sally couldn't do Shakespeare in Space alone, of course. These other astronauts have their own Ground Controls with different experiences, cultures, and risk assessments.

Let's start with Heidi. Right off the bat, Heidi has an invisible problem. She has intense childhood trauma. Her parents were not overtly abusive but emotionally checked-out. Heidi's spaceship has always been a little erratic. Don't get me wrong, she's amazing, but she's often in G-force when she needs to be sleeping, and in Preservation Mode when she needs to be connecting with other ships. This disorientation makes her feel uncomfortable in space a lot of the time. Space is just a stressful place to be.

Heidi starts playing the role of Titania. All of a sudden she feels like she's floating! What freedom. Her ship stops jerking around and for the first time she feels, "normal." She feels at home in Superplay. Her space therapist is thrilled with all the progress she's made and relieved this Superplay finally stabilized Heidi's ship— and how *creative!*

But a strange and unusual problem came up. Heidi stopped wanting to be a person (an astronaut), and now, all she wants to do is to be in Superplay. Even Ground Control was duped. They wanted to be calm and playful too. But, her ship started running out of gas. She forgot to pay the electric bill. She stopped doing her space workout and her bones started to decay from the lack of gravity. And, because she stopped interacting in "real life," the Connect Mode felt heavier than ever. She didn't want to hang out with the other astronauts unless they were playing or making art of some kind. Life felt more and more painful. She never liked it anyway, and she's determined to be in Superplay as much as humanly possible.

Heidi started winning awards and getting grants for her Superplay activities and her entire sense of self was validated. On the outside she was a famous, talented, and funny actor/astronaut, but she developed a secret addiction, a chronic illness, and had crippling anxiety anytime she was not in Superplay. This is what I call the **Connect Mode Bypass.** This is when a person with trauma is so terrified of Connect Mode that they avoid it at all cost. Ultimately, this bypass massively inhibits the artist's Connect Mode system. Of course, an artist can maintain this pattern for a long time, but eventually it will collapse, as Superplay was never intended to be a static state, but one of exploration.

Then, we have Leah. Leah was supposed to play Puck and Lady Macbeth for the late night show, but this never happened. I mean, she tried so very hard, but her Ground Control couldn't handle it. GC just kept shutting it down. It was almost as if Heidi and Leah's nervous systems were reacting to Superplay in the opposite way. Every time Leah performed her monologue, Ground Control gave her a jolt of G-force or shut her ship down. Leah's Ground Control had **no capacity for Move Mode.** Even offstage, she hated G-force and her Ground Control avoided it. When she was a kid, her parents were almost always in G-force and it scared her. It would take her so long to find her Superplay state again after feeling completely overwhelmed that— she just quit. It was too exhausting. She had what I call **Move Mode Bypass.** Plus, her Ground Control felt safer in Connect Mode anyway. The sad part was, Leah dreamed of being on space-Broadway, but when she even thought of the arts, Ground Control sent her a shot of shame just to ensure she never tried it again.

Since Superplay is the 4th state, the issues that come with it are more and more complicated. Before we move on, I need to tell you about the third astronaut.

Finally, we have little Brian. Like Sally, Brian was born in space and doesn't have any idea about Ground Control yet. He's too young and the concept is just too out of reach. Brian lost his sibling Fin when he was five to a devastating and rare space-cancer. Brian's parents were so absolutely crushed they both went into Move Mode constantly. Since they couldn't connect with his tiny growing spaceship, Brian's Ground Control put him into Preservation Mode almost all the time. Ground Control began to panic because a spaceship can only survive in space if it's in Connect Mode during childhood. So something wild happened. Brian found the nervous system's secret backdoor. Instead of moving up the polyvagal ladder, he dissociated into Superplay mode to cope. Since Sally and her friends were already playing, he joined his first theater production and covered for Leah as Puck! His Ground Control loved it because here he could grow and explore without the danger of his ship becoming developmentally stunted. In Superplay he could learn to connect, and grow developmentally with the other actors. Unfortunately, as Brian grew up, theater was all he ever knew, and had almost no tolerance for the Connect Mode state. He too had the **Connect Mode Bypass.**

The Superplay state is a revelatory, transcendent experience that is new to humans and is still evolving. And as it's evolving, it's colliding with AI at staggering speeds. For any artist to safely ride the Superplay state, they must know that:

1. **Superplay is not a permanent state and should only be visited for short stays for our survival.**
2. **Superplay is a natural ecstatic state that our species uses to explore the risks of our cultural landscape with less risk.**
3. **Superplay is the state of pretend role-play as opposed to real role-play in the Connect Mode (ketchup vs. blood).**

* I want to note that the nervous system states are spectrums and that there are some art forms that bridge Superplay and the Connect Mode state and purposefully disrupt it. They include artists and theaters like the Living Theater, Lady Gaga, The Bread and Puppet Theater, Joaquin Phoenix, and The Open Theater. This would also include Guerilla Theater, the work of many performance artists like Marina Abrimovich, Banksy, Salvador Dalí, and of course the long lineage of surrealists who followed. These artists are playing in the liminal space between these two states of being.

Anytime I play with this liminal space between Connect and Superplay, I call it "Guerilla Superplay.**" This would be like taking on a persona in real life, like when Beyonce took on "Sasha Fierce." It's not necessarily pretend, but a form of pretend that helps a person move into a Connect Mode role with more ease.

Superplay Harmonics:

Mapping the **harmonics of the Superplay state** in the Fox Method, specifically the **state of pretend**, can be a fascinating exercise in understanding the unique dynamics of this weightless state. **Superplay** is characterized by its ability to blend elements from all nervous system states, allowing an artist or individual to engage playfully with reality, incorporating elements of defense held within a safe, exploratory framework.

Let's break down the harmonics of Superplay:

1. Fundamental (C note): Core of Superplay – The Act of Pretending

- The fundamental tone represents **pretending itself**, the core experience of Superplay. This is where an individual consciously chooses to engage in a playful, imaginative space, blending reality with fiction. It's the foundation of this state, where the person feels safe enough to explore new roles, characters, or scenarios, but with an understanding that it's a form of play. The basic **freedom to pretend** is what makes Superplay distinct from other states. This must be rooted in **transparency and consent.**

2. 1st Harmonic: Emotional Fluidity

- The first harmonic (C, one octave up) represents **emotional fluidity**, a key feature of Superplay. In this state, emotions are not rigid but malleable, easily shifting between laughter, surprise, sadness, or even fear. The ability to play with emotions without being overwhelmed by them—much like how a harmonic emerges naturally from the fundamental—allows for a creative dance with one's feelings.

3. 2nd Harmonic: Playful Engagement with Threat

- The second harmonic (G) reflects **engagement with threat, but from a place of safety**. Superplay allows for flirtation with fear, risk, or challenge, but always under the umbrella of pretend. It's like the mock-growl of a playful animal: the body recognizes elements of threat, but they are reframed within a safe context.

4. 3rd Harmonic: Imaginative Expansion

- The third harmonic (C, two octaves up) symbolizes **imaginative expansion**, where the individual can transcend the usual boundaries of self and reality. In Superplay, the mind opens to new possibilities, exploring various personas, roles, and stories. Imagination is limitless in this state, much like a harmonic that resonates far beyond the fundamental note. This harmonic is what gives Superplay its power to transform both the self and the environment in creative ways.

5. 4th Harmonic: Interpersonal Connection through Play

- The fourth harmonic (E, major third) represents **interpersonal connection**. Superplay often happens in a shared space, where pretend and play facilitate deeper bonds between individuals. There's a collaborative joy that emerges in this state, similar to how harmonics blend together. This harmonic highlights the social aspect of play, where individuals build trust and intimacy through shared imaginative experiences.

6. 5th Harmonic: Resilience through Role Flexibility

- The fifth harmonic (G) could signify **resilience through role-flexibility**. In Superplay, one can switch between different roles or identities easily, trying on new ways of being without attachment. This creates a state of adaptive resilience, where challenges can be approached from multiple angles. Just like harmonics, which shift and blend with the fundamental note, individuals in Superplay can move fluidly between different "selves," adapting to the needs of the moment.

7. 6th Harmonic: Creative Problem-Solving

- The sixth harmonic (B♭) represents **creative problem-solving**. In Superplay, individuals can approach real-life problems through the lens of pretend, which opens up unexpected solutions. By pretending, one is free to think outside of conventional constraints, leading to creative insights. This harmonic adds a layer of intellectual play, where novel solutions emerge as part of the imaginative process.

8. 7th Harmonic: Joyful Mastery of Contradictions

- The seventh harmonic (C, three octaves above) represents **joyful mastery of contradictions**. Superplay, by nature, allows individuals to hold paradoxes lightly—combining safety with risk, seriousness with laughter, and structure with freedom. This highest harmonic ties back to the fundamental, showing that Superplay is an advanced state where seemingly opposing elements are integrated joyfully. It's the capacity to "play" with the rules of reality without being bound by them.

The Fox Method as an Extension of the Polyvagal Ladder

If we consider **Superplay** as an extension of the **Polyvagal Ladder** in neurophysiological terms, it would represent a state that transcends the typical fight, flight, freeze, and safe-and-social states, while incorporating elements from all of them within a framework of safety and exploration. Here's what that might look like:

1. Base of the Polyvagal Ladder: Defense States (PVT's Freeze, Flight, Fight)

At the foundation of the Polyvagal ladder are the defense states: **freeze, flight, and fight**. These are the body's responses to danger, activated by the dorsal vagal and sympathetic nervous systems. In each of these states:

- **Freeze**: The body shuts down, immobilizes, and dissociates to protect itself.
- **Flight**: The body prepares to escape danger, activating the sympathetic nervous system.
- **Fight**: The body prepares to confront the threat, using adrenaline and aggression to survive.

2. Middle of the Ladder: The Survival State (PVT's Safe and Social State)

The middle of the ladder is the **ventral vagal state**, often called the **safe-and-social** state. This is where connection, calm, and engagement happen. In this state:

- The body is **regulated**: Heart rate, breathing, and muscles are in balance.
- There is **open communication**: Facial expressions are relaxed, *and* there is an ability to engage in reciprocal social behavior.
- **Creativity and emotional flexibility** are present: The individual feels free to connect, explore, and engage in cooperative, playful interactions.
- This is a **high risk** area of play.

3. Superplay: An Extension of the Safe and Social State

Superplay, as an extension of this ladder, would represent a **new rung**, transcending but including aspects of all the states below it. Here's what the neurophysiological state of Superplay might look like:

1. Integrated Safety with Playful Risk

- **Core Ventral Vagal Activation**: At its foundation, Superplay would rely on a **strong sense of safety**, rooted in the ventral vagal system. The body is in a regulated, safe state, but unlike typical calm, Superplay encourages the exploration of boundaries, and includes activation.
- **Flirting with Defense States**: In Superplay, individuals can **playfully engage with elements of freeze, flight, or fight**, but with the full knowledge and experience that they are safe. For example, one might pretend to be afraid (mimicking flight) or engage in playful stage combat (mimicking fight), but it's all done with the understanding that no real threat exists.
  - Neurophysiologically, this could involve **momentary activation of sympathetic responses**, but with rapid regulation back into a ventral vagal state.
  - **Dorsal vagal influences** (freeze) may also surface, but instead of immobilization, they appear as controlled stillness or "pauses" in play, representing moments of dramatic stillness before leaping into action.

    * It's still to be determined whether or not a dorsal vagal influence could happen in Superplay. I will leave this to neurobiologists to study and go to the mat with.

2. Fluid Emotional and Behavioral Flexibility

- **Shifting Between States**: In Superplay, the individual can **move fluidly between different emotional or behavioral states**, mimicking aspects of defense responses (fear, anger, tension), but always returning to the core safety of ventral vagal engagement.

This is a kind of **nervous system dance** where elements of high arousal (fight/flight) are blended with calm regulation. Playful exploration of shutdown (freeze) happens in a safe context.

- Neurophysiologically, this might manifest as **quick transitions between sympathetic activation and parasympathetic regulation**, without lingering in either extreme. It's a **dynamic balance,** where the individual can "pretend" to experience intense emotions without being overwhelmed by them.

3. Amplified Creativity and Imagination

- **Broader Prefrontal Cortex Activation**: In Superplay, the **prefrontal cortex**—responsible for imagination, creativity, and higher cognitive functions—is fully engaged. The safe and social system allows the individual to use higher-order thinking to create new realities, explore roles, and problem-solve through pretend.
  - This higher cognitive engagement reflects the **absence of threat**, allowing the brain to engage in **abstract thinking, imaginative storytelling, and creative problem-solving**.
  - **Neuroplasticity is maximized**: Because the nervous system isn't in a state of survival, it can **reorganize and experiment** with new patterns, behaviors, and ways of being.

4. Joyful Engagement with Contradictions

- **Dopamine and Oxytocin** Release: Superplay would likely involve the release of **dopamine** (associated with reward and pleasure) and **oxytocin** (linked to social bonding and connection). These chemicals help support the joyful, social, and imaginative aspects of the state.
  - The presence of these neurochemicals suggests that Superplay would feel **pleasurable**, deeply rewarding, and socially connective.

- **Integration of Contradictory States**: In Superplay, the individual can joyfully hold **contradictory states**—such as seriousness and silliness, safety and mock-fear, control and chaos. This fluidity of holding opposites could be a **neurophysiological balance** between **sympathetic arousal** (high energy, action) and **ventral vagal engagement** (regulation, connection).

5. Resilience through Play

- **Increased Vagal Tone**: Superplay builds **resilience** in the nervous system by constantly exercising the ability to **return to safety** after flirtations with defense. This builds **vagal tone**, the nervous system's capacity to recover quickly from stress or arousal. Through repeated cycles of playful engagement with potential threats (real or imagined), the system strengthens its capacity to remain flexible and adaptive.
- This is a **low risk** to the brain, or else the brain would default to dysregulated states.

In Summary: Superplay as an Extension of the Polyvagal Ladder

If **Superplay** were to be represented as an extension of the Polyvagal ladder, it would sit **above the safe and social state**, integrating all lower states but infusing them with play, creativity, and imaginative flexibility. It could be described as a **"meta-state"**—one that transcends survival—while incorporating its elements within a safe, exploratory framework. Neurophysiologically, this state would:

- Be rooted in **ventral vagal regulation** but allow **playful engagement with sympathetic and dorsal vagal influences**.
- Involve **quick nervous system transitions**, demonstrating fluidity and flexibility between states.
- Activate the **prefrontal cortex**, supporting creativity, imagination, and higher-order problem-solving.
- Release **dopamine** and **oxytocin**, creating feelings of pleasure, reward, and connection.

- Build **vagal tone**, fostering resilience and adaptability especially in new areas and especially in children's imaginary play could contribute to new neural wiring.

Superplay, in this model, becomes the **ultimate creative state**, where nervous system mastery allows full engagement with life's complexities, contradictions, and possibilities in a way that is joyful, imaginative, and deeply regulated. And, the Fox Method acknowledges that the entire nervous system, and all of its states, is a creative evolutionary force. But all nerdery aside, Superplay is as intuitive as screwing in a lightbulb.

Too many people feel they aren't worthy of it, even though they're already doing it. An accountant who comes home to their five-year-old and creates the character voices that illuminate a bedtime story—that's Superplay. You see, Superplay is a human birthright. Superplay is not an inaccessible state for a chosen few. It is simply a person's conscious decision to role-play for the purpose of nervous system exploration to amplify and deepen the human experience. Unlike other nervous system states, it is uniquely revelatory because to enter this state from Connect Mode, we do it with consent and intention. Let this be an invitation back into a world of playfulness that you may have long felt was inaccessible by a parent who said you were too loud, or a teacher that gave the lead role to some other kid. And to those like astronaut Brian who found shelter in Superplay as a child and are just now finding their footing in Connect Mode—I see you too.

It's showtime.

Acting is an illusion of Superplay...

Role 1:
All states,
feelings,
sensations

Role 2:
Craftsperson
with many skills
and training

Role 3:
The pretend role
(Hamlet)

The pretend role is an
illusion. This means a
person is always juggling
the needs of all 3 roles.

Letter #15: The Theory of Constructed Emotion

Dear Artist,

While we have extensively offered a lens to understand the nervous system, how can we play a role without asking, **"What is emotion?"** I found this terribly embarrassing considering I had an acting degree from a top-notch university. How could I not have an answer to this very basic question? Well, it turns out that the truth of the anatomy of emotion is a mind-twisting endeavor that to understand fully, your whole relationship to emotion would have to change. When I took in this new information, I was on a mini-tour from Nashville to Boston, and heard myself say out loud, "NOOOO," many times as I took in the truth about emotion and its ingredients. My resistance came from the fact that neuroscience and acting schools are not on the same page about what emotion is, and it challenges everything I was taught. While PVT went down like a cool glass of water, the Theory of Constructed Emotion felt like an intellectual assault to my reality,

Luckily, I came across a few unexpectedly complementary ideas developed by neuroscientist and psychologist Dr. Lisa Feldman Barrett, in her book *How Emotions Are Made*. Unlike Porges' work, in which I felt a sense of immediate recognition, Barrett's arguments felt less intuitively and less experientially accurate. Her ideas were much thornier to grapple with, much more resistible than Polyvagal's core tenets. Ultimately, though, I found I not only agreed with her theory but also saw how it enhanced both Polyvagal's foundation *and* my theory of Superplay, as well as the Fox Method. I say all of this because if you too experience resistance to what Barrett calls the Theory of Constructed Emotion, just know that I have been there. Stick with me. There are wonders ahead still.

So, Barrett's theory goes like this: for thousands of years, we've come to believe that our emotions are inherent and involuntary physiological responses to various stimuli—what she refers to as the "classical view of emotion"—and that these emotions are universal and distinguishable. Basically, when you are triggered, an emotion like "sadness" squirts from your brain, and you express it in predictable ways. It's so obvious that it's just the way things are. But, the evidence for this concept is murky at best and damning at worst. No matter how natural an idea the classical view is, when researchers and scientists attempt to empirically prove it, they find that many people interchangeably use the same words to describe very different sensations and feelings. It turns out each emotion has an endless variety of characteristics and body responses that make it difficult to define. Individuals are not particularly exacting in distinguishing nuances between emotions, and thus aren't the most trustworthy sources. Yet, unfortunately, these are often the *only* sources in many studies undergirding the classical view. Basically, your "mad" isn't anything like my "mad," and the farther we are from each other culturally, the wider the gap. So, this language we use to describe emotion is a very rough abstraction of basic sense-feeling (affect) in the body.

Remember when we thought the Sun revolved around the earth, that is basically where we are with emotion. This is why it took me so long to accept without my nervous system pushing back. It appears that every time we try to prove the "classical theory of emotion" right, it falls apart in researchers' hands.

In Dr. Lisa Feldman Barrett's book *How Emotions Are Made*, she discusses how humans are not as adept at accurately reading emotions in facial expressions as commonly believed. Research suggests that people can correctly identify emotions from facial expressions only about **20-30% of the time**. This challenges the traditional view that facial expressions universally convey specific emotions, showing instead that context, culture, and individual differences play significant roles in how we interpret facial expressions.

This means that you likely can't read the faces of your audience. It means that most of the assumptions you make about how other people are reacting to you are incorrect. I don't know about you, but I initially found all of this disturbing to my basic sense of reality! But as you know,

I am committed to embodied science, and worked to stay in the ring long enough to feel and live this science. The good news is that we actually get more control over our environments by living this truth than by ignoring it and bungling our idea of what is real.

Barrett notes that the reason we think my "irritation" is the same as your "irritation" is that, ironically, we *feel* this to be true. But just as Einstein's theories of relativity and quantum physics seem to describe a universe we don't recognize, so too does Barrett's theory read as if it's describing an alien species. Here's Barrett's summary of her argument:

> In short, we find that your emotions are not built-in but made from more **basic parts.** They are not universal but vary from culture to culture. **They are not triggered; you create them.** They emerge as a combination of the physical properties of your body, a flexible brain that wires itself to whatever environment it develops in, and your culture and upbringing, which provide that environment. Emotions are real, but not in the objective sense that molecules or neurons are real. They are real in the same sense that money is real—that is, hardly an illusion, but a product of human agreement.

That's quite a lot to take in, right? They are not triggered? We create them? The idea that how we were raised informs the idiosyncrasies of our emotions seems intuitive, but that we "create them"? How do we do this exactly? And how is *creating* emotions functionally different from *triggering* them? If it's the body doing it, isn't the framing of their emergence almost semantic? I'll be frank, one of the reasons I had a tough time accepting this framework was that as a person with a narcissistic mother, all I ever needed was to have my emotions validated, and now you are telling me that I "construct" them?? No way, dude. I have emotions, and I'm not making them up!

But, Barrett herself admits that she too experiences emotions in the classical way, writing, "If I were not a scientist using experiments to reveal that emotions are in fact made and not triggered, I too would trust my immediate experience." But as I calmed down to understand this science more and more, I realized that she's not saying we "make up" emotions and they aren't real. She's saying an emotion is a poetic abstraction of our base senses (pain to pleasure and activation to calm spectrum). And those base sensations, the ones somatic therapists are always trying to get is to connect with, are very, very real.

Imagine a blueberry muffin. A big fluffy thing. Now for a second, think about this as an emotion-object. A blueberry muffin is made of a couple basic ingredients that all mix together in certain conditions and when we bake them (filter them through the mind), we get a blueberry muffin. But your blueberry muffin might be someone else's scone! Or, if it's someone's birthday with frosting on top, it's cake. Make it the shape of a circle and it's a donut. So, the contextual situation around the muffin changes it despite being made of the same ingredients. What we call this mix of things is an abstraction so that we can hold on to it like a donut and know what to do with it! Emotion is made up of various sensations and when they are "cooked"--sent through our mental and cultural filter–we can *feel* them as an emotion-object. We are not tapping into some shared pool of human emotional essence-emotion any more than we are tapping into some shared pool of wealth when we earn money—these are illusions of unity created by our brains and reinforced (over and over again) by art, politics, and media.

Here's why it matters: when we are allowed to look at what the muffin is made of, we have more freewill, more awareness–and more control over how we express emotion, hold emotion, and deal with emotion. For a performer this seems like a vital skill. Just as a football player knows every texture of grass and every brand of football, we must have what Barrett calls **"emotional granularity," which is the foundation of not emotional intelligence but emotional mastery.** For me, as a coach and teacher, I never assume I know how someone is feeling. And even when they tell me an emotion, **I will ask them about levels of activation and pain in their body.** This helps us *Sherlock Holmes* our way back to the body (core-affect) and away from mental analysis, which I leave to your therapeutic analyst. We are in the business of peak performance through understanding our primary instrument, with the level of nuance any professional athlete would have.

Let's take a second to break down the blueberry muffin even further to show you why we need to live inside this new theory and throw away the

Classical Theory of Emotion: I have a gig tonight. Which means I want to get my body and mind in the best position to perform. I walk to the kitchen to get coffee. As my partner talks to me, I'm immediately overwhelmed. And as I pour my cup I think, "I feel sad. Why am I sad??" My sadness is the blueberry muffin. The only thing in my sightline is my partner. I immediately think, "What is he doing to make me sad?" That question I could easily spend an hour with in therapy, or worse, unconsciously use to start a fight. But instead, I follow the Theory of Constructed Emotion. Ok, if sadness is the muffin, what are the ingredients? I scan my body. I notice my activation is low (about a three), but my pain is high (about a 10). Where is the pain? It's behind my right eye socket. I have a migraine! I realized that the construction of sadness came from being overwhelmed by pain I wasn't even aware of. I've come to know that pain translates to the emotion of sadness in my body. I was always the one on the softball field who would sob if anything or anyone hit me too hard.

Instead of fighting with the love of my life or wasting an hour in therapy, I say, "Hey babe, I'm going to go lay down, I have a lot of pain in my head this morning." I take three Motrin, take a nap, and that sad muffin poofs right away. Thank god I didn't follow the emotion or analyze it instead of tracing my "ingredients." When I know what I'm dealing with, I can address the issues much more practically than I can at the level of constructed emotion. If basic sense-feeling is light, culture and the brain are like the prism, that makes the colorful emotion object.

Going back to the importance of co-regulation, I had the luxury of doing this because I know that if I do squabble with my partner or I "start some shit," there are deep levels of lived, somatic trust between us as a safety net. This trust carries me through the moments I've projected an emotion onto my partner that simply needed to be parented or soothed. In order to explore our neurobiology, we also must know we can make mistakes in relationships that are capable of repair. Co-regulation is always a key piece in the dance of safety and another reason why we want to be discerning with who joins our nervous system's web of connection. If my relationship was not secure, I would have no access to this level of exploration and curiosity (thank you, baby).

Another example: I went back to Boston for a visit and was driving around town. Naturally, I was infuriated! My old Boston-driving survival tactics came back and I aggressively made my way through the labyrinthine cow paths. But, as I broke the emotion of "Boston anger" down into its parts, my pain was low and my activation was very low too. *I wasn't actually dysregulated or mad.* I was just doing the thing you do when you are driving in Boston. I giggled at my own "performance" of emotion. I wasn't making it up, but to me "rage while driving in Boston" is its own emotion (which you would imagine would be awful) but if I was honest with myself, it was a form of playful and pleasurable aggression. Other countries have words for this, but we don't in English!

Ok, so why does this matter? Firstly, we can be less spooked by emotion when we need to use it in our art because we have a way of understanding emotion from a base-sense level. Or, when we are triggered, we can trace our emotion from abstraction to sensation so that we can address emotion practically. I don't know what to "do" with feeling flummoxed but I do know how to deal with activation and pain. I can nurture, soothe, or metabolize those sensations. Finally, when we work on building our capacity for holding deep love and appreciation for the entire spectrum of nervous system harmonics, we have the two handlebars of the pain and activation spectrum to hold onto.

How could emotions be universal if they are experienced and defined so variously throughout the world? We've all heard of those incredibly specific names for emotions other languages have that we might recognize from our own lives but haven't ever thought of before. For instance, the German word "torschlusspanik" refers to the worry that life's doors have closed on you as you age. Japanese has a term, "shinrin-yoku," for the comfort that comes from bathing in the forest. The Arabic word "tarab" is a feeling of enchantment caused by music.

Does this demystify emotion and make it a little less witchy and sparkly? Sure. Am I glad I have this knowledge to guide my life, absolutely.

I know this idea is a mind-fuck, but I think it's important to acknowledge and define, as I believe it's important for us to see ourselves in new ways–ways that deepen our understanding of our inner lives *and* give us agency in the management of those inner lives. The Fox Method is founded on doing exactly that.

Throughout the book, I've saved a lot of the embodied exercises for the tools section. But this is such an essential skill, I don't even consider it a tool. I consider it a foundation process to reclaim your emotional agility.

"Breaking Down the Blueberry Muffin"

Objective: This exercise is designed to help artists engage with the concept of constructed emotion as proposed by Dr. Lisa Feldman Barrett. It's a guide to enhancing their emotional granularity and awareness of their body's sensations. It encourages artists to break down complex emotions into their "ingredients" of bodily sensations and environmental context, rather than reacting to a predefined emotional label.

Duration: 5–20 minutes

Step 1: Prepare Your "Blueberry Muffin"

- Find a quiet space where you won't be disturbed.
- Sit comfortably and take a few deep breaths to center yourself.

Prompt: Close your eyes and think of a recent moment when you felt a strong emotion. It could be anything: sadness, anger, excitement, anxiety, etc. This is your "blueberry muffin"—the fully formed emotion.

- Take a moment to mentally *see* this emotion as an object. Imagine it as a literal blueberry muffin sitting in front of you.

Step 2: Identify the Ingredients

Now, we will break down this emotion into its fundamental ingredients, moving beyond the label (e.g. "sadness") to uncover the underlying sensations and contexts.

- **Body Scan**: Slowly scan your body from head to toe. Where do you feel sensations? Are they tight, soft, tingly, heavy? Jot down where you feel tension or any noticeable sensations in your body. For example:
    - "Tightness in my chest"
    - "Heat in my face"
    - "Pressure behind my eyes"
- **Pain/Activation Level**: On a scale from 1–10:
    - How much physical *pain* are you experiencing (if any)?
    - How *activated* do you feel? Calm or jittery? Sluggish or energized?

Example: "I feel a 3 in activation (a little tired) and a 7 in pain (headache behind my eyes)."

Step 3: Contextual Ingredients

Reflect on the environment or situation in which this emotion occurred:

- **Where were you?**
- **Who were you with?**
- **What was happening?**

Ask yourself if the emotion you felt might have been shaped by the context. For instance, you might have thought you were angry at a partner, but you were really overwhelmed by loud noises in a crowded room.

Step 4: Reframe the Emotion

With these ingredients in mind, consider what this "muffin" is really made of:

- Could this emotion be more about a physical sensation or environmental factor than the label you initially gave it?
- How does seeing your emotion as a construct help you better understand it?

Example: "I thought I was feeling sadness, but actually I was feeling physically drained and overwhelmed from a migraine."

Step 5: Name Your New "Muffin"

Create your own label for the reconstructed emotion. This can be playful or serious. Just like other languages have unique words for feelings, what would you call this mixture of sensations, context, and reactions?

- For example, you might label the feeling of minor frustration mixed with tiredness as "Sleepy-Irritation," or the nervous excitement before a performance as "Spark-Jitters."

Step 6: Reflection

Journal about your experience, jot down:

- How did breaking down the emotion help you understand it differently?
- How might this exercise help you as a performer or artist to better understand and convey emotions in your craft?

The End of Critique

Since we got a taste of why emotion is not what we thought it was, we might as well take a sledgehammer to critique too! When in Rome…I mean "The Barrett Lab."

As artists, how on earth do we deal with feedback and critique? Many artists don't. They simply quit from the devastation this causes. *And, don't forget my devastation is different from your devastation.* It turns out there is absolutely no such thing as objective critique, ever.

Barrett uses the idea of something she calls *simulation* to illustrate the human brain. If I were to ask you to think of an apple and all of its sensory details—its taste and smell, etc.—you could do so automatically. You can even kind of "taste" it right now, as you're reading this—or at least you can *approximate* the taste in your mind. And your body could respond to that approximation by your mouth watering, your stomach rumbling, or if apples aren't your thing perhaps a mild shiver of disgust. This is your brain's *simulation* of what it expects the word 'apple' to suggest. When your mind conjured the apple, Barrett writes, "your brain responded to a certain extent as if an apple were actually present." Just thinking of the word causes your body to act as if it had seen or touched it. This is also known as **affective realism,** and if this were not possible the craft of acting would not work!

Your brain's eagerness to prepare for an apple that isn't there demonstrates how fickle our brain's activities can be when it comes to reality. Our minds don't always initiate the correct protocols. There was no apple and yet your mouth watered. When the idea that's brought up isn't an apple but something much more complex, like a situation in one's life that involves numerous parties and contexts, your brain does that same thing as it does for the apple. But this time your mind takes in all the various stimuli and comes up with an internal match for it.

This is the "simulation" that Barrett refers to. It solves a major metabolic problem as well, which is that we simply only have a certain amount of energy every day. If we were using that energy to see everything new for the first time, we would all seem totally stoned and in wonder, completely overwhelmed with stimulus and unable to get the resources we need to survive.

This means the brain is mostly the past, hallucinating. I always tell my clients that once I see their face, a lot of what I see after that is a construction of their face in my mind. Barrett calls the brain a "black box" of the past that sometimes is responding to new stimuli.

This means that when someone is giving you feedback on your work, they might not even be seeing it! Isn't that wild? If a person goes to see a production of Hamlet, but has seen 13 other productions of Hamlet, their brain is not responding just to this show but their contracted hallucination of it as well.

It turns out that when you share your work, you are not the vulnerable one. The person giving critique is. **When someone is giving you feedback, they are showing you their brain!** It's not some perfect assessment of your worth or talent. That's why one person can say, "I got chills!" and another can say, (direct quote about one of my songs) "What is this even?"

Holy Holarchy

As we move into the shifting chapters, I want you to remember that not all sense-feelings need to be shifted, metabolized, or zapped! Sometimes we need to just hold our emotions like babies. As a Holarchy, the human body and psyche responsible for caring and loving every single one of its parts. A cell doesn't judge its parts but its intelligence sure as hell will direct them if things are not right. Sometimes those parts need some shifting for the distinct purpose of peak-performance and nervous system leadership onstage. But many times, we need that Mr. Rogers kind of love. We need to embrace the absolute worst of our sense-feelings. For many of us, our blueberry muffins feel like they are made of cocaine (activation) and razor blades (pain). We hate our exiled and delinquent muffins. We can't figure out where the threat is coming from or figure out how to nurture our wounds until we stop eating this scary muffin and start responsibly caring for its ingredients. Do not shift your system into a "positive vibes only" oblivion.

Things to remember about emotion if you are a performer:

1. Happy faces will look neutral, and neutral faces look grumpy when you are dysregulated.
2. We humans are really bad at reading faces. Opt for asking instead of assuming.
3. We need more names for emotions that don't exist in English.
4. Never assume your audience hates you. They are probably concentrating.
5. Critique does not exist in the ways you think it does. It reveals the other more than it reveals you.

Theory of Constructed Emotion

Pain level 10
Activation 2 $+$  $=$

" Sadness "

Letter #16: Nervous System Shifting

Dear Artist,

While we've been diving into the fundamentals of Polyvagal Theory alongside my own insights into nervous system states, I understand why we're truly here: to equip ourselves with practical tools to improve our performing lives—playing shows, nailing auditions, and managing dysregulation when we're on stage. Let's get practical and answer, "Ok, but what do I *do* about it?"

There's something crucial I want you to keep in mind when thinking about nervous system shifting. Firstly, nervous system flexibility is our birthright. While you may choose to do this shifting with a clinician, it's not an activity that any institution owns or controls. Humans have been shifting their nervous systems way before the invention of embodied nervous system science. In fact, all kinds of musical genres have been shifting nervous systems in and out of states for thousands of years.

Next, as therapist Esther Perel wisely noted in an interview on mental health: **a protocol is only as valuable as its effectiveness.** If you've sat in therapy with the same tool for two years, and have found no progress, it's not the tool for you. Performers often encounter countless helpers that promise to fix their performance issues. Offering breathwork for hormonal issues. Telling people that fear and excitement are the same physiology (when they are not). Or telling people to reframe their thinking when they are oxygen deprived and don't have access to that kind of cognition. Those suggestions, while well-intended, are not accurately guided by functional neurobiology. They may occasionally work due to the power of confirmation bias, but leave many artists feeling shame. We deserve better than pseudo-advice from an industry that throws up their hands and says, "We just don't *do* science." Let's instead look to science-based tools that work specifically for shifting into Connect Mode for optimal stage performance. That said, I use them offstage all the time as well. Also, before I give you any protocols,

I bow to the Gods of humility. I'm always learning and always adapting. I hope that your participation in these protocols make them shaper and more useful. Much of this work has already been changed by the hundreds of MuscleMusic members who braved to tell me what really worked, and what didn't. But of course, this work is adapted for people who need to get on stage in five minutes, not after three to 10 years in therapy.

I will never tell you to only do this or do that, as if my command will magically fix your life or issues. My job is to put you in your own driver's seat and show you the biological mechanisms behind the curtain, so you can pull tools you already have! In fact when I learned this framework, a lot of old modalities like Qi Gong, Yoga, Weightlifting, Linklater, and Alexander Technique finally felt useful the way a screwdriver does when you need to hang a picture. While there is an entire tool library in this book, I want you to pay close attention to what drives each shift, instead of blindly following my tools. I want you to play close attention to how your body responds, and build your tool kit based on your experiences, not mine, or the tenets of the Polyvagal Institute.

So, let me put it this way: if a protocol is working, you'll palpably feel the difference; if it's not, you won't. If you *don't* feel it working, please remember you are not broken, you just need a tool that's a better fit for *you*.

We will start with Shifting.

I mentioned Shifting in the previous letter and noted that it cannot be your only tool for nervous system regulation. As I said, while Shifting is a useful skill to have for everyday life, it is a vital technique for performers. For ordinary circumstances, you can "shift" out of one state and into another deliberately, in order to push through a difficult experience or manage stress—a kind of therapeutic nudge. For performers, though, we aren't doing therapy; we're harnessing our biology for the stage.

So what is Shifting? And how do we do it?

Shifting is the term I use for PVT's general idea of "regulation" when applied to performers and artists. I use the more movement-oriented word because it doesn't imply, as regulation does, that one state represents a regulated self. Instead, shifting addresses more immediate needs, but it doesn't do this in a uniform manner. Each Mode requires a different Shift to move to another. Shifting is the name for the movement, whereas the tools are common activities like planking or resting or shaking. So let's again explore the physiological and psychological problems of each Mode so that we can figure out how to deal with them.

One last note before we get into specific states: Another reason we aren't just saying "regulating" is because in the context of stage performance, we are not shifting for ourselves but for the Holarchy and the honor of being a nervous system leader of that Holarchy. To remix M. Scott Peck's "The Road Less Traveled," a performer's ability to lead is the will to extend one's nervous system as a tuning fork for the purpose of nurturing one's own–or an audience's–spiritual growth. **We are not just regulating for our health and healing, we regulate because we chose leadership.** This is a calling and takes *effort,* character, and courage.

Shifting Out of Preservation (Mini-Review)

In Preservation Mode, it's clear that we need to restore oxygen. While this state seems like a complete lack of energy, it's actually both **trapped energy** that needs to be released (P. Levine) and **oxygen deprivation** (S. Porges) due to shallow breathing or bradycardia (low heart rate). Again, remember when you were a kid and wrapped a rubber band around your finger and it turned blue? That is essentially what is happening to our whole body.

So, if there's one image for how to approach a body in Preservation Mode, proceed as if your entire body was a numb limb. **It needs oxygen, but not too quickly.**

Here is a brief list of protocols (more examples will come in the Tools section) to get yourself out of Preservation Mode:

Protocol #1: Practice A Freeze Fire Drill. The most problematic part of freeze is that to follow a protocol you need your prefrontal cortex working. I made an app to help you remember called the MuscleMusic app. Or, I recommend making a list on your phone or even reminding a partner or roommate so they can remind you. Even leave a post-it or reminders in places you might look. If you are headed to a gig and you will likely go into a Preservation Mode, write them on your hand. The ability to think in Preservation Mode is so impaired that it's important to have no shame around practicing getting out of Preservation Mode like a fire drill. Why? Because in this state, you are so unbelievably physiologically different, that you are not the same person.

Protocol #2: Move, but not too fast. Since we're approaching our body the same way we approach a numb limb, we don't want to move too hard or too fast. If you are far down the ladder, restoring too much oxygen too fast can give you a panic attack. Start with gentle movements like wiggling your fingers and toes, then perhaps tapping your face, then try shaking your whole body.

Protocol #3: Light Activation. This protocol shares the goal of movement but emphasizes that anything restoring oxygen—like a horror movie, spicy food, or punk, hardcore, or metal music—can help exit Preservation Mode. Sometimes, simply being witnessed by a loving co-regulator is enough to shift out of Preservation Mode.

Protocol #4: It's Ok To Hate This. While *you* want to leave Preservation Mode, your body's survival instincts may resist. These protocols likely won't feel good or therapeutic—they may feel like a roller coaster or even terrifying. Remember, this force has kept us alive for millions of years.

Protocol #5: Grounding Techniques. Sensory Grounding brings you to the present by focusing on your surroundings: notice five things you see, four you touch, three you hear, two you smell, and one you taste. Body Awareness shifts focus to your body—feel your feet on the ground or air on your neck—anchoring you, especially in an inhospitable environment.

Protocol #6: Find a Human. After working with hundreds of artists, many prone to freeze, the truth is clear: we exit Preservation Mode best with a co-regulator. Humans didn't evolve in isolation, and self-help alone often falls short. Being present for someone, or having someone help you out of Preservation Mode, is our greatest gift.

Protocol #7: Vocal Exercises. Humming, singing, or chanting creates soothing vibrations that help you feel more at ease and in touch with yourself. This is a great way to get started with activation. Peter Levine suggests a low, "Voooooo!" sound. Interestingly enough, voice guru Kristin Linklater recommended a "Zoooooo" sound.

Protocol #8: Cold Water Exposure. A splash of cold water on your face can be refreshing and invigorating, helping you wake up your senses into a more alert and ready state. For me, cold water activates my system too much but others' nervous systems find this a surefire way to activate out of this state.

Protocol #9: Go Horizontal. When we freeze, fighting it often worsens the fear. If activation fails, try lying down to reassure your body, "I'll immobilize." Surround yourself with comforts—blankets, soft lighting, familiar sounds, or soothing scents. Surrender to the state, connect with your breath, and when ready, start activating, even by wiggling your toes or moving your arms.

Shifting Out of Preservation in the Wild

It's showtime!

You just drove 11 hours from Pittsburgh to Milwaukee through steaming Chicago traffic to make a show. You have done your best to take care of your nervous system but had to pee in a Starbucks cup in the car because your band did not have time to stop. You get to the club and the sound guy is less than friendly. You need help with your sound but everything you say seems to annoy him. During soundcheck you forget your lyrics. This seems impossible considering you wrote them. You start hearing your Preservation Mode stories in your head like, "I should just quit music" and name your state saying, "Fuck, I'm in Freeze." So, backstage you activate (bring oxygen back to the brain) by vehemently complaining to your bandmates. As you co-regulate and begin to speak, you realize you are already coming out of freeze and into Move Mode. The anger is bubbling. Just to make sure you shake your whole body and start making sound, but you know you are now in Move Mode because you, are, pissed. You think, "Ok, this is good, I'm no longer frozen."

Now, what do we do with a musician in Move Mode?…

My leg fell asleep!

Shake, pat, rub, ground,
and be slow & patient!

I'm in Preservation Mode!

Shake, pat, rub, ground,
and be slow & patient!

Co-regulation

Shifting Out of Move Mode

During a stressful Move Mode scenario, our bodies are flooded with a one-two punch of adrenaline and then cortisol. We now have too much stress hormone and glucose in our blood stream. One of the best strategies for diminishing this pulse of energy is pushing, planking, or pressing. Because it's a hormonal response, it means we need to solve it with the only way to speed up the flushing out of stress hormones in the body: **muscle contraction**.

Muscle contraction? What? You may read this paragraph and go right back to the strategies taught to you by well-meaning arts instructors, like breathing deeply or reframing (imagining your audience in their underwear). If you feel a very significant pulse of energy in your body, you need to remember that **you don't have a thinking problem, you have a hormonal one.** You wouldn't tell a woman with PMS that she needs to reframe her thoughts or should breathe it away. That would be an absolute absurdity because it's a hormone! While I understand a reframe could potentially stop the hormone influx, there is actually a neurobiological "catch" which turns off cortisol influx when it hits a threshold. So again, reframing is not the right tool. Cortisol and adrenaline are hormones coursing through your bloodstream. So, sitting in meditation means you are stewing in them. Muscle contraction is the only bathroom we have for this metabolic problem.

Peter Levine, a trauma luminary, also has a theory that, as animals, we just need to feel like we got away from the tiger by moving. I absolutely buy this and encourage my clients to imagine as they're planking that either they *are* the tiger or they have successfully found safety *from* it.

Here are some Shifting protocols for Move Mode:

Protocol #1: Push, Plank, Press. When you have nervous energy, simply asking your body to integrate that energy won't work. The most effective tool is to find a wall (make sure it's sturdy) and press on it with all your force. Press until your muscles slightly shake. Your body may just want to collapse, so remember to keep going. It's counterintuitive, but effective, just like steering *into* a skid on an icy road.

Protocol #2: Shaking. I always tell my clients to press first. But if you still have energy after the push, press, plank protocol, then do some shaking. This helps with any extra energy that wasn't dispelled while planking or pushing.

Protocol #3: Movement. This is just good old-fashioned tuckering yourself out. Do 20 jumping jacks, a 30-second plank, and 10 squats. This is called Adrenaline Matching. Repeat this three times. After you've tired yourself out and expelled the extra caloric energy rushing through you, you want to restore calm.

Protocol #4: Welcome Big Emotion. If you're experiencing uncomfortable or unwanted emotions, you're probably doing it right. This happens to all of us. Instead of attempting to immediately expel those emotions, try staying with them, acknowledging them, and considering them as a phenomenon of your life, rather than an emergency. Your emotions are not your enemies; in fact, with the right protocols, they can be your aides. "It's safe to feel rage in my body. It's safe to feel terrified. I can hold this big, big, pulse of energy."

Protocol #5: Find a Co-Regulator With Caution. This state often pits you against others, making it common to snap at a co-regulator in Move Mode. If you can't tolerate co-regulation, don't force it. But if you can, it may help.

Shifting Out of Move Mode In The Wild

Back to the Milwaukee show!

You're surprised at how quickly you came out of Preservation Mode, though your body remains on alert because of the unfriendly sound engineer. While it's tempting to blame him, the real culprit is your brain's prediction of metabolic need—not the depressed, tender, and insecure person behind the soundboard. You recognize there's still an issue: you need to lead the audience, but your Connect Mode isn't fully online yet. You are still a little pissed.

You drop into a series of planks, then settle into "child's pose" to recover. As you work through the metabolic hormones driving your tension, your brain takes notice. With your sympathetic gas tank easing off, your vagus nerve reengages, and you start to feel more and more ready. You're not perfectly calm—there's still some excess energy—but your lyrics are back on the tip of your tongue, ready to flow.

Move Mode

is a

hormonal issue.

You wouldn't tell a woman to breathe and reframe to help her PMS would you?

(no)

Muscles are the bathroom of the stress hormones.

Flush them out! Reframe and breathe after.

Remaining In Connect Mode

Here is the game-changing knowledge that can keep this particular state in connection:

Protocol #1: Expect Difficulty. This first protocol is to **expect that this state is a difficult one** and that you can tackle difficult things. Just by wanting it to be more pleasurable or fun than it really is can cause you to tumble into Move Mode.

Protocol #2: Reframing and breathwork finally work in this state! Why? Because you have enough prefrontal cortex activity for them to activate and become effective. Positive thinking or what Deb Dana would call "glimmering" totally work. Use the tools box at the end of this book to play with these. I recommend, "It's Totally Possible"[3]

Protocol #3: Calling Out Your Dog. For a stage performer, Calling Out Your Dog is when a performer incorporates their nervousness or anxieties into the performance, and acknowledges their dysregulation without burdening the audience with it. This approach softens their authority and grants others the autonomy to determine their own comfort levels with proximity, which not only helps the audience relax but also puts the performer at ease.

Protocol #4: Add Wings. In the Superplay state we need to be adding some seriousness and weight to our characters, otherwise they will be cartoonish or not compelling to an audience. To stay in Connect Mode we need to do the opposite. We need to add "wings" to our social role-play. If your role is bandleader, how can you make that more playful? Turning something heavy into a game and adding humor are powerful tools to lighten the load of this very serious proposition of trying to connect to real-play. If this real role-play gets too serious, our brain predictions often say, "TOO RISKY! Send this woman to Move Mode."

---

3. I stole this tool from comedian, pianist, and teacher Kyle Cease. Thank you, Kyle.

Letter # 17: Nervous System Leadership

Dear Artist,

You are not on stage to be loved, seen, liked, or even understood. I know that from almost every vantage point it may appear that you are—after all, a crowd of people's attention is fixed on you as you express your innermost self and try to please those in attendance. Your concert or play or stand-up act, in other words, seems to be entirely about you. But that's the sneakily wonderful thing about live art: it's actually about the audience. You are there not to be seen, loved, or understood; your job is to love, see, and understand the individuals in the crowd.

Seems impossible and counterintuitive, right? Like, how could you possibly understand anonymous people in a sea of faces, when all those people are watching and reacting to your very specific and wholly intimate performance? It's a one-way street, isn't it? You express; they digest—isn't that how it works? No, it's not.

And here's why: the reason the previous chapters dealt with pre-show issues is because by the time you're in front of an audience, you should be regulated as best as you can be. **You are not up here for regulation; you regulated so that you could be up here**. Which means that it's your job to set the stage for the audience, a random assemblage of people in varying nervous system states. **You are the Tuning Fork for your audience**. And this is what Nervous System Leadership is. It's a pact we make when we lead others, which—make no mistake—is precisely what performing is: **leading**. It's the audience's turn to benefit from your protocols, your regulation, and your artistry. You are here to tune them to your frequency, which in turn becomes everyone's frequency. This is why nervous system regulation and the Fox Method are so important for artists. You can not only find ways to stave off or relinquish nervous energy, but you can also find ways to harness it. Like some creative alchemist, you can utilize the things causing you anxiety or discomfort and turn them into tools to relieve others of the same symptoms.

It's powerful, isn't it? You've transformed your struggles into strategies that many people can benefit from. It's an amazing ability and a true testament to the power of performance, but it also means there's an equal amount of responsibility that comes along with it. The role of a nervous system leader exists because there is a power imbalance in a relationship or dynamic—so this includes performers, yes, but also teachers, bosses, directors, parents, doctors, and partners. When you take the position of leader, you must do your best to lead with regulation. And if you're in this position often in your life, you're even more duty-bound to use your leadership tools to keep your body and mind healthy. Every performer is a nervous system leader—there are no exceptions.

Please try Tool 1L: The Tuning Fork Tool in the tool library.

Back to space...

*cue John Williams

Sally is about to lead the very first version of *A Midsummer Night's Dream* in space. It's never been done before and she is the only person with both acting skills and space skills. She is the whole that brings all the parts together. But, this is a much more tricky thing to do than it seems.

Anything that transcends and includes in nature is of a "higher" order in our biological Holarchy. But this also means that whatever is holding something together also has *a lot of loving and accepting to do of the parts contained. You are not there to change your audience so they like you more.* ***You're there as a leader to accept them as they are, and to accept your own nervous system just as it is, RIGHT NOW, under the spotlight.***

Parents hold a family together, CEOs hold companies, and artists hold their audiences. That means real leadership is earned by **complete and benevolent service to the whole**. Sally's job is to take all the information about her team, including their nervous systems, and have the very first Shakespeare play go up on the moon.

A violation of this kind of leadership would be like asking your child if you're worthy of love. Or a CEO asking their company if they're competent. It's a violation of the Holarchy and that's why this energy feels so bad onstage. When it is reversed, an artist can be at ease.

Your head may be spinning right now with, "But what if I'm dysregulated as a leader?" which is totally fair. I recommend the **Calling Out Your Dog Tool** for that.

For now, think about how nervous you would feel if your young child was driving a car. You'd be insecure, sweating, your heart would race, and you would feel disoriented. Sound familiar? It's a lot like stage fright. This is what happens when we come to the stage wanting to be regulated by our audience instead of the exact opposite. **You are the tuning fork**. The second you switch the paradigm around, you will likely feel so much more in control. You may still have activation, but it will feel harnessable. This week I want you to play in three different positions.

They serve as orientation points of energetic focus, guiding how you share your nervous system with others, based on your levels of safety and position of power. The upcoming tool is one of the only tools not in the library and because it is so foundational, it must be a part of the Muscle as well as the Music.

Tool 2L: Get In Position Tool

There are three adaptable nervous-system positions on and off stage.

Position 1: Boundary-Free Flow

This kind of nervous system flow is when two people are tuning each other simultaneously. For this to work, both parties must have equal positions of power (Ex. Two friends. Ex. Two lovers. Ex. Two actors.)

You will know this is the right position because you will feel a regulated flow. **If there is not a regulated flow, you need to go into the nervous system leadership position.** There is a level of healthy enmeshment, in that your nervous systems are affecting each other but there is also a major groundwork of safety and separateness as well. Also, this gelling of nervous systems doesn't mean you don't have any boundaries. It just means you are letting your nervous system be affected by another nervous system without protection or hypervigilance. This should only take place if you feel safe. If you notice that you are not feeling this flow, ask yourself how you could feel safer and what might be impeding your ability to connect.

Position 2: Nervous System Leadership

This is when one person has more power in a relationship/role-play dynamic (Ex. Teacher, CEO, singer-songwriter, director, teacher, therapist, mom, dad, parent, doctor, etc). In this case you will always choose a nervous system leadership position, which means that you understand that the person with less power will unconsciously be tuning to your nervous system. Therefore, you must do your best to lead with regulation. If you are in nervous system leadership often, you will be responsible for using more leadership tools (more on that later). You will also carry more responsibility for keeping your body and mind healthy, and to maintain a healthy understanding of your own capacity. Any public speaker or singer-songwriter is always a nervous system leader. There are no exceptions. Use the phrase, "I am the tuning fork!" to bring you back into the right position.

When in a position of power, you must use nervous system leadership.

Position 3: Commanding Deference

I know the words commanding deference might sound contradictory, but let me explain. In Position 1, we have boundary-free flow, and in Position 2, we use our nervous system as a tuning fork to lead. Deference, on the other hand, is when you're being led by someone else in power who's holding the larger structure together.

This can be a vulnerable position, and for some, it feels too vulnerable to embrace, so we avoid it. But the ability to defer is crucial to healthy social interaction. Why is this in the leadership section? Because deference, when done intentionally, is a form of power.

How can you have power in deference? This idea comes from the work of Deb Gruenfeld, a Stanford researcher who studies power dynamics. She specifically pulls from improvisation techniques, which is why I love it. Her research shows that when someone is in a deferent role, like a child to a parent or an employee to a boss, they're not powerless. Rather, they're choosing not to use the power they have in that moment.

For example, if I'm attending a workshop, I might have the ability to lead my own, but I'm intentionally choosing to play the role of participant. Here's a story from my early MuscleMusic days: I had a participant in one of my workshops who suddenly asked to share their screen. Without warning, they started running their own mini-workshop. I had to step in and say, "We've lost the plot, let's bring it back." This person wasn't holding deference—they started to lead when it wasn't appropriate for the role.

Holding healthy deference is like role-playing. If someone is a teacher, they're playing the role of teacher in that moment. They're not always a teacher, and you're not always a student. In that specific context, you're playing those roles for a higher purpose. Your teacher might not even realize this dynamic consciously, but you can hold that perspective for both of you. For example: I'm playing the student right now, even though I could be the teacher. Or, I'm playing the audience, but I'm also a performer in other situations.

If there isn't a higher purpose or benevolence behind the dynamic, that's when you may need to question whether it's the right place to hold deference. Is this a healthy dynamic for me to be in this role?

Ultimately, deference is a power position because you are choosing to lead yourself into the appropriate role. So use this when the situation calls for it.

* A little exercise for actors: Is your character in position 1, 2, or 3 in imaginary circumstances?

Letter #18: The Dopamine Game

Dear Artist,

Dopamine is a word we casually use to explain vague pleasure, but it is actually so much more. It's a key hormone in delivering creativity and drive because it's actually the *seeking* hormone. Dopamine must be present in the brain to drive us to leave the house, go get things, or even audition for roles. It's the molecule that was abundant in the brains of early hunter-gatherers when they stepped out of their caves and said, "Bring it on! Let's go get some squirrels!"

To illustrate, consider starving mice genetically modified to lack dopamine. Despite being hungry, these mice won't eat food placed right next to their mouths. Without dopamine, their motivation to pursue food vanishes, highlighting dopamine's role in propelling us toward essential actions, rather than merely rewarding us after the fact. For so many artists, this is exactly how we feel after performances. This letter is here to finally explain why.

Dopamine is why we love making records, but when we finally release them, it's never the euphoric experience we hoped it would be. It's meant for pleasure seeking, not pleasure attaining. This post-release or post-show disappointment is not a personal failure, but more so the result of low dopamine. Let's go deep so we can harness the dopamine system with intention, instead of letting it throw us around like a helpless rag doll. We have enough on our plates as it is, let's not needlessly suffer over a hormone we just need to understand better.

But how is dopamine related to the nervous system ladder? I like to imagine it as a little sidecar on a motorcycle, that if not addressed, it can cause a major wipeout. Dopamine imbalance is the main cause of sluggishness, tiredness, brain fog, lack of willpower. With the exception of numbness and dissociation, Preservation Mode and a Dopamine Low can feel almost exactly the same. So, as we learned before, everyone needs to ask a very important question if they are feeling defeated and low. Did something feel so frightening and unsafe that I froze, or did I just do something incredibly new, pleasurable, or exciting. Because if it's the latter, you likely have a Dopamine Dip. Why does this matter? Because our protocols for moving out of Freeze and Dopamine Dips couldn't be more different. If we attribute everything to Freeze, we will use the wrong protocols for the problem.

Let's zoom out.

Why do we need to know about dopamine? It's very likely if you are reading this, you have a dopamine imbalance.

Dopamine is everywhere. According to dopamine luminary Anna Lembke, modern humans are like, "a cactus in a rainforest." Basically, we are being pummeled with dopamine and actively need to resist our stimulating environments to maintain a healthy brain.

Only 12 percent of Americans are metabolically healthy (July 2022 study published in the Journal of the American College of Cardiology). If you have insulin resistance, you have dopamine resistance, due to the stress of ingesting toxic amounts of glucose, fructose, and sugar which all spike dopamine.

You are creative or perform: Performing artists are constantly facing high highs which create low lows. If you are a performer, you will likely need to know more about your dopamine system than other populations.

What do I mean by dopamine resistance? It's the same idea as insulin resistance. If we overuse these hormones (dopamine or insulin), we need a lot more of them to do what they used to do with a lot less. For a person with pre-diabetes, insulin can't store glucose very well, so it keeps pumping it out to make sure that sugar doesn't kill us. For a person with addiction or burnout, it takes a ton of dopamine just to make us feel even, "Blah! I'm ok." We need too much dopamine to create too little pleasure. This is also what we call "addiction."

How We Cope

Everyone is dependent on dopamine, but true addiction is when pleasure sources narrow to just a few, while a healthy dopamine system enjoys a wide range of pleasures. Dopamine addiction can also isolate us from other essential neurotransmitters, like serotonin, further complicating our mental health.

The Rat Park experiment by Bruce Alexander in the late 70s highlighted the importance of environment and social factors in addiction. Rats in a stimulating and social environment chose plain water over drug-laced water, contrasting sharply with isolated rats who chose the drug-laced water. This experiment underscores that dopamine addiction is not just about exposure to drugs but also about the quality of one's surroundings and social connections. This means deep and varied social connections, plus environmental factors like food, water, and shelter, can keep us immune to addiction. So, if I'm isolated, I'm way more vulnerable to become addicted to Tik Tok.

For artists, the implications are clear. Ensuring a healthy nervous system is foundational not just for artistic success but also for overall brain health. Artists with high Adverse Childhood Experience (ACE) scores, financial insecurity, or social difficulties are more prone to dopamine-related issues. Artistic careers inherently stress the dopamine system, from the highs of performance to the constant intake of new information. I mention these things not to scare you but to empower you. While it took me a long time to quit smoking, codependence, and overworking–knowing that I was more prone to addiction due to my history–made me want to quit. I didn't want to be a victim or become a statistic based on my trauma, and instead forge my own path.

Artists must guard against the dopamine overkill from our environment—sugary foods, digital distractions, instant gratification. Our brains evolved for dopamine scarcity, not the abundance we now face. Without careful management, this leads to dopamine lows, fatigue, negative thinking, and confusion. The issue for artists is that even the most connected performer is messing with their brain chemistry any time they perform for a large crowd. We must have a new method for dopamine recovery for our population. Luckily, I have some ideas and a little dopamine game at the end of the chapter to get you headed in the right direction.

The Motivation Molecule

Now, let's delve into how various substances impact the brain's dopamine levels. Different activities and substances stimulate dopamine release to varying degrees. For example, chocolate increases dopamine by about 55%, sex by 100%, nicotine by 150%, cocaine by 225%, and speed (amphetamine) even more so. Synthetic drugs, however, spark the brain far more intensely than natural activities, making them dangerously potent and potentially addictive. The issue is, we have no way to track dopamine with wearable devices, so we actually have no idea how much performance messes with our dopamine. Looking at the amount of recovery artists need, it's likely performing releases dopamine levels that are very, very high. If we knew performing spiked dopamine 225 percent, I know we would have more reverence for the ways it can ravage us.

To truly comprehend dopamine, we must learn to embrace pain as a balancing force. Dopamine and pain exist in a dynamic balance, much like a seesaw. When pleasure is experienced, pain tips the balance to maintain equilibrium, as explained by researcher Dr. Anna Lembke's concept of "pain gremlins." For instance, a highly stimulating day can be followed by a low, depressed mood due to the pain gremlins tipping the balance back. If you have ever sobbed in the car on your way back from a performance and it felt horrible the next day, you are feeling your brain naturally tip to the side of pain.

Repetition of pleasurable activities can lead to neuroadaptation, where initial pleasure responses weaken, and the pain response strengthens. This process, known as tolerance, makes us more vulnerable to pain over time. Imagine an orange that initially yields a jug of juice when squeezed, but with each subsequent squeeze, yields less juice and becomes harder to squeeze. This metaphor illustrates how repeated pursuit of pleasure reduces dopamine's impact, leading to diminishing returns.

On the opposite end, experiences like intense meditation retreats can heighten dopamine sensitivity, making simple pleasures immensely satisfying. I once lived in a monastery in Santa Fe, New Mexico, practicing concentration meditation for several hours daily, with minimal external stimuli. This reset my dopamine system, making everyday experiences profoundly pleasurable. However, maintaining such sensitivity in a stimulus-rich modern world proved challenging.

Dopamine Dips really suck. In artists, we often feel like losers, question if we said something stupid on stage, or just feel lousy. When it leaves our brain, we are bereft. We don't want it to go. And then, we fix it with more pleasure, excitement, or novelty, when **what we need is to experience the pain**.

The Nuts and Bolts of Dopamine:

What sensations in the body tend to push our dopamine? **Pleasure,** yum! **Novelty,** wow! And, **Excitement,** eek! But what are they pushing on exactly? That seesaw we just mentioned, our brain's homeostatic reflex. This means when you feel that annoying pain, your brain is doing its job! The problem is that we think something is wrong. This may sound complicated, but just think of when the doctor hit your knee to make sure you had healthy reflexes as a kid. It's the same thing. So, when you push on pleasure, novelty, or excitement, the pain reflex immediately steps in.

Understanding dopamine necessitates exploring its relationship with pain. Our society often seeks to avoid discomfort, despite pain being essential for a healthy brain. Pain and discomfort signal necessary limits and contribute to our overall well-being. Yet, modern culture increasingly avoids pain. This culture is very damaging because it shames us for feeling slow, down, or icky and drives us all into addiction. I'm being a bit hyperbolic with my language because I want you to know that this environment wasn't created for your health. We need "regulated urgency" to reclaim what our dopamine system needs to feel clear, alert, and excited to pursue our dreams.

Again, knowing this, we can mindfully push the opposite side of the dopamine seesaw if too many of what Lembke calls, "pain gremlins" crowd one side. This also means, if we push on the pain side, we get pleasure!

Take a look at this seesaw image. What you press on will determine what your body feels, and that's whatever is highest in the air on the seesaw. Now think about how you felt the day after that big show, or book release, or comedy slam. Most artists feel like they are dying, but it's just your dopamine taking a nosedive.

One effective strategy for resetting an overstressed dopamine system is self-binding, also known as dopamine fasting. This involves temporary abstinence from dopamine-inducing activities to recalibrate the system. The process, outlined by Researcher Anna Lembke, includes tracking usage, understanding its impact on the nervous system, identifying related problems, and committing to a period of abstinence. Afterward, mindfulness, insight, and moderation help integrate healthier habits.

For artists, I just recommend a full "day of shmoo." This is a fake yiddish word I use for doing absolutely nothing but cuddling, relaxing, and resetting my nervous system. I also call this Blue Resting. Yes, you can watch Netflix but stay away from action or horror, but absolutely do not scroll on social media. Or, try Blue Walking which is taking a walk while feeling down with no phone and embracing the "ick."

Embracing boredom and reducing overstimulation are key to restoring dopamine balance. Limiting phone usage, screen time, and other exciting activities can significantly help. Practices like zen meditation can further support this process, allowing the brain to reset and become more sensitive to natural rewards. But there is a lever that must be pressed to level dopamine—pain.

Embracing the Pain Lever: The Power of Hormesis

In our quest to understand dopamine and its profound effects on our lives, we must delve into the concept of hormesis. Although Anna Lembke briefly mentions this in her book, it was Ori Hofmekler's early research on hormesis that truly opened my eyes to its significance. Hormesis is the idea that small amounts of stress can provoke beneficial responses in the body, enhancing overall health.

Imagine our pain/pleasure balance as a seesaw. Hormesis operates on the principle that introducing mild stressors can trigger a beneficial pushback from the body. For instance, brief cold exposure can significantly boost dopamine and epinephrine levels, with effects lasting for hours. This is what we mean when we say "healthy stress." Similarly, short bursts of intense muscle contractions can enhance strength and mental clarity. Exposure to extreme heat, such as in saunas, and intermittent fasting also offer substantial health benefits. These minor stressors stimulate defense systems in the body at a manageable level, resulting in increased vitality and resilience.

Think of hormesis like a vaccine: a tiny dose of the stressor prompts the body to develop a robust defense mechanism. This concept extends to practices like cold water exposure, muscle contractions, and fasting. When pushed to the point of discomfort, these activities can induce physical shaking—shivering when cold, muscle tremors during intense exercise, and slight shakes during prolonged fasting. However, the key to hormesis is moderation; excessive stress is detrimental.

Shaking, observed in these hormetic activities, is significant from a polyvagal perspective. Shaking can help prevent a freeze state, promoting movement and emotional regulation. If I were experiencing intense depression or anxiety, incorporating gentle hormetic practices like a cold shower, regular exercise, and intermittent fasting could help maintain emotional equilibrium. While I've never seen research that directly connects hormesis with preventing a freeze response, I believe the shaking induced by hormesis may also translate to an immunity to falling into a Preservation Mode state.

The Extremes of Dopamine in Performers

Performers often endure extreme highs and lows in dopamine levels. Skydivers, for instance, may experience anhedonia—an inability to find pleasure in previously enjoyable activities—after pushing their dopamine systems to the limit. Similarly, stadium performers might find their first major gig overwhelmingly exhilarating, only to feel a significant dopamine crash afterward. This dopamine low can drive musicians to seek quick fixes through alcohol, drugs, or other means.

Understanding how dopamine works can help performers manage these highs and lows more effectively. For example, a young musician performing their first stadium gig might benefit from a few days of recovery before the next show. Experienced performers, familiar with the dopamine dynamics, might manage with less recovery time but should still anticipate and prepare for these fluctuations.

To manage dopamine levels, performers can turn to hormetic practices like cold showers, sauna sessions, and intense exercise. These activities can provide a sustained dopamine boost, unlike drugs, which offer a quick high followed by a rapid crash. For example, a cold shower before a performance can elevate dopamine levels for hours, providing a steady state of readiness and energy.

However, performers must eventually allow their brains to recalibrate. Continuous high dopamine levels without periods of recovery can lead to long-term issues. Incorporating hormetic practices into a routine can help manage these fluctuations, but rest and recovery are equally important.

Radical Honesty: A Tool for Balance

One profound way to engage with pain and balance in the brain is through radical honesty. Anna Lembke suggests that truth-telling, despite its discomfort, is crucial for maintaining mental health. Alcoholism, often referred to as a "lying disease," underscores the importance of honesty in recovery and mental well-being. Onstage, honesty is essential—it's the foundation of connection and impact.

Radical honesty can activate the prefrontal cortex, promoting a sense of well-being and connection. Honest relationships, though initially challenging, often lead to deeper, more fulfilling connections. Practicing honesty, even in small ways, can improve mental health and enhance performance, making it a valuable tool for artists.

To play with the Music for this "Muscle" try this Tool:

Tool 2 (D): The Dopamine 100 Game

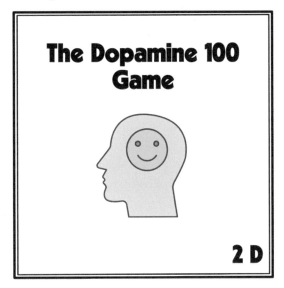

Letter #19: Capacity Building vs. Desire

Dear Artist,

Every once in a while, someone said my voice sounded "haunted." While I totally understood what they meant, there *was* a feeling like I was trying to work out something "haunted" inside me that I didn't understand. If art was so healing, and I was making art all the time, why was I plagued with dysregulation? *And, why was my desire always so, so much bigger than my capacity?* Even if I were to achieve what I wanted, I would immediately move the goalpost and make it out of reach again. I knew something was up. I had a feeling that the love of making art wasn't the only thing driving me.

It scared me to think that maybe invisible trauma-dramas could be playing out without my awareness, like ghosts. Who ya gonna call? Well, Dr. Peter Levine. His work introduced me to a life-changing and unexpected concept: "somatic memory." This refers to trauma that our **conscious mind wasn't present for.** Imagine, in those moments "you" weren't there, but your body was—and it remembers. Well, the brain remembers too, but it's left with **memory that lives as sensation without any accompanying memories.** This makes the trauma silent, mute, or unintelligible. If the trauma occurred when we were pre-verbal, or if our nervous system went into a freeze response (diminishing prefrontal cortex activity), we have no way to verbalize what happened. Of course, this makes complete sense after studying Preservation Mode.

This "somatic memory" means our unhealthy behavior (or simply intense signals from Ground Control) becomes a kind of misguided sign language, attempting to communicate to our caregivers what happened to us. The issue arises when, as adults, our cries for help are profoundly misunderstood, sometimes by the people we love the most. And, in this dysregulation, our nervous systems are driven to extremes.

If you are lost by this explanation, let me illustrate "somatic memory" with the experience of my nephew, who woke up with broken teeth after being cared for by a babysitter. He was pre-verbal and had no way of explaining what happened. The babysitter claimed he might have slipped in the bath, but insisted that nothing significant had occurred. I told my sister, "if he was hurt, he will probably act it out for you. He is looking to re-experience the trauma with a safe person." And within two days, he did. Near the park, he suddenly had a meltdown and began pointing to his teeth! My sister then comforted him, held him, and showed him that it's safe to fall. All week, they reenacted falling together as a form of play. This re-experiencing of the trauma with a safe co-regulator acts as a kind of immunity to PTSD. His unconscious dysregulation revealed to my sister precisely where the trauma occurred. Truly, the body is astonishingly intelligent, guiding us toward healing in ways we may not fully understand.

So, my nephew had a brain prediction of distress and my sister helped him discharge it! The farther we get from the inciting event, the more we need to have compassion with ourselves about behavior that is less than our values or standards. The more old and crusty the somatic memories are, often the more inappropriate they are to our current situation. There is no "bad" kid, and there is no "bad" artist. There's only activation that is looking for a compassionate space to hold it.

You don't always need to know what happened in your past when you become extremely excited from fear or agitated elation. If Peter Levine is right, it means that "you" weren't fully present during those moments, and therefore, you likely can't remember them. While psychoanalysis has its place, regulation is about retuning the nervous system without always needing to know the reasons why. Why? Because "we," our prefrontal cortex, might not have been active at the time, which also means you could force a memory that wasn't even there. So, I don't need to know why I'm so excited after an audition that I can't sleep or eat. But I do need to take responsibility for recognizing that it's time to tune myself to safety. It could be trauma, it could be something very new to me! Either way, it's time to tune.

What hit me like a freight train was that a lot of my art was a cry for help to a mother that was never coming. My mother was an evangelical Christian who spent most of my life with her depressed, mourning the death of my younger sister to Leukemia. It's no wonder I used my audience and music itself as a second mother to hold my healthy sadness and grief.

This artistic ritual was my way of telling the world that something bad happened to me in safety.

So, back to why my capacity was so far from my desire, and why my desire was like an insatiable black hole. For those with complex trauma, all you know is nervous system chaos. That becomes your home, and while it's not comfortable, it is familiar. When things are a little too good or stable, you miss the chaos. You miss the zoo. Stress and chaos were a part of my identity and comfort zone, so I glued them to my artist identity as well. Also, building a life around trying to get a mother to hold my grief was not the life I wanted.

I see many artists hiding in the comfort of dysregulated ambition and excitement, which keeps them locked in cycles of highs and huge crashes. For many of us, that instability is where love resides, and for some, it's their earliest memories of connection. I had no idea of the levels of connection that could exist outside of chaos. So when these patterns emerged in the performing arts, I couldn't conceptualize how damaging they were.

I am not advocating that we stop making art. But I am advocating that we don't hide inside of art. Unless your therapist is extremely, extremely talented, they will miss this due to the collective fetishization of art-making, fame, and the "genius creative." I've had clients admit that, after talking to their therapist about this pattern, the therapist asked for concert tickets. Artists need to be invited back into the safety of Connect Mode, not continually praised for their Superplay missions. As a protocol, and I recommend this for all therapists working with artists, if you are working with an artist who has had a lot of success, do not google them, fan girl, or become transfixed by the art.

We don't consciously intend to "feel" unworthy; our nervous systems are expressing their somatic memory. Unworthiness becomes your brain's prediction of how you can best survive. It's like my nephew falling repeatedly to indicate where the accident happened. Some people hurt others, but many, many people choose a much safer route: hurting themselves instead. I have done both. We all want to value ourselves and feel good without self-harm, but unless we can stop compulsively reenacting the theater of our childhoods, we remain stuck in a cycle of dysregulation.

The performing arts are a heavy weight on any nervous system that needs balance because they are inherently unbalanced. Auditions are thrilling, getting cast is exhilarating, not getting cast is devastating (which is also a kind of excitement). That "big break" is exciting, going viral is exciting, being seen on stage is exciting.

Now, let's get practical for those who have big pulses of energy inside them that are getting in the way of their dreams. How do we live and work while concurrently healing?

The concept I'm about to share is the most valuable idea in this book. So I saved the best for last. For any healing artist seeking to retune their nervous system to safety (aka homeostatic balance), here it is:

We must learn to be neutral with our big moments. By this, I mean that we need to manage our body's excitement, to make huge amounts of love, success, and achievement feel normal. If we are constantly dysregulated by events, wins, losses, and unhealthy foods, we deplete our metabolic bandwidth. Achieving a level of neutrality is crucial for persistence and overall success.

A former version of myself would have shouted, "Boring!" from the back of the room. And in some ways, I will always miss chaos, but I will not miss the enormous amounts of pain, brain fog, depression, and limitations that followed. In the world of the nervous system, we must train our bodies to find new levels of regulation with the big things in life. **The bigger the life event, the bigger the challenge to make it feel safe in our body.** This may be unthinkable to you right now, but it's not only essential for growth, it's totally possible. And it's not always about finding neutrality with good things.

It is safe to land a big audition. It's safe to bomb an audition. It's safe to take a risk. It's safe to ask for more money in a casting contract. It's safe to desire and ask for what we need. But, our bodies don't always know this, *so we train them.* And in the nervous system world, we "tune" them.

So let me be clear: being neutral is about reigning in our excitement when it occurs, not trying to avoid the human experience. In fact, the only way you can regulate is by experiencing dysregulation. This is a "tuning" event we will practice our whole lives, not something we will achieve permanently. Why? As you evolve, there will always be new things that seem exciting, and making them safe and neutral is our cool rocketship of evolution and growth. This is specifically important to understand in the arts, because we are trained to think the more excitement we feel, the better we are doing—then we shame ourselves for having the natural and inevitable crash.

If an Olympic athlete wins a gold medal in one event but has five more races to go, they won't have a huge celebration yet because they can't afford the dopamine dip. We're just like this, except our "Olympics" span our entire lives. The more we can stay neutral, the deeper our anchor of ascendance can reach. When we are trying to do extremely hard things, we don't let our nervous systems spike, we regulate and bring it back into balance. To me, this is exciting, and I hope it is for you.

St. Vincent calls this "monk mode." It means that when she is undertaking extreme tasks, she ensures her environment is extremely balanced to support her nervous system. This approach is incredibly wise for any musician preparing to make a record.

I am still tuning and neutralizing my system, just now on bigger levels. I'll never forget the first entrepreneurial win I had. My partner found me in bed with my hands firmly on my chest and tears running down my face and he said, "Heyyyyy babe, what are you doing?" I said, "I'm teaching my body it's safe to have success. I'm just overwhelmed." Finding neutrality was my way of claiming my worthiness, while extreme excitement was my body's way of saying, "This isn't meant for you, this is too much for you."

It's hard to imagine that it could be normal for things to be really, really great and to feel really good, but it's possible. It's also safe for things to feel really, really bad. We're not ignoring our emotions or energy; we're feeling them fully. But we know that balance is what keeps our capacity big enough to handle positive or negative excitement. If you have a lot of desire, it's crucial to ensure that your capacity for that desire isn't collapsing. And, most artists have a lot of desire.

Managing excitement spikes is essentially about conserving energy. Many artists struggle with capacity (you could just call this bandwidth) issues, so this approach can increase our energy so that we can accomplish what we need to do. The challenge is that regulating your nervous system and finding your center can seem boring for someone addicted to cortisol. It might be so boring that you feel disappointed by this chapter. If that's the case, it's okay! I promise that the benefits of regulation, connection, and increased bandwidth far outweigh the thrill of constant dysregulated excitement. It's like leaving a toxic relationship that always leaves you in tears for the love of your life. This time, it's your relationship with the arts. The very bottom line is that if you want a rocketship of growth, you need to learn to find balance.

In some families, it may seem selfish or indulgent to focus on regulation. In some families, extreme work and achievement is the only "safe" thing to do. There is often a rush of guilt around healing. It is not selfish, it is the most essential part of firing up the engine of movement behind your desire. Choosing your nervous system first can be a huge transition. So, be wary of excitement. It's like a treat that you can indulge in from time to time, but as performers, we must keep it in check.

Be neutral with the big moments. It's a powerhouse of growth and personal evolution.

My entire company and this book would not exist without the tool below. Please use this to expand your capacity when it is not yet as large as your desire. Another way to think about what we are doing here, is **daring to dysregulate**. But instead of leaving that like a helpless child, we love it, embrace it, and make it feel safe in our bodies.

When I push myself to new heights, my motto is: if I'm too excited, my body might not know if it's safe, deserving, or both. This uncertainty offers us a chance to upgrade our nervous system and boost our sense of worthiness. Imagine standing on stage for the first time, heart racing with excitement and fear.

My job is to transform that stage into a place of safety, and welcome in:

"...all the dragons in our lives who are princesses only waiting to see us act, just once, with beauty and courage. Perhaps everything that frightens us is, in its deepest essence, something helpless that wants our love." - Rainer Maria Rilke

To play with the Music for this "Muscle" try this Tool:

Tool 4 (A) Capacity vs. Desire: It's Safe to Feel

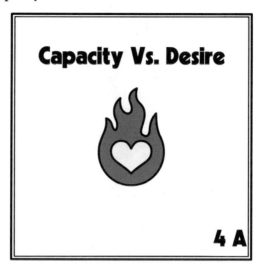

"It's Safe to Feel In My Body"

Step One: Put one hand under your armpit and the other over your shoulder, offering some compression. Or two hands on your chest.

Step Two: Take two quick breaths in and then a long breath out, trying to tune into the sense feelings inside (pain/pleasure and activation/calm). Then I say, "I am beginning to create space in my body for it to feel safe to feel heartbroken and angry with someone who has more power than me."

This invitation doesn't mean it does feel safe yet. It's an invitation to give your body a new experience of safety with feelings that used to be intolerable. If this is too much to do alone, that is a sign that you must do this in the presence of a loving co-regulator or therapist.

Here are some more examples:

"I am beginning to create space in my body for it to feel safe to feel unliked."

"I am beginning to create space in my body for it to feel safe to feel secretly judged."

"I am beginning to create space in my body for it to feel safe to feel rage that I will sooth in my body."

"I am beginning to create space in my body for it to feel safe to feel humiliated.

Ok, I get it. Who would *want these feelings* in their body? We are inviting them in to be parented and seen by us, sometimes for the very first time, and it's enormously powerful.

Imagine the feeling you are inviting in a tiny child who is raging. We are telling that part of us that it's safe for them to be in our body. We are the parent to them, we can handle them, and we can guide them.

Normally we shame these parts. We tell the parts of ourselves that are scared to go onstage to just, "be brave" and then we shove them on stage. Instead, we welcome these feelings, to find safety in our bodies, saying, "It's safe for me to feel terror in my body about being seen, I can hold that for both of us!"

The Music

I've hand-selected some of my **"top hits"** when it comes to tools. Some are repeats from the Muscle section and some we didn't have time for.

To purchase the Master Toolkit please train with us on

www.muscle-music.com

The Mini-Nervous System Toolkit

Welcome, everyone! I've handpicked some of my favorite coaching tools for unshaming and shifting the nervous system. We're starting this toolkit with foundational exercises to build your capacity for unshaming and shifting your nervous system and slowly building them. There's no right way to use these tools or engage with them. Dive in, let it be messy.

Neuroception and Co-regulation (F: Foundational Tools)

TOOL 1F: Thank You, Ground Control!

When to use: *Any time you are working in the arts and feel out of touch with your body and want to check into what your brain predicted for you. When you need acceptance for a feeling that seems out of control.*

Your next assignment is to practice taking the wheel of your spaceship. We have established the basic idea that whatever you feel in your body *right now* was predicted by your neuroception (Ground Control). This feeling doesn't have to be a major metabolic event that shifts your nervous system to a new state. While it can be a distinct state, it could also just be thirst, tiredness, exhilaration. For example, today walking back to the dog park, I thought,

"Wow, based on my blood sugar, my vitamin levels, my hormones, and all the other signals in my body, Ground Control is sending me the feeling of being tired."

So, the tool is to say, **"Thank you, Ground Control! I'm in the driver's seat now."**

Ok, now I have options. I go take a nap or meditate and lean into what my body needs. Or I can say, "You know what? I just need to power through, get that workout in, or finish up a project." I am the rocket wo(man), and I also deeply honor the 300 PhDs (my brain) who are sitting down on the ground making decisions based on the past–my body, my environment, and my mental theater–to see what I should *feel* to survive.

You see, Ground Control has one mission and one mission only: To keep your body living and surviving on this planet as long as possible. The part of you that is conscious of Ground Control is the leader of the mission to Mars! You are responsible for reaching those high, hard goals. Ground Control is here to keep the lights on. You are here to explore, play, adventure, and make discoveries.

Again, your autonomic nervous system, which is the part of you that runs automatically with no conscious control, keeps you alive. But it's not here to help you thrive. This is such an important distinction because in the arts, we must often take the wheel when our neuroception detects danger that is not present. At the same time, we are challenged to honor it and speak from our truth when it is accurate, even if that truth is hard or even devastating to admit. This tool is one of the few ways we can have contact with Ground Control because it is always predicted about a half second before conscious awareness.

The second you say, "Thank you, Ground Control!" I'd like you to imagine you are putting your hands back on the steering wheel. Imagine Sally, eyes gleaming, determined to get to her destination. Now is the moment to assess whether there really is danger in your environment or if you need to make a shift.

If you are incredibly numb or find this exercise baffling, don't worry! You may be struggling to be in tune with your senses inside your body (interoception). That is normal for a lot of trauma survivors. Take it slow. And don't forget, if **you** are feeling it, it's a human experience.

TOOL 3F: Building Your Minyan

This tool is inspired by the Jewish concept of a "minyan," which requires at least 10 humans to come together to talk to God. While I personally don't participate in organized religion, as poetry, I think this ritual is a gorgeous metaphor. To talk to the art-gods safely, what if we slowly and carefully chose 10 people to be in our "minyan"? They don't have to know, or you can tell them.

This is so that when you go off into the woods, you feel safer. Why? This is the biological design of the nervous system. When we start shifting with the wind of our biology, instead of pushing against it, we can reach all those big, beautiful dreams faster.

I keep my minyan on my phone. And yes, this is unbelievably embarrassing and uncool. But if you want a healthy nervous system, this group of co-regulators is crucial. I often text them right before I go onstage, audition, or venture into a new project. It's a way of saying, "I'm going hunting now. Keep an eye on me." This lets me know I can take more risk because if I come home with a tiger wound, I know that I have a crew to sew me together.

Let's take this game a step farther. You need people who you trust, but you also need people who get how hard it is to be an artist, and the dedication it takes. Make sure one to three of your co-regulators deeply understand you—and why your art, your voice, or your music is important.

And finally, don't wait to move forward until you find the "perfect" co-regulators. Just consider it an ongoing project of nervous system resilience. And do not feel shame if you have a small group or you are still building your co-regulatory crew. It's important to know that we cannot have entitlement when it comes to connection. Adult relationships are not handed to us, they are based on attention and investment. Many of us feel like they should fall into our lap because that's what happened—or didn't when we were kids. It's: if it's hard and as my fitness trainer says, "You don't have to like it."

These words you are reading are built and supported by my co-regulators. We don't build in a vacuum. Be careful who you let in your life. They are the scaffolding of your biological art-life.

Finally, if you grew up with secure attachment (healthy co-regulation), art is all about connection. If you grew up without healthy co-regulation, art is about survival. The sneaky part of this equation is that you can totally make a career out of both. But only the former, connection, can endure for decades and decades.

Tool 6F: Stop, Drop and Roll

This exercise is another way to experience how neuroception predicts our nervous system states for us, not the other way around. In this exercise, we have a decision to make. Now that we know Ground Control has made a choice, and we have found our state on the map, we get to decide whether it's a helpful state and is guiding you toward your safety, connection, and dreams. Or if it's a neuroceptive mismatch.

The Stop (1 minute):
Find a quiet spot to sit or stand.
Take a moment to pause and disconnect from any distractions.
Close your eyes if comfortable or maintain a soft gaze.

The Drop (1 minute):
Start by dropping your attention into your body.
Focus on the sensations you are experiencing within your body, without judgment.
Notice any physical discomfort (pain) or pleasure. Acknowledge it without trying to change it.
Observe whether you feel calm or activated, without labeling it as good or bad.

The Roll (2 minutes):

Blend the two assessments you made (sensations of pain/pleasure and calm/activation) to create a unique emotional state or "nervous system color" and put a name to it.

Reflect on how your body is reacting to your current circumstances and environment.

Based on your assessment, decide whether you want to "roll with it" or make a change in your current state.

If you choose to "roll with it," accept your current emotional state and allow yourself to experience it without resistance. If you decide to make a change, consider appropriate actions or strategies to shift your emotional state in a positive direction (whether activating or deactivating).

Until we get to the shifting section, I just want you to use this exercise to feel into the idea that you have a choice, now that you have named your state and its particular flavor.

Orienting: (O: OrientingTools)

Tool 1(O): The Physiological Sigh

This is a powerful tool because it's one of the few ways we can intentionally slow down our heart rate. I find that incredibly empowering, given how much of our autonomic nervous system operates beyond our control. So having even this small amount of control is truly wonderful.

Now, let's explore the physiological side of how we feel. Our heart rate will naturally speed up when we take two quick breaths in, followed by one long exhale. On the exhale, the heart rate slows down. **So, two quick breaths in and a long breath out.** This process engages what's called the vagal brake, activating the ventral vagal nerve, which helps keep us in a playful and calm state. Imagine riding a bike downhill—you don't want to go too fast, so you gently press the brakes to control your speed. The vagal brake works similarly, allowing us to slow down, feel safe, and stay socially connected.

Tool 4 (O): It's Totally Possible

Here's another orienting exercise for you, and it's one of my absolute favorites. It's a simple way to stop rumination by shifting our focus to task-positive thinking, rather than letting our default mode network run on autopilot. We're going to turn this into a game called "It's Totally Possible."

Now, let me be clear—this isn't about manifesting or magical thinking. It's not about making the night perfect by acting like a Matilda-like character who wills everything into existence. **No, this is about quieting the brain's natural negativity bias.** Our negativity bias, which you can look up, isn't something that needs fixing—it's a built-in part of our physiology. It's what happens when we're in new situations or meet new people. It's completely normal. That said, if we leave it running, we are prone to the anxiety that comes with affective realism.

Let's equip you with the tools to quiet that endless barrage of self-talk that can massively, whether it's off-stage, on the way to an audition, or during a voice lesson you're overthinking. Rumination is your worst nightmare on the way to an audition or after a social event. Often, you don't even realize it happened until you find yourself frozen or spiraling in anxious worry, thinking, "Did I say something I shouldn't have?" This usually happens at a #7 or below on the nervous system ladder due to the amount of risk and uncertainty you take on. It can occur in isolation or, even worse, with the people you love. Most minds cannot bear this weight of risk and begin to spin inner movies in an attempt to control what they cannot. Again, this is not a sign of a "weak" nervous system; it's just what humans do under stress.

You can't notice subtle changes in your nervous system when you scream, berate, guilt, or shame yourself. Tuning into your nervous system with constant mental noise resembles trying to hear a voice memo right next to a speaker at a music festival; the speaker always wins. By managing the weight of endless chatter, you make your excitement more manageable.

The idea for giving performers this tool did not come from the trauma world. It came from the peak-performance world, thanks to a brilliant coach named Trevor Moawad. He conducted an experiment similar to the movie "Supersize Me," but with country music and network news. Despite being mentally strong, as mental fitness was his job at the University of Alabama, he wanted to see if someone as strong as him could be affected. It turned out that this protocol of depressing country music and network news dysregulated him so much that he had to end the experiment and seek mental health support. His thesis was that removing stressors often far outweighs all positive protocols.

Dr. Steven Porges' polyvagal theory emphasizes that connection helps us feel safe. He posits that adding connection allows us to tolerate more fear and uncertainty. This holds true, but we also need to remove what damages or drains our nervous system. For artists, nothing could be more draining than the negative movies we play in our heads on the way to gigs, auditions, or performances.

So, let's embrace both perspectives. Strive to build meaningful connections and take time to eliminate harmful habits. This dual approach will empower you to perform at your best, both mentally and physically. You have the power to create a balanced and fulfilling artistic journey.

I'm about to give you mental exercises that will affect your body. You might think, "Huh? I thought this was an embodiment book. Isn't mental stuff from the other camp?" First, remember that the brain and body are one. As neuroscientist Lisa Feldman Barrett says, "The brain keeps the score. The body is the scorecard." This means the body reflects everything happening in the brain. The body also talks to the brain, telling it how to feel, and indicating if you are low on magnesium, water, or even human touch. So, understand that the brain is the body and the body is the brain.

When it comes to stress and rumination, which most artists need help with, the signals travel from the brain to the body. Think about it like this: when you watch a horror movie, your heart races, you clutch your partner, and you sit on the edge of your seat. This is self-induced stress for pleasure. When the theater of your mind starts creating that mental movie, you scare your autonomic system. The autonomic system is always at work, controlling your heart rate, body temperature, dryness of your mouth, and the sounds your brain listens for. You can consciously trigger it or calm it! So, think of your thoughts as the movie playing on a screen and your body as the audience.

When an artist comes to me struggling, they often say, "I'm ruminating and I can't stop!" This means they can't turn off the horror movie in their head, and it's influencing their body. From a polyvagal perspective, it's possible that the horror movie was induced by a nervous system state first, but this is a chicken-and-egg scenario. We will use this exercise when we have a feeling that our body may be stressed because of our mental movie.

Also, let me be clear about what I mean by horror movie-like thoughts that scare your body constantly. These thoughts might sound like:

"I'm not as good as other artists, what's the point?"

"I never have the energy I need."

"My art is shit."

"I made one good thing, but will I ever make something good again?"

"I'm an imposter."

Firstly, anything you say to yourself in passivity, is true to the body. Anything. The body isn't programmed to filter truth or non-truth, it's just meant to be a direct sounding board. So if you say, "I hate myself. I suck as an artist," the body has to feel slightly bad. It's really that simple. It's also why acting works. Language and mental imagery is powerful.

While everyone's body serves as a sounding board for the mind, actors and musicians show hypersensitivity to this connection, which likely drew them to their profession. This sensitivity means their thoughts influence their nervous system significantly, increasing their need to control rumination. By mastering this control, they can better manage stress and enhance their performance.

If you work with your "parts"—which simply means thoughts, sensations, or aspects of yourself that aren't your whole being—they will likely pop up in rumination. When a "part" of you from childhood feels cruel or scared, it tends to speak up in stressful situations. But what are these "parts" exactly? They are networks of neurons in the brain, more like electrical pathways than little people. That little kid or punishing parent in your brain is a physical neural structure that you strengthen every time you engage with it.

Working with your "parts" with a therapist can be incredibly healing, but I don't recommend engaging with "parts" on the way to an audition. Why? We don't heal on stage or while performing, ever. Bringing your therapeutic work onstage or on the way to the stage is a huge mistake and dangerous. I've seen therapists advise the opposite because they view art as a healing modality—and in the world of healing, it is! But this kind of advice leaves artists tumbling in the ocean of attention, feeling dysregulated and disconnected from their audience. There is art and there are performance therapies, but stage performance is a leadership craft that must be respected for the safety of everyone.

Furthermore, if you feel like this is therapy, it's not. This work is specifically designed for performers. You can't perform well when your mind is playing horror movies offstage. You need to focus, overcome challenges, and effectively reach out to collaborators and directors. I will leave clinical analysis to professionals, but we need to address the problems that prevent us from connecting with our audiences. Mental noise is a major culprit.

Just remember, this exercise is not about new-age manifesting, which often overlooks both embodiment and reality. Instead, it's about pulling your brain out of mental hell. Most of our thoughts about ourselves are not accurate, so if you feel these thoughts are untrue, you're likely right. We don't need to debate the science behind water when there's a fire; we just need to hose it down.

Also, if you're thinking, "I didn't come to this work for you to make me do positive thinking," hang in there. It's a long journey. We need to secure the fort before we plant flowers. Also, if you have pain coming up during these mental exercises, don't push it away, feel it.

One of my clients recently said, "I mean, this isn't supposed to work, but it weirdly does." As you move into the next exercise there is one specific requirement that also separates it from positive thinking. For it to work the best, you must speak it out loud.

So, when you're in a new venue, switching environments, or on tour, and you notice you're starting to ruminate, that's your cue to turn on the "It's Totally Possible" game.

Here's how it works: You'll want to go fast—quick enough that you don't have time to overthink or add doubts. It's a stream of positive possibilities, one after another. For example:

It's totally possible this night's going to go great.

It's totally possible my guitar will stay in tune.

It's totally possible it won't, but I'll embrace the moment, unshame my nervous system on stage, and the audience will cheer as I tune my guitar.

It's totally possible my band will feel connected because I'm leading with a calm nervous system.

It's totally possible we'll sell lots of merch after the show.

It's totally possible that even if we don't, we'll still have a great experience, meet new people, and build a relationship with this venue.

It's totally possible my new song will resonate with the audience.

It's totally possible I'll get feedback on my songs like I've never received before.

It's totally possible this show isn't even about me—it's about helping a room full of stressed-out people who need this moment of music and connection.

It's totally possible that I belong on this stage.

See how it works? You're creating a rapid stream of positive possibilities that interrupts the pattern of rumination. It's important to remember that rumination isn't a sign something's wrong with you. It happens naturally to almost everyone in stressful situations. The mind and body dysregulate together, in a sort of harmony, like they're rhyming with each other.

By playing the "It's Totally Possible" game, you disrupt that cycle, giving your body a break from the stress created by rumination. Not only does this mental pattern dysregulate you. It can also lock you into that state, making it harder to get out of. This game allows you to step out of the default-mode network and focus on your vision for the night. It's a simple but effective way to give your body and mind a pause.

Tool 7 (O): WEEBSS

While this could easily be in the foundational section, we must have our basic needs met to orient properly in a room. If any of these elements below are lacking, it is very easy to fall into distraction due to our own body's pain and activation. We must care for our physical homeostasis. This is often the last thing artists prioritize. But for anyone trying to heal or strengthen their nervous system, improving just one of these elements a month is my biggest recommendation. I created the absolute worst acronym but my students have clung to it so we are going to go with it!

The acronym for your nervous system fundamentals is WEEBSS:

Water

Energy

Exercise

Body Temperature

Sleep

Social Connection

Tool 8 (O): Your BMWs

I want you to now expand your cues of safety and danger to three realms or environments:

1. The Body: Safe or unsafe feelings or sensations in the body. Anything IN the body. Things like physical pain, sensations, hot, cold, etc.

2. The Mind: Safe or unsafe thoughts and images of the imagination. Your moving theatrical show upstairs

3. The World: Safe or unsafe cues through the five senses deriving from the present physical reality. Ex. That big guy coming towards you walking funny and carrying a knife.

I want you to identify a couple of cues of safety and danger in each category to practice recognizing your own cues. For example, a cue of danger in my body might be pain in my right shoulder, a cue of danger in my mind might be a negative thought, and a cue of danger in the world might be a threatening-looking person. I call these cues your "BMWs" to help you quickly categorize where they come from. To quickly scan for danger, ask yourself, "Is there anything in my body, mind, or world that does not feel safe?" This is especially helpful when you feel bad and don't know why.

So protocol is:
Step one: Why do I feel so weird and anxious?
Step two: What are my BMWs?

I want you to think about your last performance and write down five cues of safety and five cues of danger. A cue of safety might have been that the venue had friendly staff, a cue of danger may have been that the room was too cold. These cues could come from your Bs, your Ms, or your Ws. When you write these down also indicate whether it is a B, M, or W cue:

CUES OF SAFETY:
1.
2.
3.
4.
5.

CUES OF DANGER:
1.
2.
3.
4.
5.

Tool 1 (C): Wings and the Weight

Let's explore the top of the nervous system ladder! The safe and social state is all about risk. We should never try to lessen this risk by shrinking our lives. To truly thrive in this state, we need to add play. As adults, we often dismiss play as childish or silly, but it's essential for navigating the complexities of the safe and social state.

The "Superplay" Mode is when you're fully immersed in pretending or playing a character, like imagining ketchup instead of blood. For singer-songwriters, this means separating risk from reality, adding stakes to make the art feel real. Acting teachers often emphasize "raising the stakes" for this reason. In "The Actor Prepares," Stanislavski focuses on creating authentic experiences through "given circumstances."

These two states require opposite elements. One needs risk, the other play. Let's use this concept of "wings and the weight."

When to Use This Tool: Use this tool when life feels heavy or if your art feels lifeless.

The Weight

Add **Weight** To SUPERPLAY MODE

In the Superplay state, you're immersed in play. Adding risk gives play its excitement. Just as adding weight makes things grounded, adding gravity or risk brings Superplay closer to real life. If your art feels flat, add weight—inject gravity and risk into your work. For instance, if you're an actor and asked to "raise the stakes" in a scene, the performance becomes more compelling.

Tip: Are you in the Superplay Mode? Ask yourself, "Am I playing pretend?" Writers working with characters, actors playing roles, or singer-songwriters reflecting on past experiences are all engaging in Superplay.

The Wings

Add **Wings** To CONNECT MODE

This is the fun part. In Superplay, the characters are not real. But in the safe and social state, the roles we play are very real and carry risk. Many try to eliminate this risk, but it's essential, like gravity. The key is to lighten the risk through play—this is where the "wings" come in. We don't reduce the risk; we add play and connection.

For example, when teaching nervous system regulation, I won't pretend to be someone else. I'll fully embrace the role of Ruby Rose Fox, with all its risks. But I'll infuse my teaching with play. This could mean setting up the classroom in unexpected ways, using humor, or making slides colorful and engaging.

Tip: Are you in a safe and social state? You have one role—teacher, brother, friend. If you have two roles (e.g., actor and Macbeth), you're in Superplay.

Use wings and the weight for a full week. When life feels heavy, add play without giving up your leadership role. When you're in a playful state, add some weight by increasing the stakes. Use strategies like creating personas, reframing situations, gamifying tasks, embracing spontaneity, and acting with speed.

Tip: Simply rooting the body into the "ground" onstage can help dispel energy. Make sure you always feel like you have solid "roots" into the floor (but don't lock the knees).

Tool 3 (M): Push, Plank, Press

Even if you are aware you have nervous energy, simply asking your body to integrate that energy doesn't usually work. The most effective tool is to find a wall (make sure it's actually a sturdy wall) and press on it with ALL your force. As you press, speak or sing your text or lyrics. Pressing this hard may cause you to temporarily forget them and that is okay. Refocus and try again. I want you to press and press until you are tired. This also forces you to deeply breathe out.

Tip: If you are at a show or a performance, do this in your dressing room, closet, or bathroom for privacy. Otherwise, people might think you are in distress or have lost your mind!

This is by far the most immediate and effective tool for managing energy leaks. The pressing sends the extra energy into the wall, allowing you to feel relaxed and free. It does take significant effort though if you truly press hard; like you are trying to get through the wall.

This is one of my favorite exercises because it seems to be the most immediately effective and relieving for people. The logic behind it is that if you have a crazy child that is hyper before bed, it works to tire them out rather than just try to force them to sleep.

Another reason for actively trying to exhaust yourself is because Move Mode can cause anxious thoughts (mental triggers) which can retrigger the adrenaline and cortisol over and over. You don't want to stew in those hormones all night or you will find yourself depressed and exhausted the next day.

The reason for expelling energy is to cut off the cycle. Yes, you may be exhausting yourself short-term, but the goal is to restore to play mode.

Tool 4 (M): Shake It Off

Always press first. Use this if you still have energy after you did the push, press, plank protocol.

1. Shake your right leg, left leg, right arm, left arm, and head ten times. Shake gently.

2. Now repeat the above exercise, but for nine times each. Then again for seven times each, six times, etc. until you get down to one shake per part. That is a great shakedown.

3. Gently jump up and down on your toes to freely shake out your whole body

4. After the shaking exercise, pretend you have crumbs on your arms and pants and swipe them down and away from your body.

Tool 5 (M): BIG MOVES Tool

1. 30-second plank
2. 20 jumping jacks
3. 10 squats

Tool 3 (P): Shake and Surge

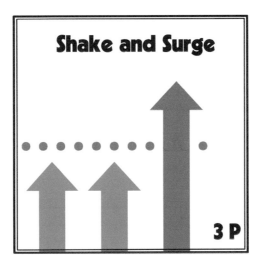

Shake your whole body. If you are super frozen, you may only be capable of moving your toes. Expect a medium to large surge of energy soon after. Do not be precious about this because all we need to do is get oxygen back to the brain. Be gentle and trust your body.

Tool 4 (P): Horror and Spice

The way out of freezing is activation. Communities in Preservation Mode have used non-traditional ways of getting oxygen back to their brains, like watching horror movies, listening to punk, hardcore, metal, EDM, House. Also, very spicy food and cold showers can knock a person right up their polyvagal ladder due the amount of oxygen it pushes into the system. Painful activities like acupuncture and tattooing can also have this effect, although these will increase your dopamine level as well.

Nervous System Leadership Tools:

Tool 1L: "I am the tuning fork."

Hey everyone, welcome to Nervous System Leadership. This is a major paradigm shift for many artists who step on stage seeking to be loved, seen, or liked. We're moving away from that childhood fantasy and shifting toward the right orientation: leading with your nervous system.

The first mantra I want to introduce is **"I am the tuning fork."** This is a simple yet powerful tool to remind you that you set the tone for the entire room. Now, don't panic—I know what you might be thinking: "If I'm the tuning fork and I'm not feeling great, won't I dysregulate the whole audience?" Don't worry. We have tools to help you in those moments. But for now, focus on this primary concept of leadership: I am the tuning fork.

You're here to give, not to search for, validation or approval. You're not asking "Am I loved?" or "Am I liked?" Instead, you *are* love. You are the source of your own joy, curiosity, and power. And you'll share whatever you have with your audience tonight.

So, remember: I am the tuning fork. That's your tool. Then sign off: Thanks, everyone. See you soon!

Tool 3L: The Marilyn Monroe

This exercise might feel like I'm asking you to mask. In the world of the nervous system, masking is compulsively and unconsciously using appeasing, nice, or safe and social cues. To get your survival needs met. And to hide a dysregulated state that you are terrified to reveal. This is not that.

Masking doesn't include consent, as it's an unconscious and compulsive response. Glimmering is masking that is conscious, consensual, and playful in nature. This is simply something leaders do to show goodwill to a group of people they are leading.

It is not fake or misleading. It is genuine. It's harnessing your biology so that a group under your leadership can feel connected and secure.

SHIFT ONE (WARMTH):
While there is no single emotion of safety that can be conveyed to trigger co-regulation, warmth is essential for communicating goodwill. Imagine you are wearing a mask that covers your face, revealing only your eyes. Now, I want you to "warm" your eyes or smile with your eyes, so that anyone walking past would sense—without seeing your mouth—that you are friendly and safe. This doesn't mean you have to be smiling. Next, count to 50 while keeping your eyes as warm as possible. Maintain this warmth for the full 50 seconds, and as you count, notice that this requires extra energy. Release any extra tension in your body and, if possible, move around, look around, or walk around. Imagine you are a twinkling source of light. If you hold this position for the entire 50 seconds, you should feel a shift. This nonverbal cue signals to your audience that you are not a threat, and even if you're nervous, you are consciously showing benevolence. Why? Because you want to use your power effectively.

SHIFT TWO (POWER):
Now I want you to open your shoulders. Think about pressing your elbows back and together. Pull your shoulders back and support your body with your core. Feel this shift and take a deep breath. Imagine you have a Superman logo on your chest. You should feel open and expanded. If you're having trouble, think of your scapulae as two angel wings pressing down and into your back. Also, as you open, let your head float up to the sky as if it were a weightless balloon.

This will make you feel more vulnerable. If you can't hold it very long, do it in tolerable amounts and keep coming back to it. Gentle is the way.

SHIFT THREE (PRESENCE):

Finally, imagine a tiny mouth where your belly button is and take a big breath in. Try to breathe without letting your shoulders rise at all, instead focus on the expansion of your belly. Another helpful image is to imagine your feet as roots of a tree, allowing the breath to flow in from the deep earth. For this shift, let go of any tension in your belly and back so that air can move freely.

Engage all three areas and ensure they are working simultaneously. To check, turn everything off (flatten your face, roll your shoulders, and move your breath into your upper chest). Once you feel completely "off," turn everything back on again. Notice how it feels to shift from off to on. The purpose of flexing this "nervous system muscle" is to realize that switching is no big deal.

Now, we are turned on and ready to learn and perform!

Tool 6L: The Mississippi Staredown

The Mississippi Staredown
A tool for singer-songwriters, musicians, and speakers

Again, when you first encounter a room full of strangers, they don't know you, and you don't know them. And yet, we are constantly coached to ignore this truth. But, it's the truth. That's a pickle.

The truth is that in a room full of strangers, feeling danger is not unhealthy and doesn't need to be pushed away. In fact, the only thing the stage really demands is your nervous system's truth. That's why a dog can walk onstage and the crowd goes wild. The only thing the stage really fundamentally rejects is shame, which is what a lot of "bad" acting actually is.

As a leader, your nervous system acts as a tuning fork for the entire room. After that trust is established, and the audience's hearts begin to sync—not metaphorically, but literally. I'm just going to take a little pleasure right now imagining that our nervous systems are synching through literary time travel.

For this to happen though, you must be willing to take on the responsibility of being that nervous system tuning fork. And, a pulse of fight/flight energy in your body, if accepted and not pushed away, is simply energy that glues the audience to their nervous-system leader. Adrenaline is the neurotransmitter of emotional glue. So, think about this pulse of energy as a honing of an invisible web of connection, propelling your audience on a nervous system ride of music and art. Do you now see that shooing away this precious energy like a shamed animal is a mistake?

As you practice this, I want you to keep an idea in mind. When we get a big pulse of energy we often think it's against us. But most of our characters are dysregulated and most of the songs we sing are sung by characters in pain. What if the energy your body gives you is the exact amount your character needs to express themselves. Of course, we will still need craft and technique to support all this energy. But trust your energy, even if it's a big wave.

The Mississippi Staredown unshames the idea that we shouldn't feel like strangers. We are strangers just getting to know each other's nervous systems—and we need to take a little time to non-verbally connect. Let your audience take the time they need to see and take in an entirely new human.

Tip: Practice this exercise first in your room, as it's very likely too overwhelming to try on stage first. While it's incredibly simple, many people find this exercise difficult. This can be done at the beginning of a performance or an audition.

Instruction:

Step one: Pick three points on the wall above the heads of the audience (try to do this at sound check so you know where your points are). This delay of direct eye contact respects the fact that your body needs a moment to orient to safety just as much as the audience does. They need some time to see you too! Before you start singing or talking, send your breath to the first point. Make sure the breath is long and relaxed as it takes to say the words, "Mississippi One."

Step two: Soft gaze at the audience, and send your second breath to the second point. Make sure the breath is as long and relaxed as it takes to say the words, "Mississippi Two."

Step three: Soft gaze at the audience, and send your third breath to the third point. Make sure the breath is as long and relaxed as it takes to say the words, "Mississippi Three."

If it's a loud bar, you will often hear people start to shush themselves. Don't have an agenda for how the audience must interact with you though. You are showing that you are a powerful tiger that will not use its teeth, and that you can use power well. You are showing you are capable of focus and presence. You are showing that silence will be just as much a part of your performance as sound. I recently did this at a show in Chicago and someone asked me if I was an "energy witch." I chuckled because we all have the power to grab an audience, we just have to dare to embrace silence and presence on a new level.

It is so rare that a person is willing to show up and choose presence first without anxiously beginning. This is how you will earn the trust of total strangers, while respecting that your body must also orient towards safety in a new environment—and that is not a weakness. Silence plus adrenaline plus focus is total power.

Tool 7L: Calling (Out) Your Your Dog

If a person loses the biological ability to connect when dysregulated, what can we do? This seems like a nightmare scenario for any performer, especially if an audience could "catch" a performer's nervous-system state. A regulated state undoubtedly gives a performer a much better chance at connecting with an audience. But what if you find yourself in fight, flight, or freeze mode? With this exercise, you can unlock connection—even in those moments. It may go against everything you've been taught. There are also variations of this exercise depending on whether or not you're working with a "fourth wall" (the imaginary barrier that separates the audience from the performance).

First, we must establish this foundational principle: if you are on stage, you've made an unspoken agreement to lead the audience with your nervous system. You hold power, and they are trusting you to use it benevolently. The first rule of this exercise is simple but profound: **truth is one of the only things the stage requires.** As long as you hold the truth, you will have the audience in the palm of your hand.

Let me illustrate this with a story. A world-class actor is in the middle of a play when suddenly, a stray dog walks on stage. Because animals can't lie, they are instantly mesmerizing on stage—they will "out-real" any actor. The audience becomes glued to the dog, aware that the actor has no lines or preparation for this moment. The tension builds.

The actor has two choices. They could ignore the dog, becoming increasingly stressed and ashamed while the audience becomes more fixated on the unplanned visitor. Or they could acknowledge the dog, perhaps by looking at it, then glancing at the audience with a knowing smile or wink. By doing so, the actor integrates the dog into their reality, signaling their control and presence. The audience laughs and applauds because the actor has passed the test, maintaining truth on stage within the parameters of their art form.

In this story, **your dysregulation is the dog.** Your role as the performer is to unshame it under the mantle of leadership.

It's important to note that this exercise must not collapse your role as a leader. If you treat the audience as your therapist, it will have the opposite effect. Your job is not to overshare or seek validation but to make your dysregulation *safe* for the audience. You must frame it, warm it up, reveal it–and unshame it.

The best way to practice "Calling Out Your Dog" is to start when the stakes are low. Try it offstage first. For example, my partner and I were at the dog park the other day (ironically, given the metaphor). He casually said, "I'm feeling kinda anxious today." I asked if he needed anything from me, and he said no. I had sensed something was off, but when he voiced his anxiety, it freed me from decoding his subtle signals or worrying that I was to blame.

Artistic environments are often high-pressure due to tight budgets and time constraints, which can easily strain anyone's nerves. The more openly you can communicate, the better. Notice how my partner didn't blame me or external circumstances—he just "called out his dog."

Tool 8L: The Truth Portal: Start From Where You Are

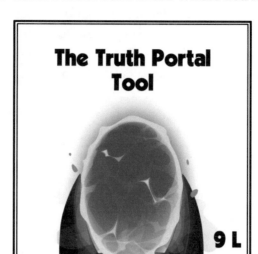

To lead an audience effectively, we must first figure out how to begin. But what happens when we're not feeling how we think we should feel? As actors and singer-songwriters, we often strive—sometimes anxiously—to "be in character," trying to achieve a specific nervous-system state–of activation or deactivation, of pain or pleasure–before we even speak. This approach can be deeply problematic.

The only acting method traditionally claiming to make this possible is Method Acting, but it can be dangerous. It asks us to decide how a character should feel—when, truthfully, we often have no idea. This is one reason reckless Method Acting is increasingly criticized in the acting world. As performers, our responsibility is to convey truth, while remaining physically and emotionally safe, both for ourselves and our fellow artists.

Trying to be "in character" often leads to nervous system dysregulation and incongruence because it forces us to aim for a place we aren't naturally inhabiting. To an audience, this disconnect registers as "bad acting." Why? Because our bodies are sending mixed signals: we're not embodying the nervous-system state we're aiming for, and we're anxious about not getting there. This compounds into an anxious feedback loop that reads as inauthentic.

Humans are wired to notice nervous system incongruence. If someone appears friendly but their body's cues suggest otherwise, we sense it immediately—and it feels unsafe. Likewise, audiences can detect when a performer's emotional cues are misaligned with their words, breaking the spell of the performance.

So, what do we do when we feel we're "not there yet," but we have to play the role anyway? Director Tim Douglas offers a solution that honors the nervous system while embracing the imaginative power of words and circumstances.

His instruction is simple yet profound:

Memorize your words or lyrics thoroughly. Focus only on the words— don't prescribe exactly how you will say them.

Begin speaking from wherever you are in your body, not where you think you should be.

To build on Tim's method, we can use insights from The Theory of Constructed Emotion, the latest neuroscience on emotion. Instead of trying to construct a specific feeling, assess your current state by rating two factors:

- ☐ Pain: On a scale of 0-10, how much physical or emotional discomfort are you experiencing?
- ☐ Activation: On a scale of 0-10, how much energy or stress is present in your body?

Notice how these two sensations mix in your body. Speak or sing from that sensation. You don't need to label the feeling or name the nervous system state—just let it guide your delivery.

In a class discussion, someone asked, "But what if I can't stop laughing and I have to play Hamlet?" Tim's response: "Do you think no one has ever laughed while contemplating the end of their life?" Rather than controlling emotion, he encouraged us to ride the emotion that was already present, like a wave. The results were astonishing. I watched classmates who had struggled with acting transform into performers with electrifying presence and charisma.

Since lines and lyrics naturally evoke emotion, follow the wave as your nervous system shifts. Or, if there's no shift, respect that too. Often, we feel pressure to grieve "better" or express anger "better," even though our faces might show nothing. There is no single "right way" to portray emotion*.

(*For deeper insights, I highly recommend Lisa Feldman Barrett's book, "How Emotions Are Made.")

This exercise requires performers to do two challenging yet transformative things:

- Do less.
- Trust their bodies.

Both are acts of vulnerability. But trust that your body is giving you exactly the right amount of pain, pleasure, and activation to work with in the moment. This is both the easiest and hardest thing you'll ever do.

By respecting the truth of your nervous system—not the state you want it to be in—you can create performances that are electric, alive, and deeply human. That, ultimately, is all the stage requires.

Tool 2 (D): The Dopamine 100 Game

Play solo or with a friend. Each activity earns you **5 points**. The goal is to reach **100 points**:

- Weightlifting for at least 20 minutes
- A hot shower followed by 1.5 minutes of cold shower
- Fasting until noon

- Waiting one hour after waking to have coffee
- Avoiding television for one day
- Avoiding social media for one day
- Meditating for 30 minutes or more
- Receiving acupuncture
- Getting a deep tissue massage
- Avoiding sugar or refined carbs
- Playing the *"It's Totally Possible"* game
- Getting 10 minutes of direct sunlight within one hour of waking
- Abstaining from a drug you might feel addicted to
- Eating a meal without using your phone or watching TV
- Sleeping 8–9 hours
- Intentionally listening to music for 10 minutes without multitasking
- Avoiding the news for one day

Tool 4 (A) Capacity vs. Desire: It's Safe to Feel

"It's Safe to Feel In My Body"

Step One: Put one hand under your armpit and the other over your shoulder, offering some compression. Or two hands on your chest.

Step Two: Take two quick breaths in and then a long breath out, trying to tune into the sense feelings inside (pain/pleasure and activation/calm). Then I say, "I am beginning to create space in my body for it to feel safe to feel heartbroken and angry with someone who has more power than me."

This invitation doesn't mean it does feel safe yet. It's an invitation to give your body a new experience of safety with feelings that used to be intolerable. If this is too much to do alone, that is a sign that you must do this in the presence of a loving co-regulator or therapist.

Here are some more examples:
"I am beginning to create space in my body for it to feel safe to feel unliked."
"I am beginning to create space in my body for it to feel safe to feel secretly judged."
"I am beginning to create space in my body for it to feel safe to feel rage that I will sooth in my body."
"I am beginning to create space in my body for it to feel safe to feel humiliated.

Ok, I get it. Who would *want these feelings* in their body? We are inviting them in to be parented and seen by us, sometimes for the very first time, and it's enormously powerful.

Imagine the feeling you are inviting in a tiny child who is raging. We are telling that part of us that it's safe for them to be in our body. We are the parent to them, we can handle them, and we can guide them.

Normally we shame these parts. We tell the parts of ourselves that are scared to go onstage to just, "be brave" and then we shove them on stage. Instead, we welcome these feelings, to find safety in our bodies, saying, "It's safe for me to feel terror in my body about being seen, I can hold that for both of us!"

Nervous System Card Index

Please note: This is an extended version of the Polyvagal Ladder, which includes the concept of Superplay, and differs from the traditional PVI ladder I was trained with. For the original source model, refer to the work of Deb Dana, who masterfully adapted Stephen Porges' work for therapeutic applications.

The Fox Method, which builds upon and remixes Polyvagal Theory (PVT), is just that—a model. If your nervous system doesn't align perfectly with it, there is absolutely nothing wrong with you; this is simply a limitation of any model. Additionally, while the nervous system is conventionally represented as a "ladder," it's more accurately comparable to Matryoshka dolls. When viewing the lines of the ladder, consider them akin to a musical staff, with each line representing a different harmony of your nervous system.

Instructions:

At any time of day—whether you're feeling tired, icky, happy, sad, angry, or defeated—take a moment to locate your nervous system on the ladder. This practice cultivates awareness of your current state, enabling you to take control of your "spaceship" and steer yourself toward a state that optimizes your biological resources. This is essential for achieving a connected performance on stage.

Superplay

11.

Role-play/Pretend
(All states
move into play)

The only non-survival state.

Safe and Social

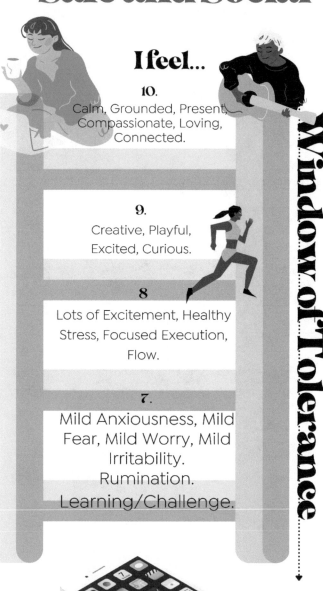

I feel...

10.
Calm, Grounded, Present,
Compassionate, Loving,
Connected.

9.
Creative, Playful,
Excited, Curious.

8
Lots of Excitement, Healthy
Stress, Focused Execution,
Flow.

7.
Mild Anxiousness, Mild
Fear, Mild Worry, Mild
Irritability.
Rumination.
Learning/Challenge.

Window of Tolerance

Sympathetic Dominant

6.
Significant Anxiousness, Fear, Worry, Irritability. (Functioning)

FIGHT

5.
Action-oriented fear, over-working, overwhelming anger, crawling out of the skin, mobilized panic, uncontrollable fidgeting, racing thoughts, Angry Fawn -people-pleasing but internally angry.

FLIGHT

4.
Wanting to Escape, Terrified, Frightened, Overwhelmed, Mobilized to Flee, Pleasing others with one foot out the door,

Dorsal Pathway Dominant

The Mobilized Freeze State

3.

Paralyzed between Flight / Freeze, Stuck, Frozen, Dissociation

The immobilized Freeze State

2.

Numb, Flat, Passive Fawn / Appeasing.

1.

"Collapsed," Withdrawn, Self-Preservation, Struggle to do anything.

MORE **Ability to feel** LESS

Acknowledgement

Dear Collaborators,

First and foremost, my heartfelt thanks to my writing partner, Jonathan Russell Clark. Your role in the creation of this book has been nothing short of essential. From being one of my earliest champions as a performing artist and songwriter, to becoming a fiercely loyal friend, your unwavering support has meant the world to me. Our three-hour conversations about science, the nervous system, and the essence of artistry are worth more than any book deal or accolade. Thank you for reminding me that art is simply a clever way to forge deep, revelatory connections between friends.

I extend profound gratitude to the remarkable individuals whose work has greatly influenced this book. To Dr. Stephen Porges, for his groundbreaking Polyvagal Theory, and to Deb Dana for her invaluable contributions in expanding upon it. To Bessel Van Der Kolk for his pioneering research on trauma and to Gabor Maté for his insights into the physical effects of stress. I owe deep thanks to Richard Schwartz for his Internal Family Systems model, Deb Gruenfeld for her work on power dynamics, and to Phil Stutz and Peter Levine for their therapeutic frameworks, particularly Somatic Experiencing®.

To my educators at Emerson College—Tim Douglas, Jennie Israel, Sarah Hickler, Kent Stephens, Robbie McCauley, and Amelia Broome—your wisdom, drawn from the traditions of Kristin Linklater, Stella Adler, and Konstantin Stanislavski, has been the foundation of the acting work presented in this book. Your teachings have deeply enriched my career as an actor, singer-songwriter, bandleader, and producer.

I'd also like to acknowledge Mika Cooper, David Halbrooks, Jen Cohen, Sarah Kornell, and Lee Bateman for your early editing work, guiding this dyslexic writer through countless drafts and moments of doubt. Without the brilliance and intuition of Patsy Rodenberg and her transformative book, *The Second Circle*, I may never have connected PVT with acting training.

Roger Metcalf, you are gold. A once in a lifetime friend. Thank you for collaborating with me on The Unstoppable Performer. I would have never been able to explore and expand without the help to create and expand that course. You are my hero and the most wonderful friend anyone could ever have.

Jennie Knott, thank you for introducing me to PVT and for your constant enthusiasm for my art and work, and for making this world a better place.

To my brave students, for trusting me with your vulnerabilities and allowing me to grow as a teacher, thank you. To my fans and family, who believed in me long before success arrived, your faith has sustained me. And to all my fellow dyslexics: if you've ever doubted your ability, felt overwhelmed by writing, or carry trauma from the dreaded red marker—know that you can do anything.

Lastly, thank you to the hundreds of MuscleMusic members (and the early ones–Nicki, Eszter, Timmy, Angela, Sara, Kev, Janey, Brian, Alison) whose honesty and transparency have reshaped my teaching in profound ways. You've been indispensable in shaping this work.

References and Further Reading

References and Further Reading

The Polyvagal Theory = PVT

ibid.

The following titles are referenced repeatedly:

Porges, Stephen W. *The Polyvagal Theory: Neurophysiological Foundations of Emotions, Attachment, Communication, and Self-Regulation.* Norton & Company, 2011.

Wilber, Ken. *Sex, Ecology, Spirituality: The Spirit of Evolution.* Shambhala Publications, 1995.

Levine, Peter A. *Waking the Tiger: Healing Trauma.* North Atlantic Books, 1997.

The rest

Prelude & Letter #1: It's Showtime

Chase, Nancy D., ed. *Burdened Children: Theory, Research, and Treatment of Parentification.* SAGE Publications, 1999.

Harari, Yuval Noah. *Sapiens: A Brief History of Humankind.* Harper, 2015.

Jurkovic, Gregory J. *Lost Childhoods: The Plight of the Parentified Child.* Brunner/Mazel, 1997.

Porges, Stephen W. *The Pocket Guide to the Polyvagal Theory: The Transformative Power of Feeling Safe.* Norton & Company, 2017.

Porges, Stephen W. *Polyvagal Safety: Attachment, Communication, Self-Regulation.* Norton & Company, 2021.

Porges, ibid.

Porges, Stephen W., and Deb A. Dana, eds. *Clinical Applications of the Polyvagal Theory: The Emergence of Polyvagal-Informed Therapies.* Norton & Company, 2018.

Schultz, Danielle. *The Parentified Child Experience: A Guide for Recognizing and Overcoming the Hidden Trauma of Parentification.* Independently published, 2020.

Taylor, Timothy. *The Artificial Ape: How Technology Changed the Course of Human Evolution.* Palgrave Macmillan, 2010.

Vince, Gaia. *Transcendence: How Humans Evolved through Fire, Language, Beauty, and Time.* Penguin, 2019.

Wilber, ibid.

Letter #2: When Life Hands You Avocados

Cohen, Leonard. *Songs of Leonard Cohen.* Columbia Records, 1967.

Dana, Deb. *Polyvagal Theory in Therapy: Engaging the Rhythm of Regulation.* Norton & Company, 2018.

Porges, Stephen W., and Deb Dana. *Co-Regulation Handbook: Creating a Balanced and Effective Therapy Practice.* Norton & Company, forthcoming.

Siegel, Daniel J., and Tina Payne Bryson. *The Power of Showing Up: How Parental Presence Shapes Who Our Kids Become and How Their Brains Get Wired.* Ballantine Books, 2020.

Letter #3: The Astronauts

Barrett, Lisa Feldman. *7 1/2 Lessons About the Brain*. Houghton Mifflin Harcourt, 2020. Extended Notes.

---. *How Emotions Are Made: The Secret Life of the Brain*. Houghton Mifflin Harcourt, 2017.

---, and James A. Russell, editors. *The Psychological Construction of Emotion*. Guilford Press, 2015.

Clark, Andy. *Surfing Uncertainty: Prediction, Action, and the Embodied Mind*. Oxford University Press, 2016.

Craig, A. D. *How Do You Feel? An Interoceptive Moment with Your Neurobiological Self*. Princeton University Press, 2014.

Danziger, Kurt. *Naming the Mind: How Psychology Found Its Language*. SAGE Publications, 1997.

DeSteno, David. *Emotional Success: The Power of Gratitude, Compassion, and Pride*. Houghton Mifflin Harcourt, 2018.

Eugenides, Jeffrey. *Middlesex*. Farrar, Straus, and Giroux, 2002.

Gleiser, Marcelo. *The Island of Knowledge: The Limits of Science and the Search for Meaning*. Basic Books, 2014.

Gilbert, Daniel. *Stumbling on Happiness*. Knopf, 2006.

Hohwy, Jakob. *The Predictive Mind*. Oxford University Press, 2013.

James, William. *The Principles of Psychology*. Henry Holt and Company, 1890.

Linden, David J. *Think Tank: Forty Neuroscientists Explore the Biological Roots of Human Experience*. Yale University Press, 2014.

Lewontin, Richard. *The Triple Helix: Gene, Organism, Environment*. Harvard University Press, 2000.

Lewis, Michael, Lisa Feldman Barrett, and Jeannette M. Haviland-Jones, editors. *Handbook of Emotions*. 4th ed., Guilford Press, 2017.

Searle, John R. *The Construction of Social Reality*. Free Press, 1995.

Smith, Tiffany Watt. *The Book of Human Emotions: An Encyclopedia of Feeling from Anger to Wanderlust*. Little, Brown, and Company, 2015.

Sporns, Olaf. *Networks of the Brain*. MIT Press, 2010.

Sterling, Peter, and Simon Laughlin. *Principles of Neural Design*. MIT Press, 2015.

Swanson, Larry W. *Brain Architecture: Understanding the Basic Plan*. Oxford University Press, 2012.

Watt Smith, Tiffany. *The Book of Human Emotions: An Encyclopedia of Feeling from Anger to Wanderlust*. Little, Brown and Company, 2015.

Letter #4: The Phones

Dawkins, Richard. *The Ancestor's Tale: A Pilgrimage to the Dawn of Evolution*. Houghton Mifflin, 2004.

Hanna, Thomas. *Somatics: Reawakening the Mind's Control of Movement, Flexibility, and Health*. Da Capo Press, 1988.

Lecointre, Guillaume, and Hervé Le Guyader. *The Tree of Life: A Phylogenetic Classification*. Harvard University Press, 2006.

LeDoux, Joseph. *The Emotional Brain: The Mysterious Underpinnings of Emotional Life*. Simon & Schuster, 1996.

Levine, ibid.

MacLean, Paul D. *The Triune Brain in Evolution: Role in Paleocerebral Functions*. Springer, 1990.

Panksepp, Jaak, and Lucy Biven. *The Archaeology of Mind: Neuroevolutionary Origins of Human Emotions*. W.W. Norton & Company, 2012.

Porges, ibid.

Wiley, E.O., and Bruce S. Lieberman. *Phylogenetics: Theory and Practice of Phylogenetic Systematics.* Wiley-Blackwell, 2011.

Letter #5: Houston We Have a Problem

Dana, Deb. *Polyvagal Exercises for Safety and Connection: 50 Client-Centered Practices.* W.W. Norton & Company, 2020.

Levine, ibid.

Porges, ibid.

Cozolino, Louis. *The Neuroscience of Human Relationships: Attachment and the Developing Social Brain.* W.W. Norton & Company, 2014.

Schore, Allan N. *Affect Regulation and the Origin of the Self: The Neurobiology of Emotional Development.* Routledge, 2015.

Letter #6: Wholearchy Vs. Hierarchy

Koestler, Arthur. *The Ghost in the Machine.* 1967.

Wilber, Ken. *A Brief History of Everything.* 1996.

Bauwens, Michel. "Holarchy vs. Hierarchy." P2P Foundation.

Letter #7: Preservation Mode

Brosschot, Jos F., Willem Gerin, and Julian F. Thayer. "The Perseverative Cognition Hypothesis: A Review of Worry, Prolonged Stress-related Physiological Activation, and Health." *Journal of Psychosomatic Research,* vol. 60, no. 2, 2006, pp. 113–124.

Epstein, Mark. *The Trauma of Everyday Life.* Penguin Press, 2013.

Herman, Judith. *Trauma and Recovery: The Aftermath of Violence—From Domestic Abuse to Political Terror.* Basic Books, 1992.

Levine, Peter A. *In an Unspoken Voice: How the Body Releases Trauma and Restores Goodness.* North Atlantic Books, 2010.

Porges, Stephen W. "Orienting in a Defensive World: Mammalian Modifications of Our Evolutionary Heritage. A Polyvagal Theory." *Psychophysiology,* vol. 32, no. 4, 1995, pp. 301–318.

Porges, ibid.

Roelofs, Karin. "Freeze for Action: Neurobiological Mechanisms in Animal and Human Freezing." *Philosophical Transactions of the Royal Society B: Biological Sciences,* vol. 372, no. 1718, 2017, pp. 20160206.

Thayer, Julian F., and Richard D. Lane. "A Model of Neurovisceral Integration in Emotion Regulation and Dysregulation." *Journal of Affective Disorders,* vol. 61, no. 3, 2000, pp. 201–216.

Van der Kolk, Bessel. *The Body Keeps the Score: Brain, Mind, and Body in the Healing of Trauma.* Viking, 2014.

Letter #8: Move Mode

Bracha, H. Stefan. *Human Brain Evolution and the "Neuroarcheology" of Psychopathologies.* University of Hawaii Press, 2004.

Cannon, Walter B. *Bodily Changes in Pain, Hunger, Fear, and Rage.* Appleton-Century-Crofts, 1929.

Cannon, Walter Bradford. *The Wisdom of the Body.* W.W. Norton & Company, 1932.

Eminem. *Lose Yourself.* Music from and Inspired by the Motion Picture *8 Mile,* Shady Records, 2002.

Helmholtz, Hermann von. *On the Sensations of Tone as a Physiological Basis for the Theory of Music.* Dover Publications, 1954.

LeDoux, Joseph. *The Emotional Brain: The Mysterious Underpinnings of Emotional Life.* Simon & Schuster, 1996.

Letter #9: Connect Mode

Bareilles, Sara. "Gravity." *Little Voice,* Epic, 2007.

Cozolino, Louis. *The Neuroscience of Human Relationships: Attachment and the Developing Social Brain.* W.W. Norton & Company, 2014.

Dana, Deb. *The Polyvagal Theory in Therapy: Engaging the Rhythm of Regulation.* W.W. Norton & Company, 2018.

Damasio, Antonio. *The Strange Order of Things: Life, Feeling, and the Making of Cultures.* Pantheon Books, 2018.

Gilbert, Paul. *The Compassionate Mind: A New Approach to Life's Challenges.* New Harbinger Publications, 2010.

Goleman, Daniel, and Richard J. Davidson. *Altered Traits: Science Reveals How Meditation Changes Your Mind, Brain, and Body.* Avery, 2017.

Levine, Peter A. *In an Unspoken Voice: How the Body Releases Trauma and Restores Goodness.* North Atlantic Books, 2010.

Porges, ibid.

Schore, Allan N. *Affect Regulation and the Repair of the Self.* W.W. Norton & Company, 2003.

Siegel, Daniel J. *The Developing Mind: How Relationships and the Brain Interact to Shape Who We Are.* 2nd ed., Guilford Press, 2012.

Letter #10-12: Houston We Have a Problem Chapters

Levine, ibid.

Porges, ibid.

Scaer, Robert. *The Trauma Spectrum: Hidden Wounds and Human Resiliency.* W.W. Norton & Company, 2005.

Ogden, Pat, and Janina Fisher. *Sensorimotor Psychotherapy: Interventions for Trauma and Attachment.* W.W. Norton & Company, 2015.

Letter #13: Roles, Risk, and Play

Gruenfeld, Deborah H., and Larissa Tiedens. "Organizational Behavior: Role Transitions and Power Dynamics." *Annual Review of Psychology,* vol. 61, 2010, pp. 517-542.

Porges, ibid.

Goffman, Erving. *The Presentation of Self in Everyday Life.* Anchor Books, 1959.

Brown, Stuart L., and Christopher C. Vaughan. *Play: How It Shapes the Brain, Opens the Imagination, and Invigorates the Soul.* Avery, 2009.

Scheff, Thomas J. *Shame in Social Theory: Symbolic Interaction, Social Bonds, and Emotions.* Cambridge University Press, 2000.

Letter #14: Superplay and The Astronauts

Porges, ibid.

Levine, ibid.

Turner, Victor. *The Ritual Process: Structure and Anti-Structure.* Aldine Publishing, 1969.

Boyd, Brian. *On the Origin of Stories: Evolution, Cognition, and Fiction.* Belknap Press of Harvard University Press, 2009.

Artaud, Antonin. *The Theatre and Its Double.* Translated by Victor Corti, Alma Books, 2010.

Grotowski, Jerzy. *Towards a Poor Theatre.* Routledge, 2002.

Letter #15: The Theory of Constructed Emotion

Panksepp, Jaak. *Affective Neuroscience: The Foundations of Human and Animal Emotions.* Oxford University Press, 1998.

Eberle, Scott G. "The Elements of Play: Toward a Philosophy and a Definition of Play." *American Journal of Play,* vol. 6, no. 2, 2014, pp. 214-233.

Barrett, Lisa Feldman. *How Emotions Are Made: The Secret Life of the Brain.* Houghton Mifflin Harcourt, 2017.

Barrett, Lisa Feldman, and James A. Russell, editors. *The Psychological Construction of Emotion.* Guilford Press, 2014.

Gendron, Maria, and Lisa Feldman Barrett. "Reconstructing the Past: A Century of Ideas About Emotion in Psychology." *Emotion Review,* vol. 1, no. 4, 2009, pp. 316–339.

Russell, James A. "Core Affect and the Psychological Construction of Emotion." *Psychological Review,* vol. 110, no. 1, 2003, pp. 145–172.

Barrett, Lisa Feldman. "Solving the Emotion Paradox: Categorization and the Experience of Emotion." *Personality and Social Psychology Review,* vol. 10, no. 1, 2006, pp. 20–46.

Letter #16: Nervous System Shifting

Porges, ibid.

Dana, Deb. *The Polyvagal Theory in Therapy: Engaging the Rhythm of Regulation.* W.W. Norton, 2018.

Levine, ibid.

Barrett, Lisa Feldman. *How Emotions Are Made: The Secret Life of the Brain.* Houghton Mifflin Harcourt, 2017.

Perel, Esther. *Mating in Captivity: Unlocking Erotic Intelligence.* Harper, 2006.

Ogden, Pat, et al. *Trauma and the Body: A Sensorimotor Approach to Psychotherapy.* W.W. Norton, 2006.

Letter #17: Nervous System Leadership

Boyatzis, Richard E., and Annie McKee. *Resonant Leadership: Renewing Yourself and Connecting with Others Through Mindfulness, Hope, and Compassion.* Harvard Business Review Press, 2005.

Carroll, Brigid, and Ruth Simpson. "Embodying Leadership: The Somatic Dimensions of Leadership Practice." *Leadership,* vol. 8, no. 3, 2012, pp. 237-256.

Hatfield, Elaine, John T. Cacioppo, and Richard L. Rapson. *Emotional Contagion.* Cambridge University Press, 1994.

Kabat-Zinn, Jon. *Full Catastrophe Living: Using the Wisdom of Your Body and Mind to Face Stress, Pain, and Illness.* Bantam Books, 1990.

Porges, ibid.

Stanislavski, Konstantin. *An Actor Prepares.* Theatre Arts Books, 1936.

Letter #18: The Dopamine Game (and References for "brain prediction")

Berridge, Kent C., and Morten L. Kringelbach. "Pleasure Systems in the Brain." *Neuron,* vol. 86, no. 3, 2015, pp. 646-664.

Lembke, Anna. *Dopamine Nation: Finding Balance in the Age of Indulgence.* Dutton, 2021.

Lieberman, Daniel Z., and Michael E. Long. *The Molecule of More: How a Single Chemical in Your Brain Drives Love, Sex, and Creativity—and Will Determine the Fate of the Human Race.* BenBella Books, 2018.

Robinson, Terry E., and Kent C. Berridge. "The Incentive Sensitization Theory of Addiction: Some Current Issues." *Philosophical Transactions of the Royal Society B: Biological Sciences,* vol. 363, no. 1507, 2008, pp. 3137-3146.

Schultz, Wolfram. "Neuronal Reward and Decision Signals: From Theories to Data." *Physiological Reviews,* vol. 95, no. 3, 2015, pp. 853-951.

Volkow, Nora D., and Marisela Morales. "The Brain on Drugs: From Reward to Addiction." *Cell,* vol. 162, no. 4, 2015, pp. 712-725.

Baumeister, Roy F., Kathleen D. Vohs, and Dianne M. Tice. "The Strength Model of Self-Control." *Current Directions in Psychological Science,* vol. 16, no. 6, 2007, pp. 351-355.

Letter #19: Capacity vs. Desire

Deci, Edward L., and Richard M. Ryan. "The 'What' and 'Why' of Goal Pursuits: Human Needs and the Self-Determination of Behavior." *Psychological Inquiry,* vol. 11, no. 4, 2000, pp. 227-268.

Porges, Stephen W. "The Polyvagal Theory: New Insights into Adaptive Reactions of the Autonomic Nervous System." *Cleveland Clinic Journal of Medicine,* vol. 76, suppl. 2, 2009, pp. S86-S90.

Barrett, Lisa Feldman. *How Emotions Are Made: The Secret Life of the Brain.* Houghton Mifflin Harcourt, 2017.

LeDoux, Joseph E. "Emotion Circuits in the Brain." *Annual Review of Neuroscience,* vol. 23, no. 1, 2000, pp. 155-184.

*For additional resources, tools, and please go to www.muscle-music.com

This is an invitation into my **work, programming, and courses.** Thank you for your precious time. you are marvelous the gods wait to delight in you.

All my love, Ruby Rose Fox

Made in the USA
Columbia, SC
21 May 2025

58249107R10154